Using iPod, MP3 and WMA with your PC

Other Computer Titles

by

Robert Penfold

Using iPod, MP3 and WMA with your PC

Robert Penfold

Bernard Babani (publishing) Ltd
The Grampians
Shepherds Bush Road
London W6 7NF
England
www.babanibooks.com

Please note

Although every care has been taken with the production of this book to ensure that any projects, designs, modifications, and/or programs, etc., contained herewith, operate in a correct and safe manner and also that any components specified are normally available in Great Britain, the Publisher and Author do not accept responsibility in any way for the failure (including fault in design) of any projects, design, modification, or program to work correctly or to cause damage to any equipment that it may be connected to or used in conjunction with, or in respect of any other damage or injury that may be caused, nor do the Publishers accept responsibility in any way for the failure to obtain specified components.

Notice is also given that if any equipment that is still under warranty is modified in any way or used or connected with home-built equipment then that warranty may be void.

© 2005 BERNARD BABANI (publishing) LTD

First Published - November 2005
Reprinted - February 2006

British Library Cataloguing in Publication Data
A catalogue record for this book is available from the British Library

ISBN   0 85934 561 0

Cover Design by Gregor Arthur
Printed and bound in Great Britain by Cox and Wyman

Preface

Portable audio is not exactly a new phenomenon. Many years ago there were battery powered record players that you could, in theory, take and use just about anywhere. Of course, these units were huge by the standards of today, and the slightest vibration would cause the stylus to jump from one track to another. The sound quality from the built-in loudspeakers was generally rather "tinny" and distorted. Genuinely portable audio started with the Sony Walkman, which was the "must have" gadget of its day. Using audio cassettes and headphones enabled these units to be genuinely portable while providing surprisingly good sound quality. I suppose that by current standards portable cassette players are not that small, and the sound quality is not that good. The size and quality of the cassettes themselves are the limiting factors.

The quality problem was solved by the introduction of portable CD and Mini Disc players. Using digital rather than analogue recording technology provides these players with true hi-fi sound quality. However, being largely mechanical in nature they were no smaller than the original Walkman players, and in some cases they were actually much larger. The early MP3 players used Flash memory to store the music, which meant that there were purely electronic devices that could be made very small and light. The iPods and some of the more recent MP3 players use a miniature hard disc drive instead of Flash memory, which in a way is a step backwards. These players are relatively large, but they are still very portable. The big advantage of using a hard disc drive is that it can store the music from dozens or even hundreds of CDs. The built-in storage is a crucial difference between all MP3 players and earlier types of portable player. An MP3 player might not be much smaller than a portable CD player, but it is very much smaller than the CD player and a stack of 20 or more CDs. When going on your travels with MP3 players and iPods you take a stack of music with you, inside the player.

A slight problem with MP3 players is actually getting the music into the player. In this respect MP3 players are unlike anything that has gone before. You can not go to the local shop, buy an MP3, take it home, and put it in the MP3 slot of your player. It is not necessary to buy any new music at all. Your existing library of music can be used with an MP3 player, once you know how. You can also download music and upload it to your player, but only if you obtain music that is in a suitable audio format. This book tells you how to convert your existing music into audio files and upload them to your player, convert files from one format to another, download music from the Internet, burn files to ordinary CDs, play files on your PC, and so on. The final chapter provides advice on choosing a player that best suits your needs.

Robert Penfold

Trademarks

Microsoft, Windows, Windows Media Player, WMA, WMV, Windows XP, Windows Me, Windows 98 and Windows 95 are either registered trademarks or trademarks of Microsoft Corporation.

ITunes, and iPod are registered trademarks of Apple Computer Inc.

Napster is a registered trademark of Napster LLC

Real Player and Real Audio are registered trademarks of Real Networks Inc.

All other brand and product names used in this book are recognised trademarks, or registered trademarks of their respective companies.

Contents

3

WMP 10 and playing files 75

4
_____

iTunes and iPods 171

5

Choosing an MP3 player 275

Formats and conversions

Beginnings

Many people seem to be under the impression that the Apple iPod was the first portable device for playing digital music to be marketed to the general public. Of course, this is not the case, and portable digital audio devices have been around for many years. Not only have they been in existence for many years, they have also been very popular. My first digital audio gadget that supposedly qualified as "portable" was a very early example of a battery powered CD player.

It was powered by ten AA size batteries that sometimes reached exhaustion point before you had played two CDs. The cost of the batteries to run it was sometimes more than the cost of the CDs being played! It was portable, but was not really comparable to a modern player in this respect. It was much bulkier and heavier than a modern portable CD player, and had no form of jog-proof technology. The slightest vibration was sufficient to make it "lose the plot". The cost of powering it from batteries was so high that its portability was notional anyway. In practice this player had to be powered via its mains adapter, which meant it was not really any more portable than an ordinary CD player for use in a hi-fi system.

I eventually replaced this player with one that was "state of the art" at the time, but would now be considered as a "run of the mill" player. It was about the size of a double CD case and obtained its power from two rechargeable AA size batteries that lasted for about five CDs before needing a recharge. Although lacking any form of jog-proof technology, this player was genuinely portable and you could use it in the garden, take it with you on holiday, or whatever. It was an expensive player that came complete with some quite pricey in-ear headphones. The audio quality provided by these headphones was superb, and my interest in large hi-fi systems rapidly waned. With portable audio you could have top quality sound anywhere, any time, with no need to fill the house with large speakers and hi-fi units. Portable CD players soon became very popular, and the prices dropped from hundreds of pounds to what can now be as little as a few pounds. Portable CD players are still popular and widely available, but are "feeling the pinch" from MP3 players.

Other players

Of course, there have been and still are other types of portable music player. Mini Disc players never achieved great popularity in either portable form or as part of a hi-fi system. The audio quality provided by these players is extremely good, and it is a medium that can be used to make your own recordings. However, the portable units were perhaps not quite as small and light as they might have been, and the relatively high cost no doubt deterred many would-be buyers. Anyway, for whatever reason, this type of portable player has never achieved true mass-market status.

The Mini Disc units were designed to replace compact cassette players and recorders. The Sony Walkman probably represents the beginning of the portable music player, and this type of player was extremely popular for many years. Although very good in many ways, the real drawback of any form of cassette player is the cassette itself. Although not very large, the size of a standard tape cassette plus its largely mechanical nature makes it impossible to make a really small and light player. Jumping to the beginning of any desired track is simple and more or less instant with most other types of player. With a cassette player it is a long and awkward process that is unlikely to justify the effort involved.

Probably the biggest drawback of the compact cassette is that it does not provide top quality results. Some would put this down to the fact that normal audio cassettes are analogue rather than digital in nature. It is not as simple as that though, and analogue tape recording has provided some top quality results. However, you have to bear in mind that the compact cassette was designed for use in dictation machines and other applications where low quality voice recording was needed. It was not designed for playing music with hi-fi quality reproduction, and trying to use it in that role was perhaps being a little over-optimistic. Despite advances in tape technology and other aspects of cassette players, they never achieved anything approaching CD quality, and this recording/playback medium is now bordering on obsolescence.

When MP3 players were introduced I suppose it was really just a matter of time before they took over from other types of audio player. Initially the cost was too high for MP3 players to sell in huge numbers, and the specifications were quite low. A conventional MP3 player stores the digitised music in Flash memory, which is the same type of memory that is used in digital cameras and numerous portable electronic gadgets.

Flash memory is a form of non-volatile memory, which means that it retains its contents when the power is switched off. When used in a portable music player this means that you do not have to keep the player switched on in order to prevent the player from getting amnesia and losing its store of music. Similarly, the stored music remains intact if the battery goes completely flat. The problem with the early MP3 players was that Flash memory was very expensive, which limited the amount that could be fitted to a player without escalating the price to a level where few would even consider buying one. Using data compression enabled longer playing times to be obtained without seriously compromising the sound quality, but most of the early players could barely accommodate the contents of one full-length CD.

Things move on, and many of the current MP3 players can store the equivalent of about 30 CDs. IPods and some other MP3 players incorporate hard disc drives that can accommodate a library containing the equivalent of several hundred CDs. You can effectively carry your entire music library and a hi-fi system everywhere you go. The MP3 players that use Flash memory can be genuinely tiny, and they have been incorporated into pens, key rings, and even watches.

On the move

With MP3 the audio quality depends on the amount of compression used during the encoding process, but true hi-fi quality is easily achieved. There is no need to worry about anti-jog systems if you use an MP3 player while on the move or exercising. Flash memory is not fazed by constant and strong vibration. You can shake an MP3 player as hard as you like and it will not "lose the plot".

Understandably, people are normally reluctant to switch to a new music format since it renders all their existing recordings obsolete. This is not the case with MP3 players, since it is possible to convert you existing recordings into MP3 format and load them into your new player. Any modern PC should be able to produce MP3 files from CDs, with no additional equipment being required. Other types of recording are more awkward because there is no suitable drive built into the PC, and most of them are analogue and not digital systems. It can be done though, and in most cases it requires nothing more than the player normally used with the recordings plus a lead to connect it to the PC.

Computer standards

Digital music based on a PC and a portable player has a lot going for it, but there are the inevitable complications. One of these is that you encounter so-called computer standards. If you say "computer standards" to someone with experience of the computing world they tend to fall about laughing. Having regained their composure they next indicate that "computing" and "standards" are a classic contradiction of terms.

I suppose that there is more than a little justification for this jaundiced view of things. In the early days of personal computing there were so many standards that this word ceased to have any real meaning when used in relation to computing. Each time a new computer was launched onto the market it seemed to come complete with its own set of standards! Some of us made good livings explaining these standards to the uninitiated.

Another problem was that few pieces of equipment rigidly adhered to the few real standards that had been agreed. Just why so many manufacturers were intent on "doing their own thing" is something of a mystery. Some of it was certainly due to ill-advised cost cutting, and the rest was presumably a case of inadequate design work. Whatever the cause, the chances of two supposedly compatible devices working together first time were not very good. It often required an adaptor, custom cable, software patch, or whatever.

Fortunately, things have improved over the years, and many of the old computing standards have now faded from use. Those that remain are mostly quite rigidly standardized. Getting computer equipment to function properly as a system is far easier than it used to be, with most of the problems due to minor flaws in the supporting software.

On the face of it, this is good news for those who use PCs for downloading and playing music. You download music in the fully standardized and only music format, and then connect your music player to the PC so that you can transfer the music files to the player. In this new and ideal world of computing there is only one interface used to connect a PC to music players, so there are no hardware compatibility issues.

Interfaces

Of course, in the real world things are never as simple as that, and they are certainly not that straightforward in the computing world. Although many of the old standards used in computing have now disappeared, some new ones have been introduced. This was inevitable, due to the large amounts of data that are routinely swapped in everyday computing. We routinely transfer hundreds of megabytes of data between our PCs and devices such as digital cameras. With some gadgets, including certain types of music player, it can be necessary to transfer many gigabytes of data.

The only common interfaces from the early days of computing that still survive are the serial and parallel (printer) types. Serial ports have never been used much with music players, if at all. Even when used some way beyond its intended maximum operating speed, using a serial interface to transfer a few hundred megabytes of data would take a few days! Some music players utilise a parallel port for data transfers, but only a few of the early and low-cost models use this method. As serial and parallel ports are now being phased out, it is probably not a good idea to buy any device that is reliant on these ports.

Serial and parallel ports have now been largely replaced by the USB variety. USB is a sort of turbocharged version of a serial port that achieves similar speeds to an ordinary parallel port. However, it avoids the thick cables associated with parallel connections, and it is rather more sophisticated than either serial or parallel ports. The original USB interfaces adhered to the USB 1.1 specification, which was perfectly adequate for most peripherals, and still is. Devices such as printers, mice, and most scanners operate perfectly well using a USB 1.1 interface.

The introduction of mass storage devices such as external hard disc drives showed up the inadequacies of their original USB specification. While it is certainly possible to swap large amounts of data via an ordinary USB interface, doing so can be quite time-consuming. This led to the development of USB 2.0, which is potentially many times quicker than USB 1.1. I say potentially, because few real-world devices can actually utilize the maximum speed available when using USB 2.0. The rate at which data is transferred is limited by the slowest device in the system. When using a USB 2.0 interface it is unlikely to be the interface itself that is the slowest part of the system. Sometimes the computer will be the limiting factor, but in an electronic music context it is more likely to be the player. To be more precise, it is the memory in the player that is usually the limiting factor.

Modern music players often have very high storage capacities. This makes a USB 2.0 interface a decided asset. Bear in mind that the higher speeds associated with USB 2.0 can only be achieved if both the computer and the music player have an interface of this type. It also pays to remember that some devices are USB 2.0 compatible rather than true USB 2.0 devices. In other words, they can be connected to and used successfully with a USB 2.0 interface, but will only support USB 1.1 speeds. Genuine USB 2.0 interfaces are now often called "high-speed" USB ports to distinguish them from the compatible variety.

Both types of USB interface fully support Plug N Play operation. In theory at any rate, this should make it extremely easy to use practically any USB device with a modern PC. Provided you are using a modern version of Windows, many music players can be used without having to install any software on the PC. The memory in the player effectively becomes an external disc drive, and it is assigned a drive letter by the operating system. Music files can be copied to the drive in the normal way, and deleted once you have finished with them. This is perhaps not the best way of doing things with a player that has a huge storage capacity, but it is simple and efficient when used with players having a few hundred megabytes of memory.

Some music players do not fit into the operating system as an external disc drive, or they do, but you would not normally access them directly. With these players it is essential to follow the manufacturer's installation instructions, and to use the software supplied with the players. The software will usually include some form of database that makes it easy to keep track of and manage the songs uploaded to the player.

In some cases the software includes a media player that enables music files to be played on your PC. Of course, all modern versions of Windows come complete with the Windows Media Player program, and this is capable of playing many types of music and video file. Therefore, the media players supplied with MP3 players may be of little practical value to most users. Sometimes the database program is combined with a media player, which is in many ways a neat solution. However, it can make life difficult if you would prefer to use a different media player program on your PC.

FireWire

These days there is only one real alternative to USB, and that is the FireWire interface. USB was designed specifically for use with PCs, but it is now used with other computers including Macs. FireWire was designed for use with Mac computers, and was primarily intended as a means of using them with digital video cameras. It has found more general use though, and many PCs are equipped with a FireWire port as standard. Practically any PC can be equipped with the FireWire port by adding a suitable expansion card.

Because it was originally intended for use with digital video cameras, FireWire provides very high operating speeds. In theory it is not quite as fast as the USB 2.0 interface, but in practice there is very little to choose between the two types. FireWire is possibly the faster of the two when transferring large amounts of data. FireWire is certainly fast enough for use with music players, including those that have high-capacity disc drives.

Where there is an option, it probably makes sense for PC users to choose USB rather than FireWire. Any reasonably modern PC should be equipped with a few USB ports, and they will be fully supported by the operating system. Of course, if your PC has both USB and FireWire ports it does not matter a great deal which one you use. The vast majority of MP3 players are only for use with USB ports, so you will probably find that FireWire is not actually an option.

Audio formats

The hardware side of things is usually fairly straightforward, with only two different types of interface now in common use with music players. Since music players are normally supplied with a suitable cable to facilitate the connection to your computer, this aspect of things is unlikely to be a problem. Unfortunately, things are less straightforward when it comes to the issue of audio formats.

The fact that music players are generally called "MP3 players" gives the impression that this is the only format that they support. However, most players can handle at least two other types of audio file. Media player programs for PCs can often handle half a dozen or more different formats, although some of the more obscure formats might require some additional software to be installed.

From the user's point of view it would clearly be better if there was just a single format. In the world of computing things are never that straightforward though. There are various reasons for rival formats being introduced. If you produce anything in the computing world it is only a matter of time before someone comes up with a better alternative. Where a format has associated licensing or royalty fees it is understandable if rivals come up with alternatives that avoid these payments. It is also understandable if people produced royalty-free alternatives that avoid the constraints of proprietary systems. Anyway, there are numerous audio formats in existence, and several that are in general use.

What is an audio format? With digital audio the signal is sampled at regular intervals, and converted into a series of numeric values. In the case of CDs for example, the signal is sampled just over 44,000 times per second. The sampling rate is important to the final audio quality because an inadequate rate will provide only a limited bandwidth. In other words, with a low sampling rate there will be a lack of treble in the reproduced audio signal.

The sampling rate needs to be at least double the maximum frequency in the audio signal. Human hearing covers a range of approximately 20Hz to 20kHz, which means that the sampling rate of at least 40kHz is needed in order to provide the full audio range. In other words, at least 40,000 samples per second must be used. The system used for CDs samples at a high enough rate, but at 44.1kHz it is only just high enough.

Another important factor is the resolution of the system. With analogue audio there is no sampling and the signal varies continuously. With a digital system a series of "snapshots" are stored in some form of memory and the signal jumps from one level to another. The nice smooth signal of Figure 1.1 (top) might look something more like Figure 1.1 (bottom) once it has been digitised.

Although a system like this gives the impression that it could never work, it can provide superb results provided it is done properly. It is not the stepping of the signal that is the real problem. Filtering used during playback smoothes the signal so that it changes in a step-free fashion. Consequently, the final output from a digital audio system is essentially the same as that from an analogue type. There are no steps in the signal, and it sounds perfectly all right provided it is technically adequate in other respects.

Resolution

The flaw in a digital audio system is that it does not provide an infinite number of levels. CDs are recorded in 16-bit digital audio, which means that the system provides over 65,000 different output levels. Each time the signal is sampled, the digital value that most closely corresponds with the actual signal level is used. This inevitably introduces errors, and the system must be able to handle a large number of different levels

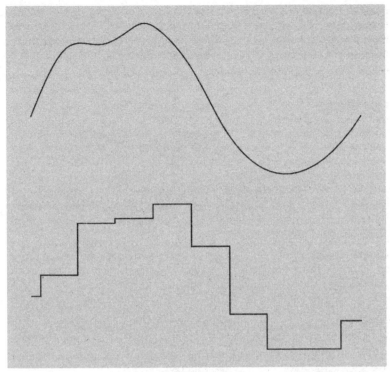

Fig.1.1 An analogue signal (top) and a digitised equivalent (bottom)

in order to keep these errors to a minimum. Very good results have been obtained from 14 -bit audio systems, but 16-bit operation tends to be regarded as the minimum that will provide true high fidelity results.

Having converted an analogue audio signal into a series of values that can be stored on a hard disc or in memory, there is the problem of storing it in a form that can be read by any hardware players and media player programs. At its most basic level, the music can just be stored as a series of 16-bit values. Even with this method it is necessary to have a standard method of handling things so that players know what each value represents. Are the values alternate samples from the left and right channels? If so, is the first value for the left or right-hand channel? Is the music in stereo at all, or it is an old monophonic recording?

Even with the most basic method of storing digital music it is essential to have a standard arrangement that players can interpret correctly. In practice matters are complicated by the fact that digital music is often compressed. In other words, the amount of data is reduced so that more music can be stored in a given amount of memory, hard disc space, or whatever. Two types of compression are used with music files, and it is important to understand the difference between the two.

Lossless

Some file formats use what in an audio context is termed "lossless" compression. This is essentially the same as the compression often used in computing when producing Zip files, etc. When the file is decompressed it is exactly the same as it was prior to compression. With an audio file this means that compressing the data does not give any reduction in the sound quality. A CD that is converted into a lossless file format should sound exactly the same whether the original or the compressed version is played.

On the face of it there is no point in using a lossless file format. You could obtain much the same amount of compression by turning a non-compressed audio file into something like a normal Zip or RAR file. In a way this is true, but the Zip or RAR file could not be played on a music player unless it was decompressed first, which would be a bit pointless. Music files that use lossless compression can be played using a suitable player or player program without having to decompress them first. The player decompresses the data "on the fly" so that only a very small part of the file is decompressed at any one time.

Compression that does not involve any loss of sound quality has a lot in its favour. It allows more music to be fitted into the memory of a player, but the end result sounds just as good as it does when playing the CD version. Unfortunately, there is a huge drawback in that the degree of compression that can be used without impairing the quality is rather limited. The amount of compression achieved in practice depends on the methods used and the amenability of the source material to these methods. It is usually possible to at least halve the amount of storage space required, and a reduction by about two thirds is well within reason.

Getting three times more music onto a player without incurring any loss of quality is worthwhile, but a higher degree of compression is very desirable. Obtaining a higher degree of compression is possible, but only if some loss in audio quality can be tolerated. In general, the greater the amount of compression used, the lower the sound quality. However, some methods of compression are more efficient than others. A five megabyte file will not necessarily be better than a four megabyte equivalent produced using a different method of compression.

There is clearly a dividing line between an acceptable amount of compression and an amount that reduces the sound quality by an intolerable amount. The position of this dividing line is to some extent a matter of opinion. It also depends on the source material, with some pieces showing up any inadequacies in the decompressed signal much more clearly than others.

Most people are quite happy with a file that has been compressed to about 10 percent of its original size provided an efficient system of compression is used. Greater amounts of compression might give acceptable results, but there is an increasing risk of the compression producing clearly audible distortion products if the compression is taken much beyond this level. With the best methods of compression it is possible to get passable results with the file compressed to about 5 percent of its original size. In other words, a player that has sufficient storage for about two CDs can accommodate about 40 full CDs when using this level of compression. The amount of memory fitted to portable music players has steadily increased over the years, but a large amount of compression is still needed in order to store a worthwhile amount of music on most players.

Compression methods

A number of compression techniques are used by most digital music formats that include this feature. These obviously include the normal compression techniques that are utilised for Zip files and the like. Most also include a system that uses reduced resolution when the music is loud. This relies on the fact that loud sounds tend to mask quieter ones. Consequently, the quieter bits can be omitted when louder sounds are present, because the listener will be unable to hear the quieter sounds anyway. Other techniques are less subtle, such as a general reduction in the resolution and a reduced sampling rate. This type of thing soon produces a noticeable reduction in sound quality.

You are not usually left in any doubt when a music file has been encoded using a level of compression that is too high. The giveaway is not usually an obvious lack of detail or high frequency content in the music. Excessive compression usually produces sounds that were obviously not present when the recording was being made. In general, we are not usually talking about the types of distortion that occur with an analogue system that is of poor quality or is being driven too hard. The distortion produced by excessive compression tends to sound very odd indeed. It sounds clearly out of place and decidedly unmusical.

The effect is equivalent to the artefacts that are produced when excessive compression is used for a digital image such as a JPEG photograph. There is often no obvious lack of detail in the photograph, but the textures in what should be plain areas stand out like the proverbial "sore thumb". Anyway, trying to get too much music into a player by using an excessive amount of compression is not a good idea. It is much better to have slightly less music that is of good and enjoyable quality than it is to have a bit more music that sounds pretty terrible in many places.

As anyone familiar with the world of computing would expect, a number of music file formats have been produced over the years. Some of these use no compression, others use lossless compression, and yet more use compression that does involve a loss of quality. Many of these formats are of little or no interest to users of portable players or to those using a computer to play digital music files. The following are the formats that are of most interest in the current context.

MP3

This is the format that has become synonymous with digital music and portable music players. It is known by a variety of names such as MPEG 3 and MPEG 1 level 3, but these days it is most commonly referred to as MP3. It is apparently based on the same fractal mathematics that is used for the JPEG image format. Like the JPEG image format, it achieves a fairly high degree of compression, but it can also give a noticeable reduction in quality.

With MP3, and some other digital music formats, you will encounter the term "bit rate". This is the total number of bits per second used when encoding and playing back the file. The 16-bit audio on a CD is at a sampling rate of 44,100 per second. This works out at 705,600 bits per second, but there are another 705,600 bits per second in the other stereo channel. This gives a total rate of 1,411,200 bits per second for the full stereo signal. A thousand bits is a kilobit, and a million bits is a megabit, so this rate would more normally be given as 1,411.2 kilobits per second or 1.4112 megabits per second.

The MP3 format supports a wide range of bit rates, but the lowest ones are only suitable for low quality signals. Most people find that 128 kilobits per second represents the lowest rate that gives acceptable results with stereo music. However, not everyone is happy with a rate as low as this, which is well under one tenth of the rate used for CDs. Higher rates of 160, 192, 256, and 320 kilobits per second are quite common, and provide superior sound quality. Bear in mind though, that higher bit rates do not provide a massive increase in sound quality, but do give a massive increase in file sizes. For example, a file encoded at 256 kilobits per second is twice the size of one encoded at 128 kilobits per second.

Some MP3 files are now encoded using a variable bit rate (VBR). As the name suggests, this method does not use a constant bit rate, but instead varies the bit rate to suit the programme material. The rate is speeded up for complex material and slowed down if it is deemed that this will not noticeably impair the sound quality. The idea of this is to give a high perceived sound quality while keeping file sizes as small as possible. Variable bit rate encoding can produce some impressive results, but bear in mind that not all portable players and media player programs support this type of MP3 file. Note also that portable players do not always support files that are encoded using a high constant bit rate such as 320 kilobits per second.

MP3 is not a format that is free of licensing restrictions. It is owned by the Moving Picture Experts Group (MPEG), as are the various MPEG video encoding formats. This is largely of academic importance to most users, since they will not use MP3 in a fashion that incurs any royalty payments.

WMA

This is the Windows Media Audio format, which should not be confused with its video counterpart (WMV). WMA was designed to be the standard audio format for use with Windows and the software that runs under this operating system. With many other music file formats in use on Windows PCs, including the ever popular MP3 format, it is has not really achieved this status. It is in widespread use though, and some portable music players will happily work with most WMA files.

Like MP3, the WMA format uses compression techniques that produce some loss of sound quality. WMA is generally regarded as being more efficient than MP3, and it can therefore be used at lower bit rates while still maintaining acceptable sound quality. Some users find a rate as low as 64 kilobits per second gives what they deem to be acceptable sound quality, but most people find that 96 kilobits per second is a more realistic minimum rate.

Fig.1.2 The free version of the Real Player is adequate for most users

There are now two forms of the WMA format in addition to the standard (constant bit rate) type. One of the extra versions is a lossless format, but as one would expect, this does not provide a great deal of compression and it is not supported by most portable players. There is also a variable bit rate version. This is well suited to use with portable music players, but at the moment there are relatively few portable players that can handle WMA variable bit rate files.

Real thing

The Real Audio format is another one that uses large amounts of compression, but can incur a significant loss of quality as a result. It can, of course, provide very high quality results provided the bit rate is not made too low. The Real Audio format can be used to produce compressed music files, but it is not used in this way to any great extent.

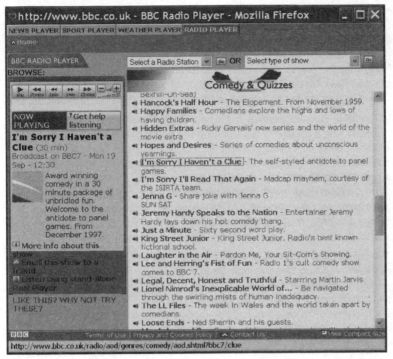

Fig.1.3 The BBC Radio Player is based on the Real Player and will only work if the latter is installed on your PC

It is a format that is often used in applications that require streamed audio. The video version (Real Video) is used a great deal for streamed video.

Streamed audio is where a web site provides a continuous stream of audio. This can be recorded material made available on-demand, or it can be a live audio feed. It is most commonly used by radio stations and in its live version is sometimes referred to as "Internet radio". Similarly, a live video stream is mainly used by television stations and is often referred to as "Internet TV". In both cases it is quite common for very low bit rates to be used, giving what are often extremely rough results. Sometimes there is an option for broadband users to use a higher bit rate, and this should provide greatly improved results.

The Real Audio format is not widely supported by portable players or media player programs. The normal way of playing a Real Audio file or material streamed in this format is to download the free version of the Real Player (Figure 1.2) from the Real web site (www.real.com). There are commercial versions of the Real Player that provide additional features, but for most purposes the free version is perfectly adequate. Note that the basic version of the Real Player is not only suitable for playing Real Audio files and streamed material. It is capable of playing CDs and media files in a variety of formats, including some video types.

In order to play streamed material via the Real Player program it is normally just a matter of left-clicking the appropriate link. The program will then be launched automatically and will start to play the streamed material. In some cases it will not be obvious that it is the Real Player is playing the material. This is where the supplier of the streamed material uses the Real Player with their own skin for the program. In other words, the player you see on the screen does not look like the normal Real Player program, and it might even have one or two features that are not found on the normal version of the Real Player program.

The BBC Radio Player is a good example of this (Figure 1.3). This does not look anything like the normal version of the Real Player, and it has additional facilities that enable users to select the required station or recorded material. However, the standard Real Player program is there under the add-on skin that is downloaded when the BBC Radio Player is launched. Unless the Real Player program is properly installed on the PC, the BBC Radio Player program can not function.

Files that are in the Real Audio format usually have an "ra" file extension. Those in the Real Video format generally have an "rv" or "rm" (Real Movie) file extension. Some Real Audio files now have an "rm" file extension. The idea seems to be that all Real files should have the same "rm" (Real Media) extension, and that the player can still sort out which type of file it is playing. Matters are not always as clear-cut for users though.

AAC/MP4/M4a

This is the Advanced Audio Coding system, which is also known as MP4 and M4a. It enables high degrees of compression to be achieved while retaining excellent audio quality. It is in widespread use because it was adopted by Apple as the normal format for their iTunes program and music download service, and their iPod players. All the iPods can be used with MP3 files as well incidentally. Unfortunately, few MP3 players can handle AAC files, although it does seem to have much more widespread support amongst media player programs. There is more than one version of AAC, and it is the LC (low complexity) version that is widely supported by hardware players.

MPC

This format is most commonly called MPC, but it is also known as the Musepack format. It seems to be aimed primarily at producing very high quality results rather than the highest possible amount of compression for a given audio quality. This is probably the reason for its relative lack of popularity. MPC is not supported by hardware players, but MPC files can be handled by some media player programs. However, this usually requires a plug-in to be installed.

OGG

The OGG format, which is also known as the OGG Vorbis format, was designed to be an open source alternative to the proprietary systems such as MP3 and WMA. In other words, it is largely free from any licensing restrictions and for most purposes this format can be used free of charge. In fact, OGG Vorbis would appear to be fully open source, which means that anyone can use it in any way they like, with no royalty payments or other charges being incurred. This has obvious attractions for small scale commercial or amateur distribution of music in a highly compressed form.

While the use of OGG is nothing like as widespread as MP3 or WMA, it is supported by a reasonable number of media player programs. It is not supported by WMP 10, but it is not too difficult to find a free plug-in on the Internet that enables WMP 10 to play OGG files. A few portable music players can handle OGG files, but this feature is still something of a rarity. It produces good results at quite low bit rates, so technically it is a good choice for portable music players.

WAV/Wave

The Wave format is more popularly known as the WAV format, and files of this type normally have a WAV extension. It is a very basic format that is lossless because it does not use any form of compression. This limits its usefulness, because it tends to produce very large file sizes. It is best suited to small sound clips and sound effects where the lack of compression will not result in huge files. It is a standard Windows format, and as such it has quite widespread support. Many portable players and media player programs can handle WAV files. It is often used as a "halfway house" when converting from one format to another or ripping CDs.

FLAC

FLAC stands for "free lossless audio codec". Codec is a term that you will often encounter with digital music and video, and it is a contraction of coder/decoder. This is simply the software or hardware device used to generate a compressed audio or video file, and to turn it back into a decompressed stream of data. FLAC is a lossless format that achieves a moderate amount of compression. It is closely associated with the OGG format and I suppose it could be regarded as a sort of lossless version of OGG. At the moment anyway, it is less widely supported than OGG, and its relatively small compression ratios are unlikely to make it popular for use with hardware players. It is supported by some media player programs, and it can be played by WMP 10 with the aid of a free plug-in program from the Internet.

APE

Believe it or not, this is a lossless format from Monkey's Audio, and it is sometimes known by the Monkey's Audio (or just Monkey Audio) name. It has probably been the most popular lossless audio format, and might still be. However, it is under pressure from alternatives such as FLAC. Relatively few players can handle this format, but there is a free plug-in for the Winamp player program. There is also a free compression and decompression program for use with Wave files. The free software and more details of the APE format are available from the Monkey's Audio web site at www.monkeysaudio.com.

ALE

ALE stands for "Apple lossless encoder", and this format was produced for users that require maximum quality rather than small file sizes. With a 40 gigabyte iPod it is possible to store large amounts of music using this format, but it has less appeal to those using iPods with much lower storage capacities. This format is little used by those that do not have Apple audio products.

MIDI

MIDI stands for "musical instruments digital interface". There are vast numbers of MIDI files on the Internet, and they can be played by many media players including WMP 10. However, this is a music format and not what could accurately be described as an audio format. The purpose of MIDI is to enable suitably equipped electronic musical instruments to communicate with each other, and (usually) with a computer. A number or instruments can be connected together to effectively form one huge instrument that can be controlled by a computer. A MIDI file consists of a series of instructions, such as turn on this note on channel 12, and switch off that note on channel 14. The file contains no sounds as such. It is up to the instruments in the system to turn the instructions into the corresponding sounds.

As pointed out previously, many media player programs can handle MIDI files, including WMP 10. You do not need a set of musical instruments connected to your PC in order to play these files. All you need is a sound card that has a suitable built-in synthesiser, or a basic soundcard plus some software that can give it this facility. In practice, most PC soundcards are able to handle MIDI files, and in some cases there are two or three types of synthesis available. Unfortunately, the sound quality varies considerably from one soundcard to another. Where two or more types of synthesis are available, there can be considerable differences in quality from one method to another. Some MIDI files and soundcards produce very good results, while others are mediocre at best.

MIDI has huge limitations as a general means of distributing music. Since it can not handle recorded sounds it can not accommodate vocalists at all, and it only handles instruments after a fashion. MIDI is not compatible with hardware players since they lack any form of built-in synthesis. It is a file format that is really only of use to those involved in music-making using electronic instruments and computers.

Changing formats

As far as possible, it is best to avoid the need to convert music from one file format to another. Where a large number of files are involved, converting them all to a different format would be very time consuming, and could be impractically so. Another point to bear in mind is that the result of a conversion is something of an unknown quantity, or perhaps that should be an unknown quality. It will certainly not give an improvement in quality, and is unlikely to fully maintain the quality of the original. It would be reasonable to expect a slight reduction in quality, although the loss of fidelity will often be insignificant in practice.

While taking a file through two or three conversions does not guarantee that there will be a significant loss of quality and other problems, it has to be regarded as asking for trouble. The more a file is messed around, the greater the chance of something going wrong. Dealing with each file can become very longwinded if a lot of processing using two or three programs is required. More than one conversion should be avoided unless there is really no alternative.

Note that it is perfectly all right to decompress a file in a lossless format and then convert it to a highly compressed format. Decompression is not really a conversion, and it restores a perfect copy of the original. The only loss of fidelity will be the normal loss caused by converting the music to a highly compressed format.

When using a media player on a PC it is not usually necessary to convert a file to a format that the player can accommodate. Most players can handle a wide variety of file formats, and in some cases even more formats can be handled with the aid of plug-ins. Many of these plug-in programs are available as free downloads from the Internet. For example, there are plug-ins that enable WMP 10 to play files in the FLAC and OGG formats, and there is an APE plug-in for the popular Winamp player program. Where you have files in a format that is totally incompatible with your normal player it would probably be more practical to switch to a different player for those files instead of trying to convert them to a compatible format.

Burning issues

File conversions can often be avoided when trying to burn music onto CDs. Few file formats can be handled by WMP 10 when burning CDs, but alternatives such as the popular Nero range can accommodate a wider range of formats. Yet more formats can be accommodated with the aid of plug-ins. Some formats seem to evolve slightly over a period of time, so it is advisable to do some searching on the Internet to ensure that any plug-ins you use are the most up-to-date versions available. If you get error messages when using a plug-in it is likely that it is an older version than the one used to create the source files. Installing the latest version of the plug-in should cure the problem. If not, it is likely that the source files have been corrupted and are unusable.

File conversions are most likely to be needed because files are downloaded from the Internet in a format that is not compatible with your hardware player. Most portable players are only compatible with a very limited range of file formats. In fact many MP3 players are strictly that, and can not play any other format. There will probably be restrictions on the types of MP3 file that can be played, with those having high bit rates or variable bit rate files being unplayable. If you play an MP3 file and it is too fast and (or) intermittent, it is a fair bet that it has a bit rate that is too high for the player.

If you are paying for downloaded files it is important to make sure that they are in a file format that is fully compatible with your player. Many of the files that these sites provide are in some form of protected format. This means that it would probably not be possible to convert them to another format, and that it would almost certainly be outside the licensing conditions if you did find a way of making the conversion.

Sometimes files are offered in two formats, one of which is protected and one that can be burned to a CD, used on an MP3 player, or whatever. The version with fewer restrictions will usually cost more, and might only be available as a complete CD with no individual tracks available. Unfortunately, unrestricted files tend to cost a lot more than the protected versions, and in some cases it is actually cheaper to buy the CD. It is important to understand exactly what you are getting before paying for any music downloads. The chances of getting a refund are not good if you successfully download files that you can not use.

Files made available for no charge might be in a form that most players can handle such as MP3 or WMA, but many are not. The free downloads are mostly provided by bands, individual artists, and even full symphony orchestras trying to obtain some cheap publicity. They will probably wish to avoid the hassle and costs associated with proprietary file formats, and often opt for APE, FLAC, or OGG files. Apart from OGG, there is little chance of a portable player being able to handle these formats, and you are quite likely to be out of luck with OGG.

Many media player programs can use plug-ins that expand their repertoire of compatible file formats, but there is no equivalent to this for hardware players. It is possible that there will be a firmware upgrade available for your player, and that this will expand its capabilities. Unfortunately, it is unlikely to give an increase in the supported file formats. In order to play these formats, or any of the other less common ones, it is usually necessary to convert them to something more suitable such as MP3 files.

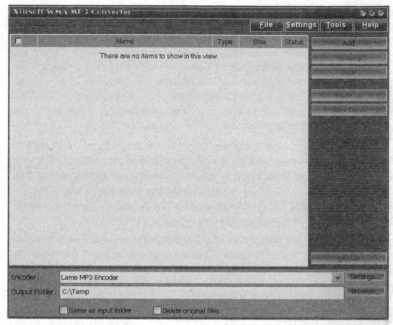

Fig.1.4 The opening screen of the Xilisoft WMA MP3 Converter

It has to be pointed out here that the fact that you can download something free of charge does not necessarily mean that you can use it in any way that takes your fancy. The copyright in the recording is usually retained by the artist or artists who produced the recording. There will usually be a ban on selling copies of it in any form, and making non-commercial copies might not be permitted either. There could also be restrictions on copying that effectively make it illegal to convert the file into a suitable format for a hardware player and upload it to the player. In effect, you can download the file to your PC and play it using a suitable media player program, but anything beyond this is not permitted. If the licensing conditions are too restrictive you have to give serious thought as to whether it is worthwhile downloading the file.

Converting

In general, media player programs do not have much ability to convert files from one format to another. Plug-ins that enable them to play a

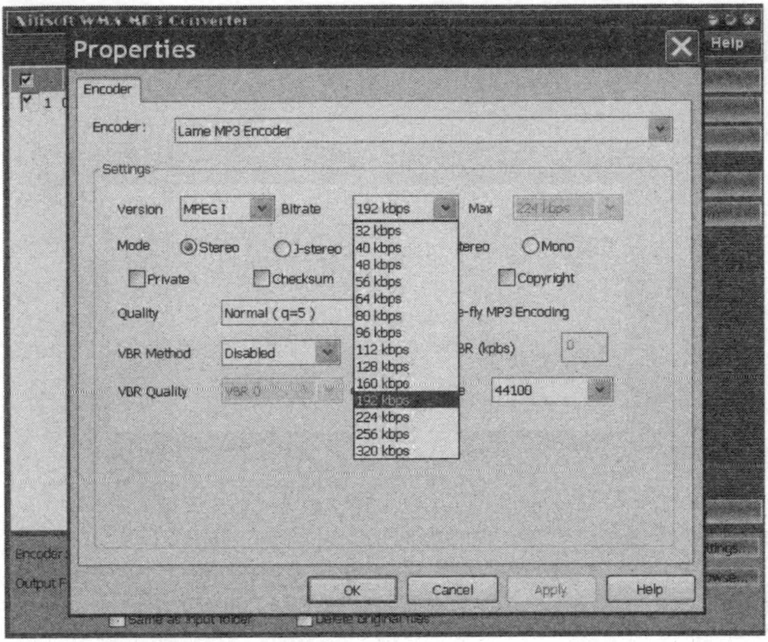

Fig.1.5 A full range of bit rates is available

greater range of file formats do not necessarily enable them to do anything else with those formats. In fact it is unusual for these plug-ins to permit anything other than the files to be played. You might even find that some of the more advanced facilities of the program do not function when using some plug-ins.

CD burning programs do not offer file conversion as such, but by burning the file to a CD it is converted into a form that is easily tured into MP3 and other formats. This is a rather slow and cumbersome way of handling things though, and it involves burning a CD that will probably be of no further use once the conversion has been made. This method is something that is best avoided unless desperation sets in.

The easy way to convert files from one format to another is to use a special audio file conversion program, and plenty of these are available on the Internet. Unfortunately, there seems to be a lack of free programs of this type that are easy to use and work well. Many of these programs are shareware though, so you can try them and ascertain that they work properly before handing over any money. I would definitely advise testing

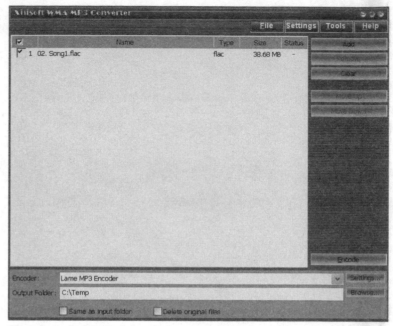

Fig.1.6 An FLAC file is loaded and ready for conversion

any form of file conversion program before buying it, since this type of software is not really known for its technical excellence and reliability. It is not aided in this respect by the occasional tweaking of some file formats.

The Xilisoft WMA MP3 Converter (www.xilisoft.com) is one of the better known file conversion programs, and despite its name it does actually handle a wide range of input formats including MP4, APE, FLAC, and OGG. However, it will only convert these to various versions of WMA and MP3. Figure 1.4 shows the opening screen of this program. There are some options available at the bottom of the screen where you can choose the encoder that will be used, the destination folder for the converted files, and whether the original file should be deleted. It is not a good idea to delete the original file until you are sure that the converted version fully meets your requirements. You might not have selected the correct settings, or the computer could glitch during the conversion. Therefore, it is not advisable to accept the option that deletes the original file unless you have a backup copy.

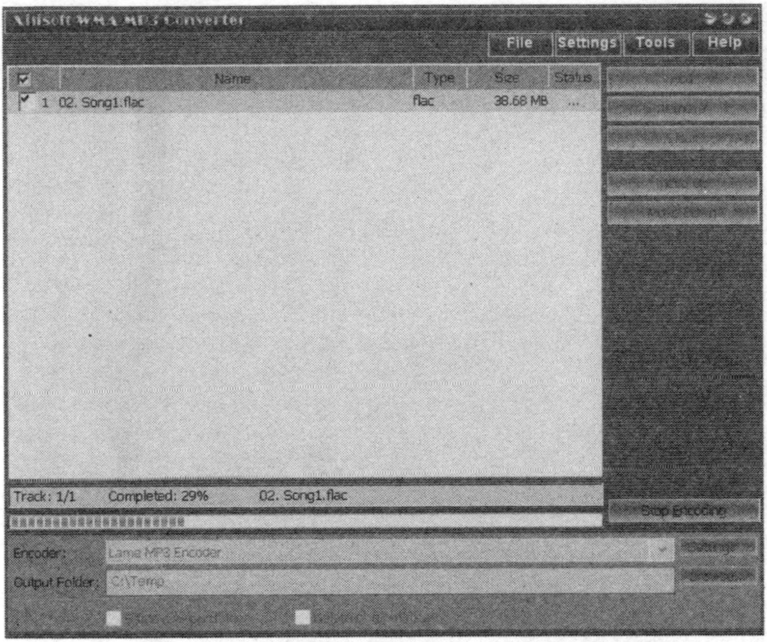

Fig.1.7 A bargraph shows how the conversion is progressing

Selecting Encoder Properties from the Settings menu produces the Properties window of Figure 1.5. Here you can select various options, but in most cases the defaults will be suitable. However, you will have to set the required bit rate and type (constant or variable). Operating the File button produces the usual file browser so that the required source file or files can be selected. In Figure 1.6 a single FLAC format file has been selected and the program is ready to start. Operating the Encode button gets the conversion under way (Figure 1.7), and the process usually takes a matter of seconds for each track.

CUE file

Files in the APE format are often accompanied by a CUE file, which appropriately has "cue" as its file extension. The main (image) file contains all the tracks for an audio CD, and the CUE file tells the burning program how to arrange these tracks on the finished CD. In order to burn the tracks onto a CD it is necessary to have a burning program that

1   Formats and conversions

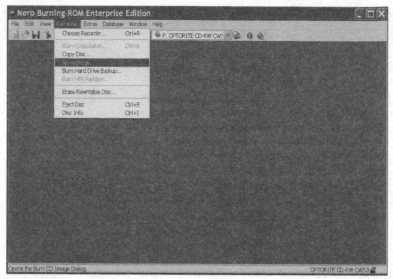

Fig.1.8 Burn Image is selected from the Recorder menu

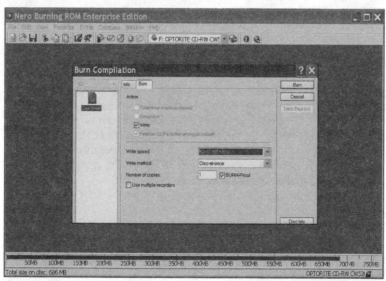

Fig.1.9 With the CUE file selected and processed, the program is
ready to burn the image onto a CD

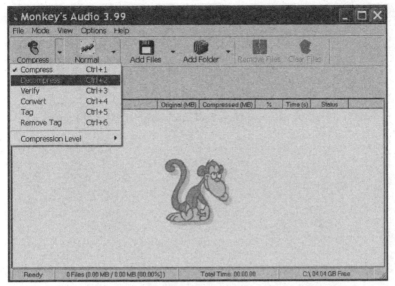

Fig.1.10 *Select Decompress from the menu*

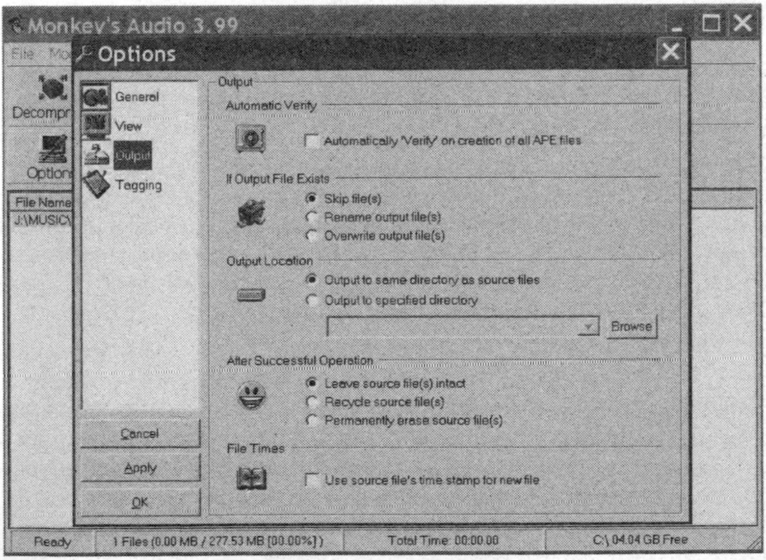

Fig.1.11 *A number of output options are available*

Fig.1.12 An APE image file loaded into the program

can handle APE and CUE files. There is no need to convert the APE file in order to burn it onto a CD. The burning program makes the conversion as part of the burning process.

The popular Nero Burning ROM program can handle APE and CUE files with the aid of a free plug-in. In order to burn a CD it is necessary to choose Burn Image from the Recorder menu (Figure 1.8). The usual file browser then appears and the CUE file is selected, not the image file. Assuming Nero can handle the files properly, a window like the one shown in Figure 1.9 will appear after the program has done some processing. You then burn the CD in the normal way.

Burning the file to CD is not necessarily the way to start if you require something like MP3 files rather than an ordinary audio CD. You can convert the image file direct to MP3 or WMA using a suitable program, or the image can be converted to a Wave file using the Monkey's Audio compression/decompression program. The program must first be set to the Decompression mode using the pop-down menu associated with the button in the top left-hand corner of the window (Figure 1.10). Next

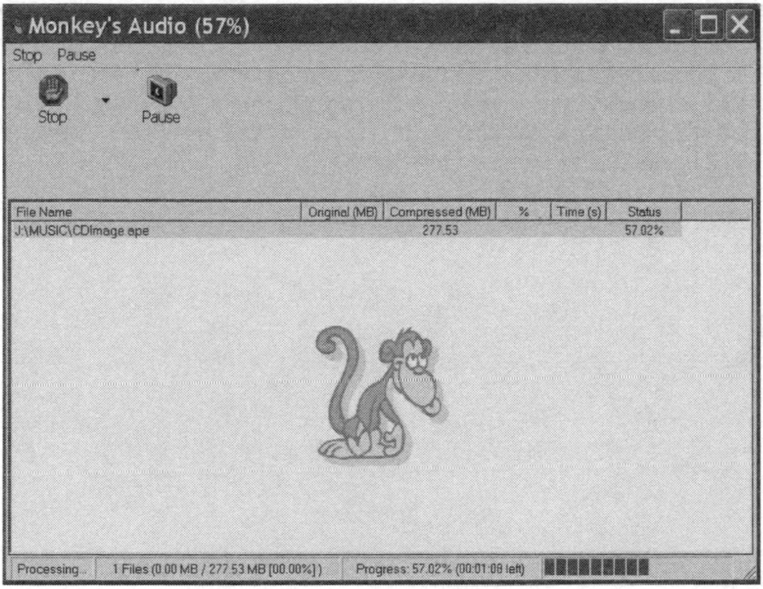

Fig.1.13 The bargraph shows how the decompression is progressing

the required file or files are selected by operating the Add Files button and using the file browser that appears.

By default the program will place each Wave file in the same location as its source file. However, a different location can be selected by operating the Options button and then choosing the Output section (Figure 1.11). The radio buttons and the Browse button in the middle part of the screen enable a different output location to be selected. There are other output options that could be useful, so it is worth looking at each section of this Options window.

With at least one APE file loaded (Figure 1.12) operate the Decompress button. The program will then start decompressing the file, and the usual bargraph will appear in the status bar at the bottom of the window to show how things are progressing. Eventually the program should report that the file has been decompressed, and the Wave file is in the appropriate location.

One slight drawback of producing a Wave file from a multi-track APE file is that the tracks are merged into a single and huge file. This is not a problem if you wish to play the file from beginning to end, but it makes it impossible to jump to any desired track. There is just one big file with no tracks to jump to. The way around this is to burn a CD from the CUE and APE image files, and then rip the CD to produce the MP3 tracks, WAV tracks, or whatever. This is a slightly cumbersome way of doing things, but it will provide the desired result. It also makes it possible to convert only selected tracks instead of the whole lot.

Points to remember

Although MP3 players are not the first portable digital audio players, they are in many ways a more practical proposition than the CD and Mini Disc players that preceded them. They can be made much smaller and lighter than the earlier types of portable player, and they are inherently jog-proof. They can be used while running or exercising without having to worry about problems with the player jumping tracks.

Modern portable players connect to the computer via a USB or FireWire port. These are mainly associated with PCs and Mac computers respectively, but many Macs have USB ports and a fair percentage of PCs have FireWire ports. USB 2.0 and FireWire are many times faster than USB 1.1 ports, but in some cases it is the speed of the memory in the player that is the limiting factor.

Superb audio quality is provided by the system of 16-bit digital audio used for CDs. Unfortunately, it takes a huge amount of storage capacity to accommodate the music on one full CD. In fact it takes about 600 to 700 megabytes of storage space, which is much greater than the memory capacity of many MP3 players. Compression techniques are used in order to get more music into the limited amount of storage capacity available on most MP3 players.

There are two types of compression, one of which is the lossless variety. This does not give any loss of sound quality, but it does not give a very high degree of compression either. With lossless compression it is typically possible to get about three times the playing time from a given amount of memory. Lossless compression is not used a great deal with MP3 players, but it is a practical proposition with players that have high capacity hard disc drives.

The other type of compression does involve some loss of quality, but a high level of sound quality can be achieved provided the compression is not taken to excess. The MP3 file format uses this type of compression and can produce a significant loss of sound quality if inappropriate parameters are used. The advantage of "lossy" compression is that it can provide greatly reduced file sizes while still providing acceptable results. The playing time for a given amount of memory can be extended by a factor of about 10 to 20 times.

MP3 is not the only digital audio file format in common use. There are various formats that do not use compression, others that use lossless compression, and some that use "lossy" compression. Many of these are not of any practical importance to users of hardware players and media player programs, but there are several formats that are. These include MP3, MP4/AAC, OGG Vorbis, FLAC, APE, and WMA. There are a number of versions and variations associated with many of these formats.

Sometimes it is only possible to play a file on a portable player if it is first converted from its original file format to one that is compatible with the player. Try to avoid multiple conversions where the conversion from one format to the other is via one or more intermediate formats. Each conversion increases the risk of a noticeable loss of sound quality or something going drastically wrong.

Downloading music

Free downloads

One way of obtaining music to play on a PC or a portable player is to use a CD as the source. Licensing conditions permitting, the music can be ripped and converted into a format that is suitable for your portable player and media player program. In practice it is highly unlikely that the licensing conditions will permit this type of activity, but in the real world there is little risk of any company suing someone who has ripped music from a CD that they have obtained legitimately.

Of course, it is not legitimate to rip the music and then sell or give away the CD. Neither is it within the rules to rip the CD and supply one or more copies of the files to other people. A CD and any files ripped from it should only be used by yourself and other members of your household. In other words, the ripped files should only be used by those having access to the CD, and who would otherwise use the CD rather than the ripped files. The ripped files are then used instead of rather than in addition to the CD, which effectively becomes a backup copy of the ripped files.

The alternative way of obtaining files is to download them from the Internet. There are numerous sources of music downloads, and some of these offer the same music that is available on CD. In effect, you are "cutting out the middle man" and buying the ripped files. In some cases you can burn the files onto a CD, but there are often restrictions that place severe limitations on the way in which the files are used.

There are also free downloads available via the Internet, and this is the aspect of file downloading that will be considered first. It has to be pointed out straight away that many of the free music downloads are illegal. The files on offer contain material that is still in copyright and the files are not being supplied by their legitimate owner.

Apart from the fact that it is illegal to download and use these files, it is also "living dangerously". Many of the sites that provide illegal music downloads are using them as bait. Users are being lured to a site where their computer will be bombarded with various viruses, Trojans, and other malicious programs. The owners of the site will then try to extract useful information from your computer such as bank account details and passwords, use it as part of a denial of service (DOS) attack, or use it for other illegal activity. Keep well away from any sites that offer illegal downloads. The freebies on offer could prove to be quite costly, if there are actually any freebies available.

Out of copyright

On the face of it, there can be no music files offered legally on the Internet, because the rights to the music will always be owned by someone. Matters are nothing like as simple as this though. It tends to be assumed that all music is governed by some form of copyright, but this is not actually the case. The rights to the music and lyrics of a song remain the property of the originators of the work (or their successors) for 70 years after the death of the originator. This means that the copyright in a song lasts at least 70 years from when it was written, and in many cases it remains in force for more than a hundred years from when it was produced. Note that the copyright used to last for 50 years after the death of the writer or composer, and it still does if he or she died in 1944 or earlier.

Since the music and the lyrics are often produced by different people, the expiry dates of their copyright will also be different. Some amateur operatic societies were caught out some years ago when they performed Puccini operas that they though were out of copyright. Puccini's music was indeed out of copyright, but the librettos were not. Note that the rules are much the same for all types of work including instrumental pieces, operas, novels, and works of art. Whoever originated the work owns the copyright unless they sell or license it, and someone owns the copyright until 70 years after the death of the originator.

In practice matters tend to be more complicated than this, especially with recorded music and songs. Laws on copyright have been unified to some extent by international agreements, but there can still be differences from one country to another. Indeed, there are still a few countries that do not recognise international copyright. The rules governing sound and video recordings are different to those for the works being performed. The copyright in the performance is entirely separate to that for the work being performed.

The copyright for a record lasts 50 years from when the recording was made. This means that the copyright in the performance has a shorter life than the copyright in the work being performed. A performance is considered to be an interpretation of an existing work rather than something genuinely new, and it is for this reason that it is given a shorter period of copyright. Of course, the copyright in a work might have already expired by the time a recording is made. In that case the copyright in the recording fully expires 50 years after it was produced. In other cases the copyright in the work will expire some time during the 50 year run of the recording. Again, all rights to the recording expire 50 years after it was made. In most cases though, the copyright in the recorded work will remain in force for some time after the recording has gone out of copyright.

Modern and Free?

One implication of this is that the chances of finding a free and legitimate download of a modern pop song are extremely slim. Even if the song is a modern version of a golden oldie, the recording will still be within its 50 year copyright period. Although the song itself may be very old, someone will presumably own the new hit arrangement of it. A site that offers free and legitimate downloads of modern hit songs is almost certain to be an illegal site that is simply lying to you.

The only likely exception is where is a site is running some sort of special. For example, there are sometimes freebies on offer if you sign up to a site that sells music downloads. This normally works on the basis that the owners of the site are paying the royalties on the tracks that you download, and they hope to recoup this money and more when you buy tracks from them further down the line. The freebie tracks you download are free to you, but someone somewhere is still paying for them.

There is some modern music on the Internet that is free to download, but you are unlikely to find the latest mega-band in this category. This type of free download is usually provided by a band or individual artist that is very much in the unknown category and using the Internet in an attempt to gain exposure. The tracks can be offered free of charge because the performers are not claiming copyright in the recording, and neither are the writers of the works that are being performed. In most cases the performers have made their own recordings of their own songs.

This means that they own every aspect of the recordings and can make them freely available if they choose to do so.

No doubt some of these groups and artists are highly talented and will move on to great things, but being realistic about it, most of them will never get beyond giving their work away. Much of this free material is worth what you pay for it, but there are some good tracks on offer. Sorting out the good, from the bad and indifferent could be very time consuming, but many people enjoy going through the material that is on offer.

It is not just pop music that is available as free downloads. Artists in other fields such as classical and jazz try to gain exposure by having web sites that include freely downloadable examples of their work. The classical artists provide performances of works by the great masters such as Mozart and Brahms, which were never covered by copyright as we know it today. Consequently, if they give up the rights to their performances, the recordings can be legitimately made available as free downloads. Artists in other fields have to make sure that they use suitably old material or perform their own works.

Modern composers of all types of music sometimes use the Internet to publicise their works. In some cases there are just short demonstration tracks posted on their sites, but some have made complete performances of large works. A few years ago one classical composer arranged for a recording of his latest concerto to be made, and it was then made available on the Internet as an MP3 file.

Old but not forgotten

A growing list of old recordings is now going fully out of copyright. Recordings have been made for around 100 years now, but the copyright in the recording only lasts 50 years. Many of the works performed in recordings more than 50 years old are still in copyright, but a fair percentage are now in the public domain. The number of old recordings that could be made freely available on the Internet must be vast, and it is growing every day. Surprisingly few of these recordings are actually available on the Internet, which could simply be due to a lack of interest in old monophonic recordings of low technical quality. There could also be a fear of legal action, since it can be difficult to determine whether a recording is still protected to some extent or is fully in the public domain.

Anyway, interest in classic performances of the past is certainly rising, and many old recordings are being released commercially. In fact some of the more choice ones are made available by two or more recording companies. Companies that were blocked from issuing what were originally recordings belonging to another company are free to issue their own version once the copyright has lapsed. Some of the fully out of copyright recordings are now starting to appear on the Internet, and it seems likely that this trend will gather pace. With the earliest stereo recordings now starting to go out of copyright, there could be an upsurge in the availability of these lapsed recordings.

An important point to bear in mind with old recordings that are out of copyright is that any processing of the original recordings will normally introduce new copyright. The technical quality of old recordings is often quite poor, and this is especially so with recordings that exist only as gramophone records. In many cases there was no master recording on tape, and the sound was transferred direct to a master disc. In other cases the tape has been lost or has simply degraded to the point where it is unusable.

Anyway, recording companies often use modern digital processing techniques to "breathe new life" into ancient recordings. Practically all the recordings that are taken from gramophone records have the "cracks" and "pops" removed, and many are given the "full works". With this type of thing the record company holds the copyright in this new version of the recording, which is then subject to much the same restrictions as if it were a brand new recording.

In the world of computer software it is now quite common for the rights in old pieces of software to lapse. This can occur for a number of reasons, but it is usually because the company that owned the rights has ceased to exist and no one else has bought the rights. Some companies and individuals simply abandon the rights to their old software, presumably because it has become more trouble than it is worth, or it is simply deemed to no longer have any worth. There are web sites that specialise in this software, or "abandonware" as it has become know.

There is no real equivalent of this in the music world. Music can become out of date, but there are enthusiasts for every type of music from every period of musical history. Any music that is still in copyright is potentially worth something to its owner, and is unlikely to be abandoned. The opposite situation is far more common, with two or three parties disputing the ownership of old songs. If in doubt as to whether some music is still in copyright it is best to assume that it is. It is likely that at least one party somewhere is claiming the rights in the work.

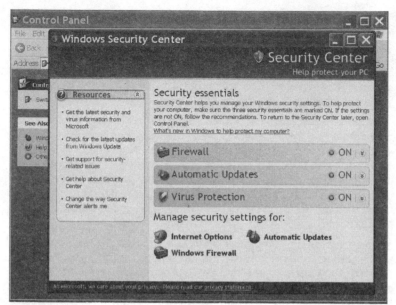

Fig.2.1 The Windows XP Security Center

Security

If you are going to search for free downloads on the Internet it is important that your PC has all the necessary security measures in place. Frankly, if you use the Internet at all it is important to take a series of precautions to protect your computer from malicious programs and various forms of attack. If you go in search of any form of download it is vital to do so. One essential is a firewall, which is a program that, amongst other things, attempts to stop hackers from gaining access to your PC via the Internet.

If you are using Windows XP and you have no additional firewall, make sure that the built-in firewall program is switched on. Go to the Start menu and select the Control Panel option, and then left-click the Security Center icon. This produces the pop-up window of Figure 2.1, which should indicate that the firewall is switched on. If the firewall is turned off, operate the Windows Firewall link near the bottom of the window. Another window will then appear (Figure 2.2), and the firewall can be switched on by activating the "On" radio button.

If you do not already have them, it is also important to install an antivirus program and a program that can deal with spyware and the like. This

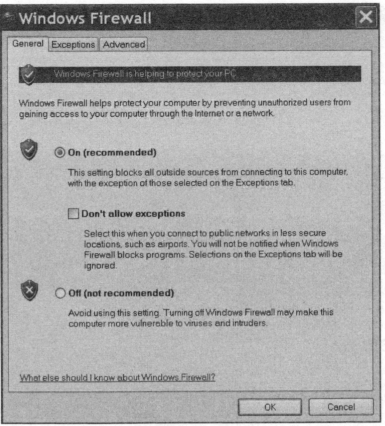

*Fig.2.2 If there is no other firewall, the On button should be active so
that the Windows firewall is switched on*

does not have to cost anything, and the free version of AVG 7.0 (Figure
2.3) is a well respected antivirus program. It is important to keep antivirus
programs up to date, and AVG 7.0 has free daily updates available via
the Internet.   The free version of AVG 7.0 is available from
www.grisoft.com. Ad-Aware Personal SE (Figure 2.4) is a well-respected
program for dealing with spyware. It can be downloaded free of charge
from www.lavasoft.com, and updates to the program's spyware definition
database are also free.

Putting likely search strings into a good Internet search engine should
produce plenty of results, but expect to spend a fair amount of time

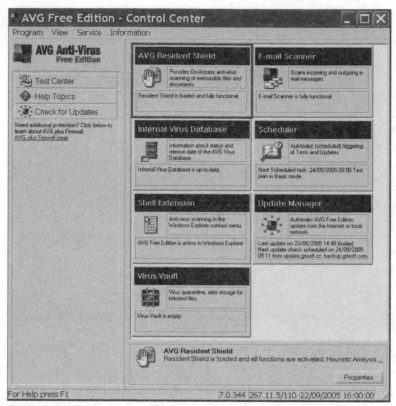

Fig.2.3 The free version of AVG 7.0 has a good range of features

searching through them in order to find some worthwhile sites. Simply using MP3 is unlikely to get you very far, as it tends to produce numerous links to dubious sites that are best avoided. It will probably produce links to commercial sites that sell music downloads, which is fine if that is what you are looking for. Avoid sites that offer unlimited and supposedly legal downloads of every type for a single upfront payment. If they provide anything at all, it is simply access to peer-to-peer networks that are available to everyone free of charge. Many of the files on these networks are actually illegal downloads.

The best search strings for wannabe artists and bands are things like "unsigned artists", "new band", and "independent band". Adding MP3 to the search string might help to give a higher proportion of useful sites,

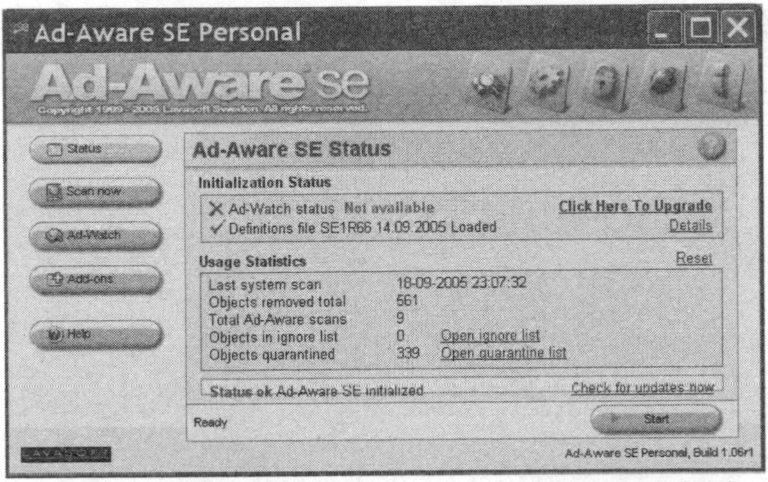

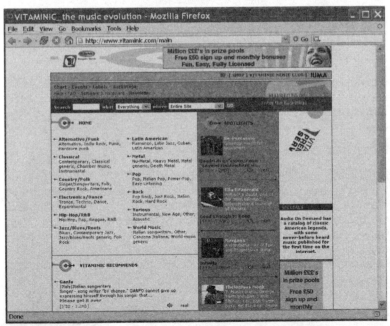

Fig.2.4 Ad-Aware SE Personal is free, but it is a highly regarded anti-spyware program

Fig.2.5 The Vitaminic site offers a wide range of free music

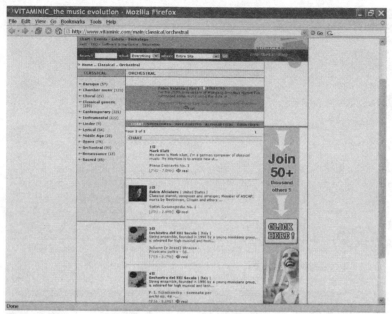

Fig.2.6 The music is divided into categories, with each of these having various subcategories

but with some search engines it can have the opposite effect. In addition to the sites of individual artists and bands, there will be directory sites that list sites that are likely to be of interest.

Popular sites

There are a couple of web sites that are worth investigating if you are looking for free MP3 downloads, and they both have a wide range of downloads. The Vitaminic site (www.vitaminic.com) is well-established site that has numerous music files available, many of which are in the Real Audio format and require the Real Audio Player. On the homepage (Figure 2.5) there are various music categories listed near the top left-hand corner of the page, and operating one of these links leads to a page that offers further choices (Figure 2.6).

The free music downloads section at www.amazon.com is relatively new, but like the Vitaminic site, music in a wide range of categories can be accessed via the homepage (Figure 2.7). They are accessed via the

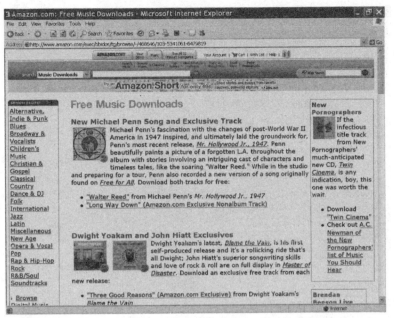

Fig.2.7 Amazon now has a section with free music downloads

links down the left-hand side of the page. Operating one of these links produces a page that provides subcategories and a list of popular choices (Figure 2.8). Operating the link for a file produces a page that gives some technical information such as its size and file format, and there is also a button that can be used to download it (Figure 2.9). Note though, that you must be registered with Amazon in order to access the free download facility. If you are registered with the UK version of Amazon (www.amazon.co.uk) you can use you normal user name and password to sign in.

Assuming that you are using Internet Explorer, operating the Download button will produce a small pop-up window (Figure 2.10) that enables you to open the file or save it to disc. If you operate the Open button the file will be downloaded and then played using the default player for that type of file, which will normally be the Windows Media Player in the case of MP3 files. The usual file browser will appear if you opt to save the file to disc, and you can then select a destination for the file. Either way, the usual bargraph will appear once the download is under way (Figure 2.11).

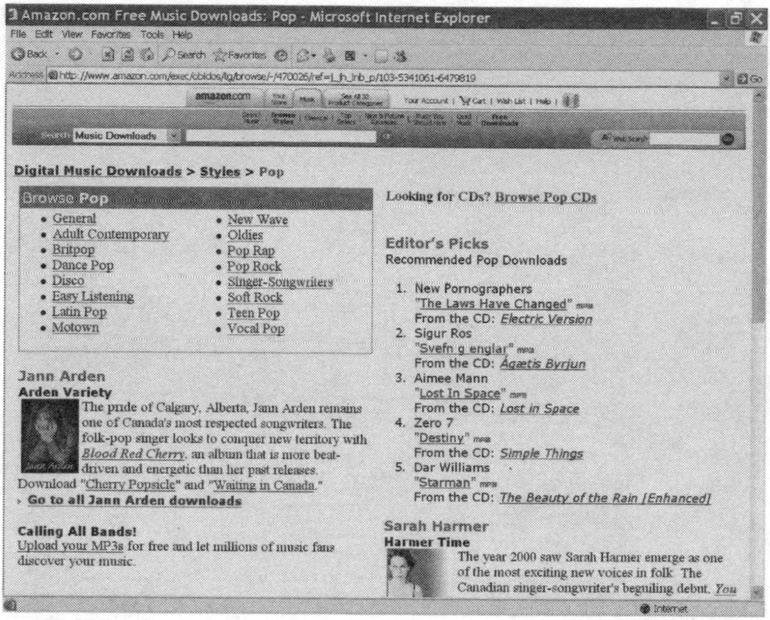

Fig.2.8 Each category has subcategories and "Editor's Picks"

This window also shows the current download rate and the estimated time it will take to complete the download.

Some of the free downloads on the Amazon site are quite short, which renders them of little real use. There are some full tracks, and some quite long tracks are available. It seems likely that an even wider range of music will gradually appear, with longer tracks perhaps becoming the norm rather than the exception.

There are plenty more sites that offer free but legal music downloads, and these are worth investigating:

www.purevolume.com

www.soundclick.com

www.peoplesound.com

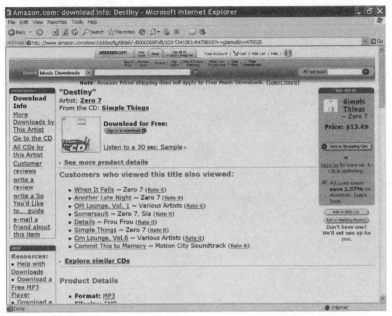

Fig.2.9 Each download has a page that provides some basic details such as the file size

Peer-to-peer

Vast amounts of data are swapped over the Internet using peer-to-peer (P2P) networks. MP3 and using a computer to play music first became big news when the original Napster site was launched. This enabled users to look at the music available on the hard disc drives of other users and download anything that took their fancy. The problem with this system, or any similar system, is that there is no reliable way of preventing users from illegally swapping material that is protected by copyright. After a number of legal wrangles the original Napster was taken over and eventually turned into a site providing legal music downloads. Note that the original site at www.napster.com is only for US residents. However, there is a UK version at www.napster.co.uk.

Napster was an early example of a peer-to-peer network, which is a term used to describe any system that enables users to share each others' data via the Internet. Although the original Napster no longer exists, there are plenty of peer-to-peer file sharing programs available, and some

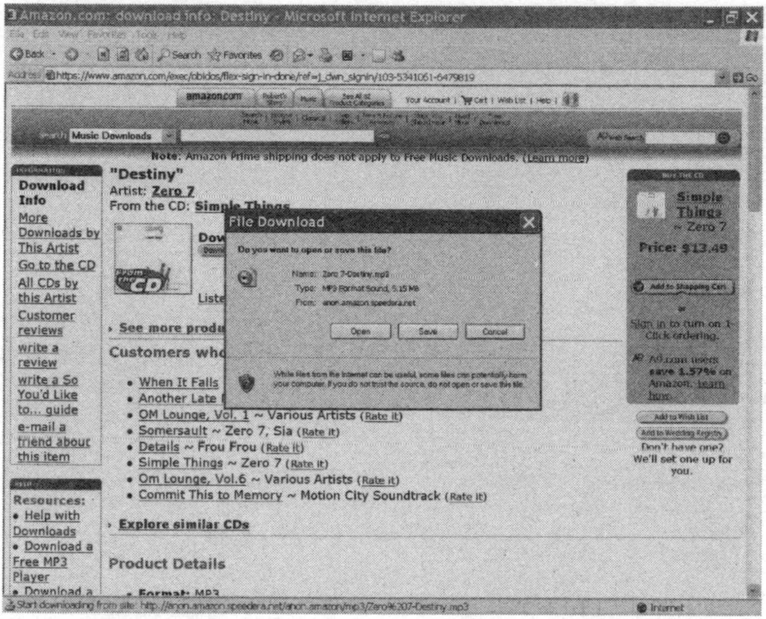

Fig.2.10 Operate the Save button when the pop-up window appears

of them are available as free downloads. The companies behind some of these programs are embroiled in ongoing legal disputes with the recording companies and organisations that represent them. A peer-to-peer program can be used for legitimate file swapping, but it can also be used for illegally swapping material that is still in copyright. This has made peer-to-peer systems something of a "grey area", since they are legal or illegal depending on how they are used.

If you use a peer-to-peer file sharing system it is important to bear in mind that there are potential problems. A substantial amount of the material available on the popular systems seems to be within copyright and downloading it is illegal. Perhaps of greater importance, making this type of thing available for others to download from your computer is also illegal and has resulted in prosecutions in the US and the UK. When using peer-to-peer systems it is important to make sure that you do not download or make available anything that can not be swapped legitimately.

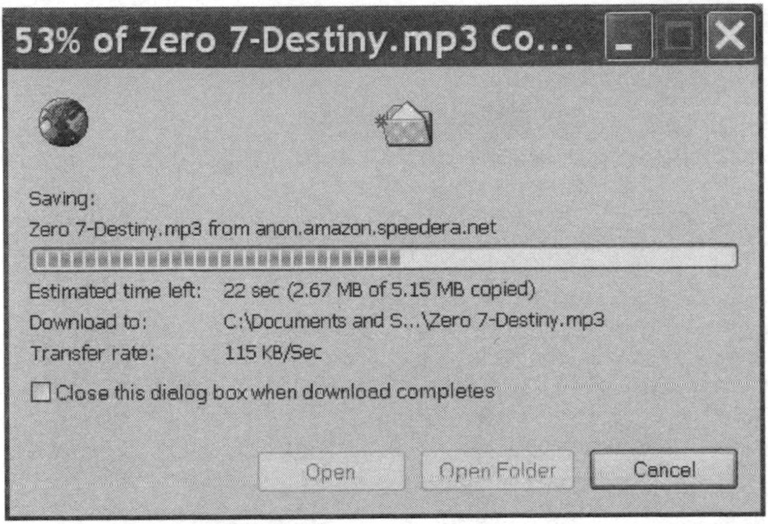

Fig.2.11 The usual bargraph is provided to show how the download is progressing

Downloading files via a peer-to-peer network can be problematic. It is very easy to end up with an incomplete file that can never be fully downloaded or a complete but badly corrupted and useless file. There are plenty of jokers operating on these systems, and one of their tricks is to put files on the system that are not what they are purported to be. Sometimes this is relatively innocent, with the downloaded file actually being a piece of music, a picture, or whatever you were trying to download, but the wrong one. In other cases the downloaded file is pornography, a file that is infected with a virus, a backdoor Trojan, or something of this general type. You need to be on your guard if you use one of these systems, and they are not probably something that newcomers to computing should get involved in.

Torrents

Should you decide to try peer-to-peer systems there are plenty of programs to choose from. Probably the most popular peer-to-peer system at the time of writing this is the Torrent method of file sharing. The original Torrent file sharing program is Bit-Torrent, but there are now others such as Bit-Comet and Bit-Lord. The popular download sites such as www.download.com should have Bit-Torrent and a fair selection

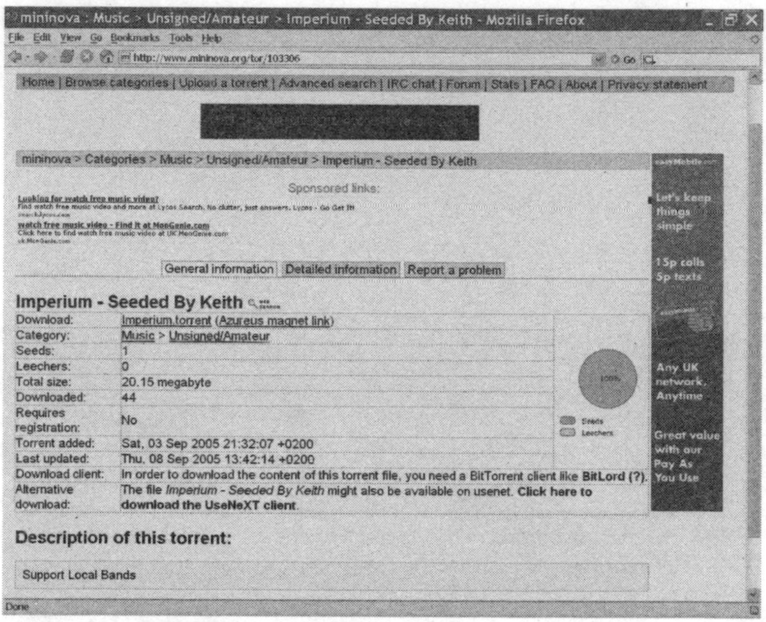

Fig.2.12 *In order to download a file using a program such as Bit-Torrent you must first locate its Torrent file*

of alternatives. Note that the free versions of some peer-to-peer programs are supported by adware. It is therefore advisable to check this point before downloading any of these programs if you are not happy with adware that might, for example, produce pop-ups when you use your web browser or the peer-to-peer client itself.

The Torrent way of doing things is a bit different to most other peer-to-peer systems. It is generally regarded as being more efficient at sharing large files and at avoiding corruption of files. In a music context the files will often be relatively small, but a system that maintains the integrity of the data is clearly advantageous with any type of file. For users, the most obvious difference between a Torrent system and traditional peer-to-peer systems is that there is no built-in search facility. In order to download something using this system you require a Torrent file. This gives the peer-to-peer program the information it needs in order to contact sources of the required material and download it. There are various web sites that have databases of Torrent files, and some of the Torrent programs can access a range of these sites.

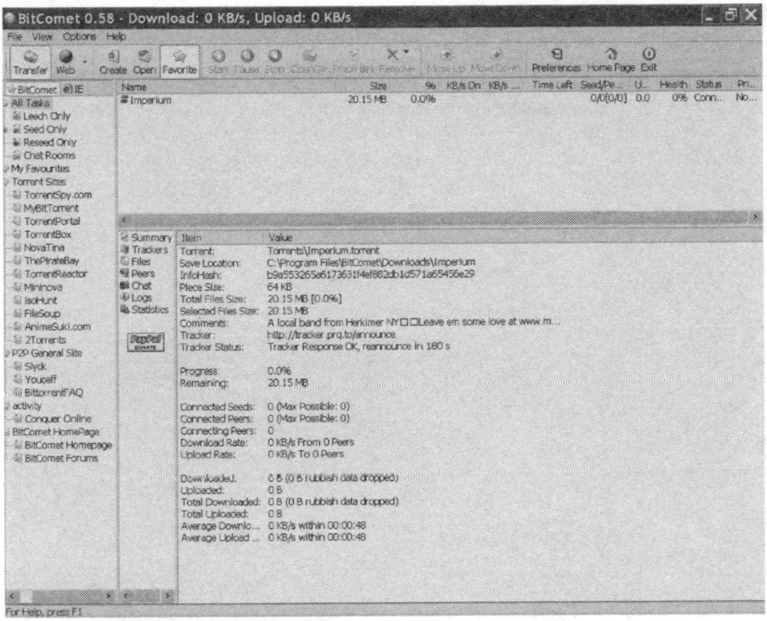

Fig.2.13 The Torrent file has been run and Bit-Comet has been launched. Unfortunately, on this occasion there are no sources for the file

Having located a Torrent file for a music file that looks interesting, it is just a matter of running it. The operating system will then launch the default Torrent application which will then set about downloading the file. In Figure 2.12 I have located a likely looking Torrent file, and left-clicking its link on the web page resulted in it being run in Bit-Comet (Figure 2.13). Unfortunately, the selected Torrent file was quite old, and the requested file failed to download because there were no sources available

This is another way in which the Torrent system differs from some other peer-to-peer systems. With most other methods of file sharing it is only possible to find a file if at least a fragment of it is available on the system. Without all or part of the file in the system there is nothing for the search engine to find. With the Torrent method, the fact that you have located a Torrent file does not mean that the target file is still present on the system and downloadable. Most Torrent sites do their best to remove out of date files, but there will inevitably be a significant percentage of files that are "past their use-by dates".

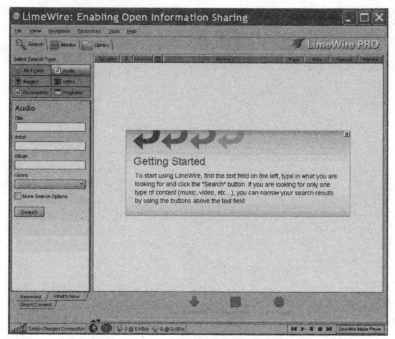

Fig.2.14 *Limewire Pro is a more conventional peer-to-peer program
that has a built-in search facility*

With any peer-to-peer system it might be worthwhile trying again later if
a file either fails to start downloading, or it partially downloads and then
stops. A blockage in the distribution system might have been corrected
by the time you try again, or someone with the missing part of the file
might have joined the system. However, it is a fact of peer-to-peer life
that some files prove to be impossible to download. It is another fact of
peer-to-peer life that many files download only very slowly and
intermittently. It is up to you to decide whether the more awkward files
are worth the time and effort involved in downloading them.

Limewire Pro (Figure 2.14) is a more typical peer-to-peer client that has
a search facility in the left-hand section of the window. Here you can
select the type of file required (audio, video, software, etc.) and add
search strings to help the search engine find suitable files. Any suitable
matches are then listed in the main panel to the right of the search facility

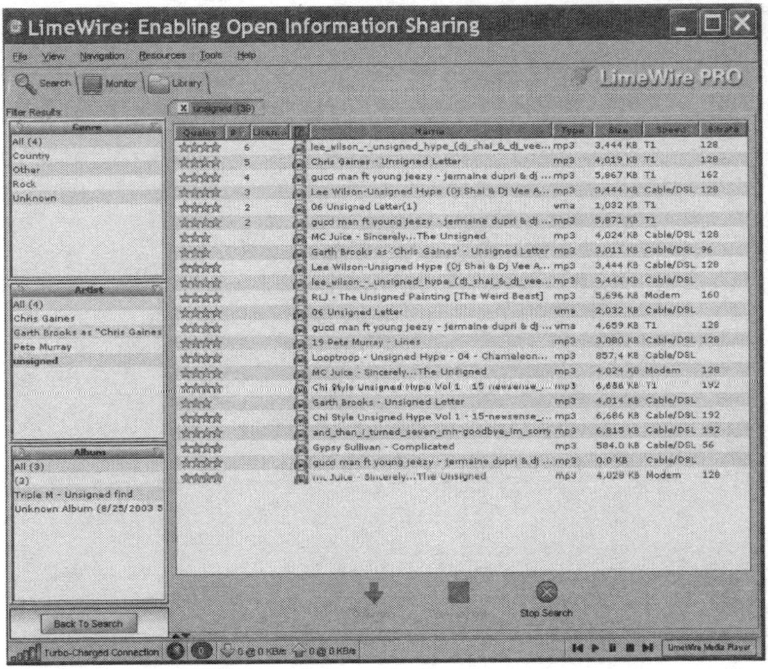

Fig.2.15 The search has produced a list of matching files

(Figure 2.15). To download a file it is just a matter of selecting its entry, operating the Download button, and hoping.

A warning message (Figure 2.16) will be issued if the program can not verify that the file can be downloaded legitimately. This does not necessarily mean that it is not legitimate, and there is the option of continuing with the download anyway. The decision is yours. The bottom section of the window is used for monitoring downloads. It shows the number of sources, the percentage that has been downloaded, the download speed, etc. With luck, before too long it will show that one hundred percent of the file has been downloaded (Figure 2.17).

Paying for downloads

In order to obtain the latest hits it is necessary to go to a pay-site, and one that is run by a reputable company. In fact most of these sites provide

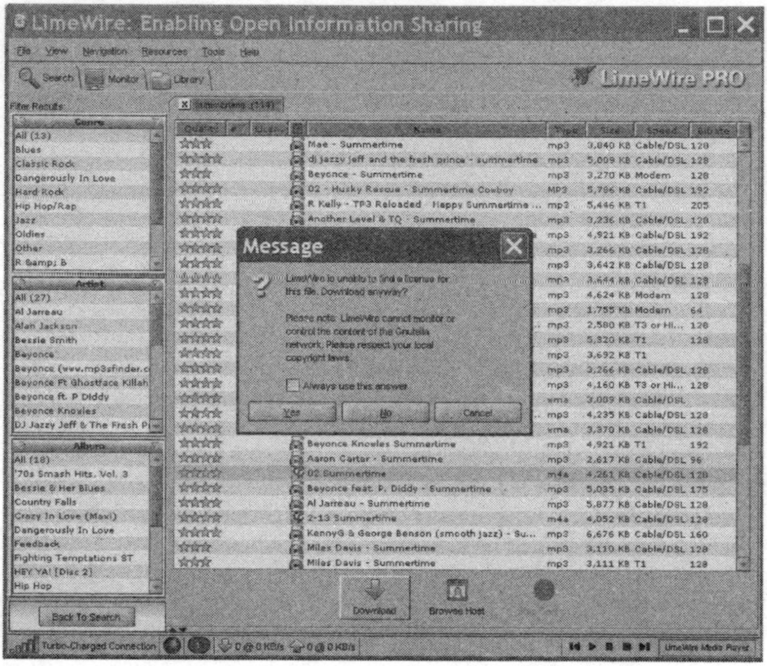

Fig.2.16 *The warning message indicates that no licence has been found for this file*

a lot more than the latest hits. There is usually a wide choice of music including "golden oldie" hits, jazz, classical, world music, and so on. Whatever the type of music you require, it should be possible to find several sites that can sell you legitimate downloads. The range of music on offer via legitimate downloads is growing steadily. Some record companies have made discontinued CDs available on their download sites or via other sites. It is not worthwhile reissuing and promoting these CDs in the normal way due to the high costs involved, but it costs very little to make them available to buy as downloads.

The choice of suitable sites could be more limited if you require tracks from a specific artist. As far as I am aware, there is no single site that can provide downloads from every record company, or even a very high percentage of record companies. Consequently, if you are very specific in your requirements, and you are interested in a number of bands or artists, it will probably be necessary to use the services of two or more music download services.

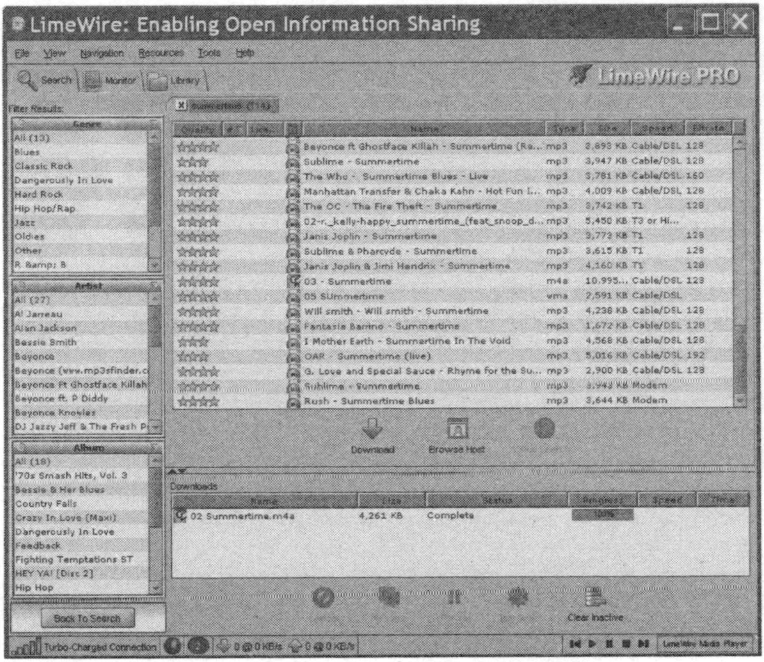

Fig.2.17 The file has been downloaded successfully

When buying music downloads it is important to ensure that you know exactly what you are buying, and that they are suitable for your requirements. First and foremost, is the download in a format that your player can handle? There is no point in buying a file that is in a protected format that your hardware player can not handle. In general, there is no legitimate way of converting a protected file into a format that is compatible with your player.

It is also important to check on the precise nature of any restrictions that limit the way in which downloaded files can be used. Some download services offer a bewildering range of options. Ideally, you should be free to load the file onto your hardware player, burn it onto an audio CD, and use it in any way you like other than supplying copies to other people. In other words, you would be able to use it in much the same way as if you bought the same music from a shop on a CD.

There are download services that provide files that can be used in this way, but the prices tend to be relatively high. Also, selling tracks in this form seems to be going out of fashion. Most downloaded files have some form of protection and attendant restrictions. Competition is helping to tame prices somewhat, and you should no longer find that buying music downloads over the Internet costs more than buying the same music on a CD. On the other hand, the cost saving is often quite small, and in such cases you could reasonably decide that you would be better off paying a little extra to buy the CD.

A point worth bearing in mind is that in most cases you do not have to download complete CDs. With downloaded music it seems to be the norm for music to be sold on the basis of so much per track, possibly with the option of buying the entire CD as well. If you are only interested in a few of the tracks on a CD you can save a fair amount of money by only buying those particular tracks. Note that some tracks will probably cost more than others. As with CDs, you might find that the latest releases cost more than those from some years ago. Also, some tracks only last a couple of minutes while others can last half an hour or more. If you are buying classical music or music from some other genre where tracks tend to be long, expect to pay a relatively high price per track.

Copy protection

With the illegal copying of music taking place on a massive scale it is understandable that the recording companies have taken steps to counteract the problem. It is also understandable that this type of thing is not popular with legitimate users since they tend to find that they are blocked from using the protected material in certain ways. Copy protection is not only encountered with music files, and a form of it has been applied to some CDs. These CDs can not be played on a computer and, therefore, can not be ripped to produce files that can be played on an MP3 player.

In a music download context, the copy protection is based on a technology such as Microsoft's DRM (Digital Rights Management). Technologies of this type operate on the basis that a file will only be played if the player finds a valid licence for it. This is the same whether the player is a hardware device or a program running on a computer. Perhaps of more importance to many users, file conversion programs will not usually work with protected files. It depends on the licence you have, but if you try to convert a protected file you are almost certain to be greeted by an error message pointing out that the program can not process the file as the necessary licence has not been found (Figure 2.18). Trying to burn protected files on an audio CD is likely to be equally unsuccessful.

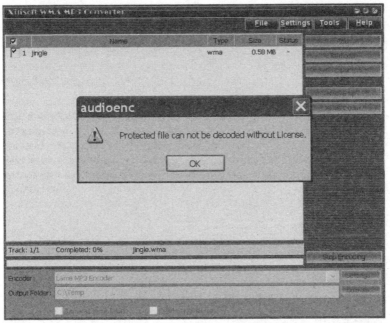

Fig.2.18   Trying to convert a protected file will probably just produce an error message

Copy protection is perhaps not the most apt term in the current context. Copying files to an audio CD is not usually possible, and neither is a conversion to another file format, which is a form of copying. However, normally there is nothing in the protection technology to prevent users from make as many "straight" copies of the files as they like. Doing so is pointless though, because the copies will be unplayable unless they are used with a player that is licensed to handle that particular file. The files are encrypted and can only be decrypted if the appropriate licence is present. Making and distributing copies of protected files is a pointless exercise because the recipients will be unable to use them.

Many of the protected files that you can buy and download use the DRM method of protection and are therefore in the WMA format. A practical consequence of this is that they can only be played on MP3 players that can handle WMA files, which many can not. None of the Apple iPods are compatible with WMA files. Even where an MP3player can handle WMA files, it will not necessarily be able to play any that are protected by DRM technology. They can be played on any PC using the Windows

Media Player program, but going portable with them could prove to be problematic. The Apple iTunes download service uses protected AAC files that are, or course, compatible with iPods and the iTunes program. Unfortunately, apart from iPods, few portable players can handle this format.

In most cases the licensing conditions and protection system do not prevent the downloaded files from being used on more than one machine. The word "machine" in this context means a portable player, a PC running a media player program, or anything that can play the file. Of course, there will be a limit on the number of machines that are covered by your licence, and to be of any real use the licence should cover at least two machines. You can then use the file with (say) a computer and with a portable player.

Backing up

There is a potential problem with a licensing system in that you could find your downloaded music unusable if a fault "zaps" the licence. Where this is allowed, it is important to ensure that licences are properly backed up. Of course, it is essential to make sure that all computer data is properly backed up, and the music files themselves are no exception to this. Some methods of licensing more or less guarantee that you will no longer be able to use the files at some time in the future, but they should still be usable for many years. In fairness, there is no recording medium that is guaranteed to last indefinitely, although it is theoretically possible to extend the life of non-protected digital files indefinitely by periodically copying them to fresh media.

Some download sites provide a sample file that you can download and try with your equipment. It is definitely a good idea to download and experiment with any available files of this type so that you can make sure that any downloads you buy will be fully usable with your equipment. Failing that, there might be some sort of free trial that you can use to check the suitability of the service before you spend any money. If no trial period is available, it will probably be possible to buy a few tracks at low cost and them try them out. Are the files of a type that your player can handle, and are they recorded at a compatible bit rate? If the bit rate is too high, is it possible to convert them to a lower rate or are you blocked by the protection system. You certainly need to confirm the suitability of the files supplied by the download service before parting with significant sums of money.

Music hire

There is a recent trend towards what is effectively the hiring of music via downloads. The basic idea is that you have access to a huge library of music tracks that you can download and play. Rather than paying a certain amount per track, you pay a monthly fee. With some sites that charge a monthly fee you can only download a certain number of tracks per month, but the new idea is to permit unlimited downloads per month. This sounds too good to be true, and it is. The music tracks you download are protected and are only usable if you have valid licence to use them. The licences will remain valid provided you keep paying the monthly subscription fee. If your subscription lapses, so do your licences, and the downloaded tracks become unusable.

This way of doing things has its advantages and drawbacks. The main advantage is that you have instant access to a huge library of music that would cost a fortune to buy. There is no need to spend substantial sums of money over a period time as you build up a library of CDs. The obvious drawback is that you are effectively left with nothing if you let the subscription lapse. You only have a huge library of music while you keep paying the monthly fee. This is fine provided the subscription is set at a reasonable price. You could otherwise be left in the position where the money spent over a period of years would have been sufficient to build up a massive library of CDs. The CDs would represent then represent a much better deal in the long term. In order to be worthwhile this type of service must also provide the vast majority of the music you require. It would be a bit pointless if you end up going to other providers for many of the tracks you need.

The fact that there are a number of companies providing different types of music download service makes things a bit confusing, but it does mean that there is a good chance of finding at least one that is well suited to your requirements. However, it might take a fair amount of searching, reading of "fine print", and experimenting with some downloaded files to check their suitability. Probably the best advice is not to reach for the credit card at the first download service you find. Look carefully at a range of services and if possible try them out before you actually pay for anything.

Buying and downloading

The exact method used when buying and downloading music files varies significantly from one company to another. The example provided here

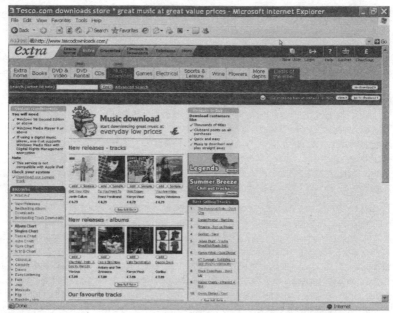

Fig.2.19 *The Tesco download shop has music in various categories*

is representative of the way in which it is done, but buying tracks from other companies will inevitably be different in a least a few points of detail. With most suppliers you buy the tracks in much the same way as you buy anything else online. This is certainly the case with the Tesco's music download service (www.tescodownloads.com). There are various music categories to choose from on the homepage (Figure 2.19). You browse the available goods and having found something you wish to buy it is just a matter of operating a button in order to add it to your virtual shopping basket (Figure 2.20).

Having ordered everything you require (or can afford) it is then a matter of going through the checkout system. Here you will normally have to supply an email address and a telephone number so that you can be contacted if there is a problem with the order. In some cases it is necessary to register with the company before you place an order. This can save time on each occasion you place an order since the company will already have some of your details on record. Some users are not happy with this type of thing and consider it to be an invasion of privacy. Registering is optional with the Tesco site. Having completed the

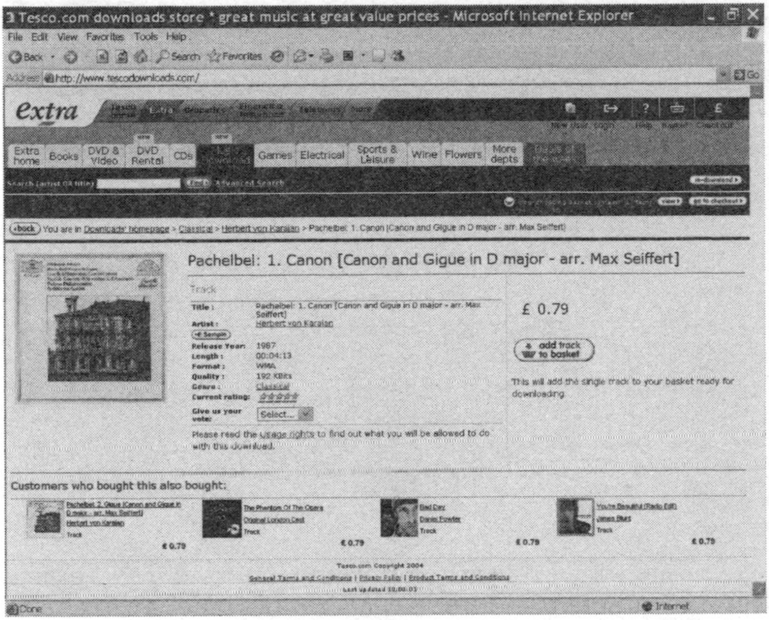

Fig.2.20 *Having decided to buy a track or CD it is just a matter of operating the button to add it to the virtual shopping basket*

preliminaries, it is then a matter of paying for the downloads using a credit or debit card.

These days many sites use the service of a company that handles online payments, and these services are mainly provided by the large banks. The idea is that because the deal is handled via an intermediary, the company you are buying from does not have access to your card details. This is

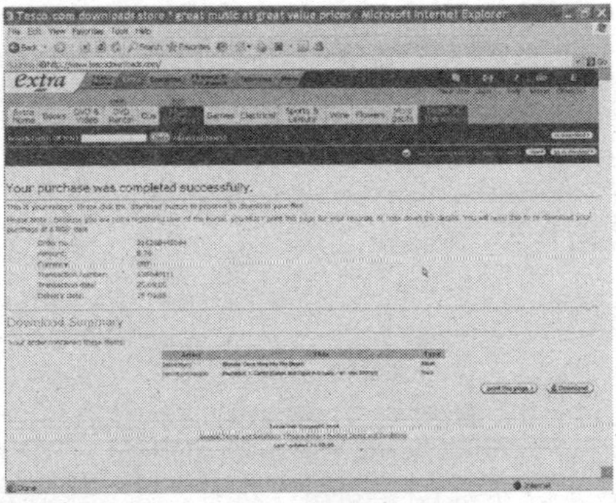

Fig.2.21 *The order confirmation page*

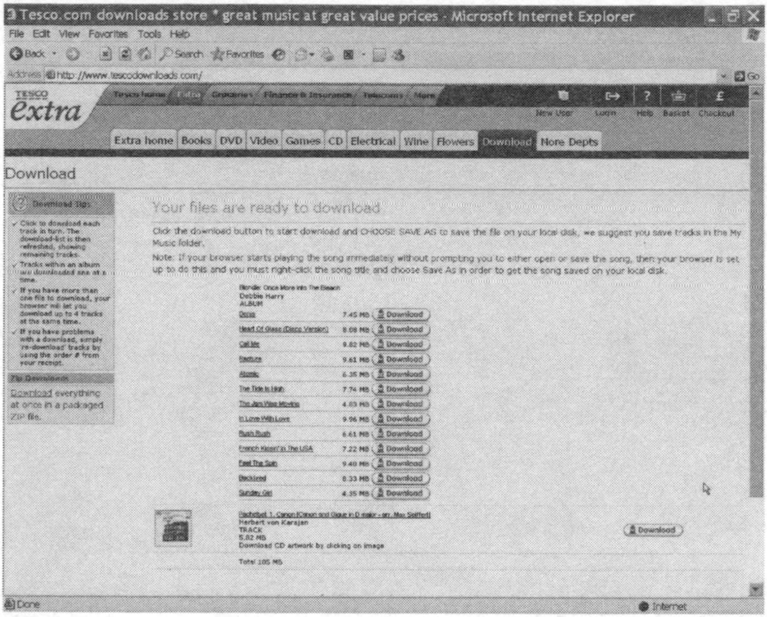

Fig.2.22   There is a separate Download button for each track

not really of any significance when buying from a household name like Tesco, which is presumably at least as trustworthy as one of the large banks.   On the other hand, it can give peace of mind if you are buying from a company that you are not familiar with.

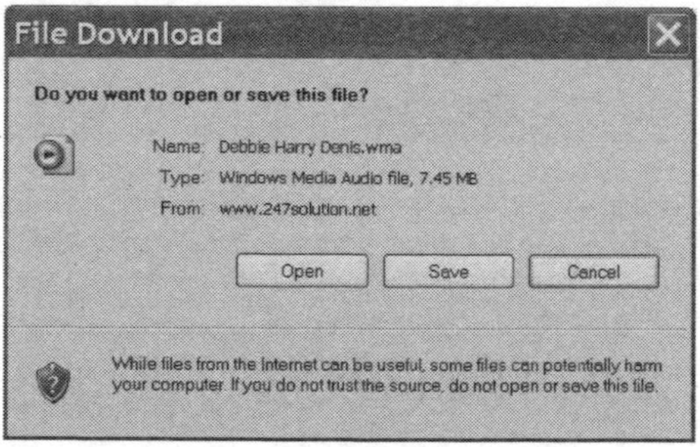

Fig.2.23   Operate the Save button in the pop-up window

Having completed the ordering and payment processes, a page confirming the order appears (Figure 2.21).   Operating the Download button moves things on to the next page (Figure 2.22) where you can actually start downloading the files.

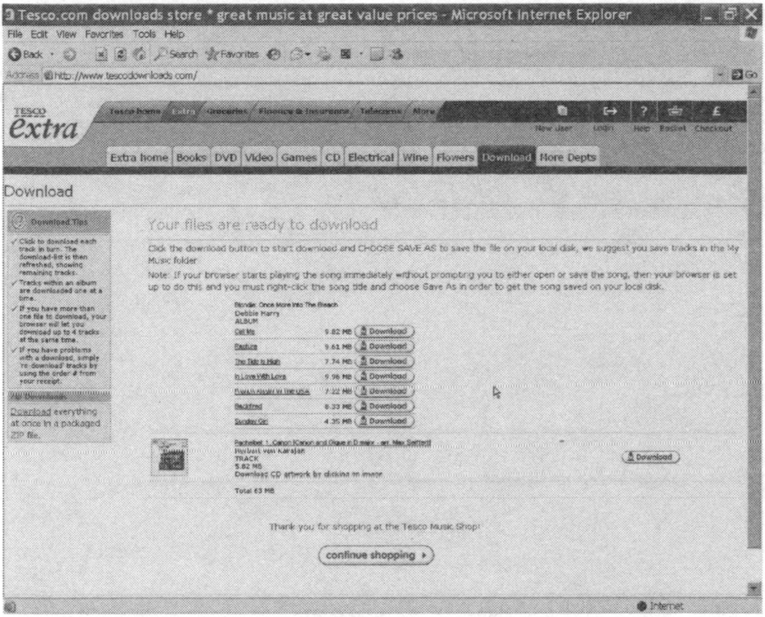

Fig.2.24 As each track is downloaded, its button and entry in the list
are removed

In this case it is necessary to download everything track by track, which
is the way most music download systems operate. There are fourteen
tracks to download plus the CD artwork for one of the tracks. It may
seem slightly strange that there is the accompanying artwork for a single
track, whereas the complete CD of 13 tracks is not supplied with any at
all. Whether you get any CD cover designs, notes, etc., seems to depend
on the policy of the particular record company concerned rather than
the number of tracks purchased.

Operating one of the download buttons produces the usual pop-up
window (Figure 2.23) where you can opt to open or save the file to disc
once it has been downloaded. Left-click the Save button and then use
the browser to select a destination folder. The obvious destination is the
My Music subfolder that is placed in the My Documents folder when
Windows is installed, but you can select any folder. Many users like to
have a folder specifically for newly downloaded files so that it is easy to
check that everything has been downloaded correctly. The files can be
moved to their proper destination once it has been established that they
are all present and correct.

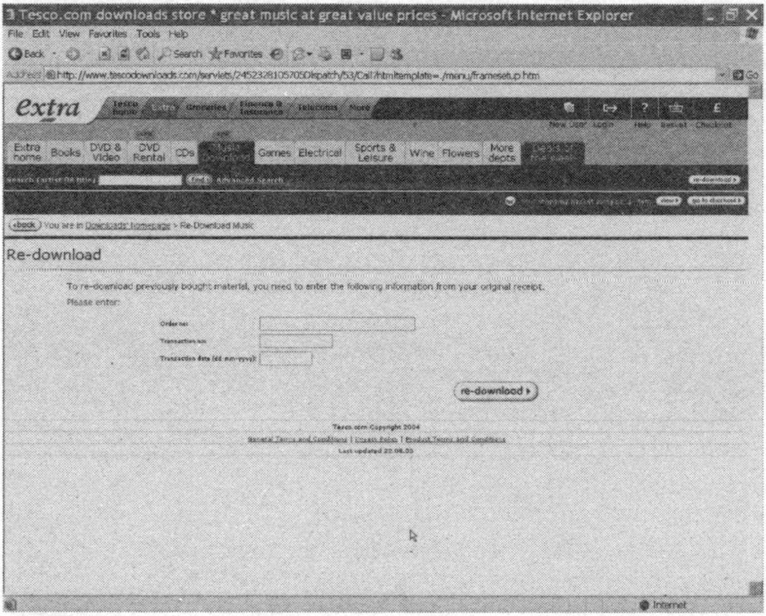

Fig.2.25 *Providing the requested information enables the download page to be accessed again*

As files are downloaded they are removed from the list so that you do not waste time trying to download a file that you already have (Figure 2.24). Eventually you should end up with everything on the computer's hard disc drive, and a page that has no Download buttons left. Things can go wrong though, and with big downloading tasks they often do. In this case the download page failed to refresh properly after about ten of the files had been downloaded. The Tesco solution to this problem is to go to the homepage and operate the Re-download link. This produces the page of Figure 2.25 where you have to supply some details from the receipt that is emailed to you when the order is placed. Operating the Re-download button then takes you to a rebuilt version of the original download page where any of the files can be downloaded.

Archive file

The Tesco download page does actually provide a link to an alternative download page where the tracks can be downloaded as a single Zip file.

The downloaded file must be processed using a suitable decompression program such as WinZip, which will extract the individual files from the Zip archive. For those using an ordinary dial-up Internet connection it is probably better to opt for downloading the files one by one. Downloading huge files via a dial-up

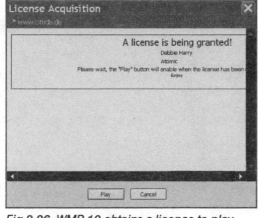

Fig.2.26 WMP 10 obtains a licence to play the file

Fig.2.27 In order to find licence information, right-click on the file's entry and select Properties from the pop-up menu

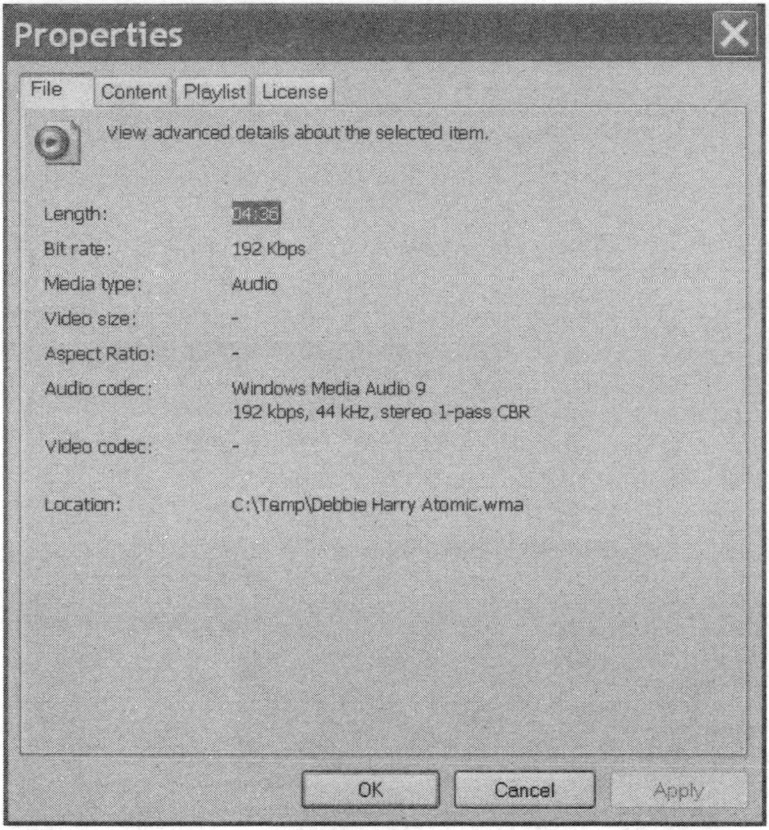

Properties   ☒

| File | Content | Playlist | License |

View advanced details about the selected item.

Length: 14:36
Bit rate: 192 Kbps
Media type: Audio
Video size: -
Aspect Ratio: -
Audio codec: Windows Media Audio 9
                 192 kbps, 44 kHz, stereo 1-pass CBR
Video codec: -

Location: C:\Temp\Debbie Harry Atomic.wma

| OK | Cancel | Apply |

Fig.2.28 The File section provides some basic information about the file

connection tends to be problematic, and a number of smaller files are usually an easier option. Do not get carried away and order dozens of files if you are using a slow Internet connection. It could take days to download them! With a broadband connection a single Zip file is probably the more practical option, since large files usually download without any problems.

In theory, the download time can be reduced by opting for individual files and downloading several at once. Not all sites permit more than one file at a time to be downloaded, and your web browser will probably set a limit of four files. In practice it is by no means certain that using

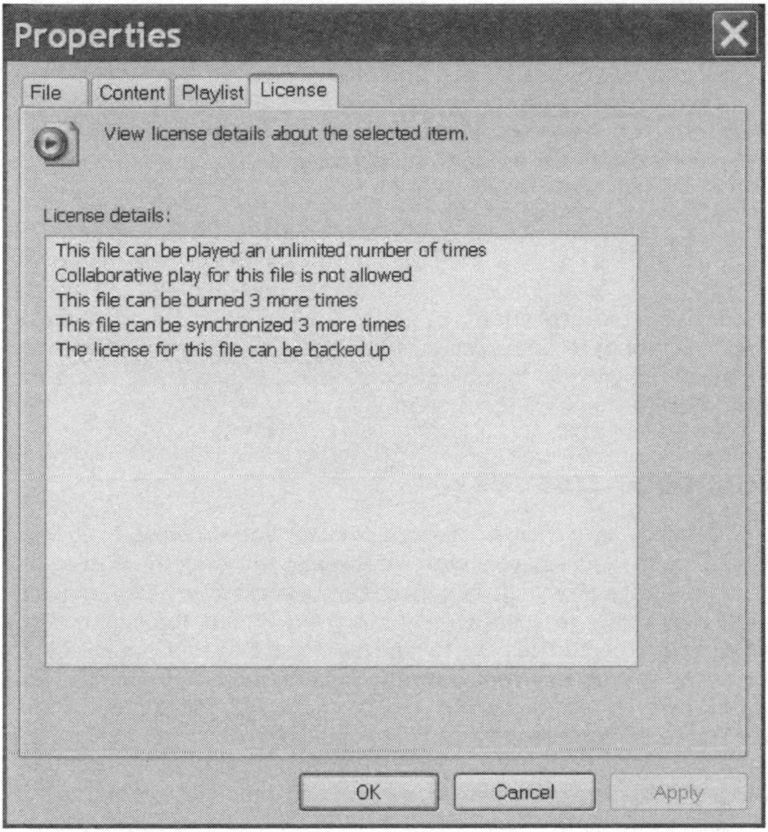

Fig.2.29 The License section gives a list of all the licence conditions

multiple threads will substantially reduce the download time. Most of the companies that sell music via downloads have high-speed servers that will supply data close to the maximum rate that your Internet connection can handle. However, it might be worth trying a few simultaneous downloads if the speed obtained with a single file seems to be well below the maximum rate that your connection can handle.

Playing

Having downloaded the files, trying to play one using WMP 10 produced the pop-up window of Figure 2.26. The file is a WMA type that has DRM protection, and WMP 10 is obtaining the necessary licence to decrypt and play it. Note that this only happens the first time the file is played. Once obtained, the licence is stored on the hard disc drive so that there is no need for the player program to go online and obtain it again. The Play button becomes active once the licence has been obtained, and operating it closes the window and plays the file.

The restrictions on the use of files are not always made crystal clear when you buy them. It is easy to check on the restrictions from within WMP 10, and the first step is to right-click on the file's entry in the playlist (Figure 2.27). Selecting Properties from the pop-up menu produces a window like the one shown in Figure 2.28. This gives some basic information about the file such as its bit rate. Operating the License tab changes the window to look something like Figure 2.29, where the restrictions on the file's use are listed.

Analogue sources

If you already have a large collection of music you will presumably wish to use it with media players and portable players rather than taking the alternative route of buying it all again! Ripping tracks from CDs to produce audio files is very easy, since practically every PC has some form of CD ROM drive. This can be used to read the digital data from audio CDs so that it can be processed and converted into the required file format. You do not even have to buy any conversion software. Ripping audio CDs can be carried out very successfully using free software such as the Windows Media Player that is part of Windows, and Apple's free iTunes program. Ripping audio CDs is covered in chapters 3 and 4 and will not be considered further here.

In order to convert music from non-digital sources into digital audio files the music must be fed into the PC's audio card as an ordinary audio signal. The computer's soundcard then converts it into a series of corresponding values which software can convert into a standard file format. There will inevitably be a slight loss of quality, compared to the original analogue recording, but this loss will usually be too small to be of significance. The main problem with this method is that it has to be done in real-time. In other words, it will take an hour to digitise and convert each hour of music. When ripping CDs the process is much faster, because a modern CD-ROM drive can read the data from the disc at a very high rate. Digitising an hour of music typically takes just a few minutes.

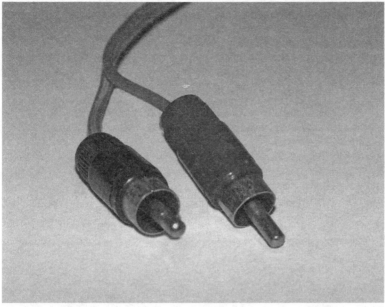

Fig.2.30 The lead will normally need two phono plugs at the end which connects to the amplifier

One way of getting analogue music into the computer is to connect a microphone to the relevant inputs of the computer and use them to record the sound from the loudspeakers of the hi-fi system. While some people do the recording this way, it is not really a method that can be recommended. There is some loss of quality through the loudspeakers, and a further loss of quality is produced by the microphones. Also, any sounds in the room or coming in from outside will be picked up by the microphones. This system will work, but not well enough to satisfy some people.

Much better results are obtained by feeding the audio signal direct into an audio input of the soundcard. Cassette and tape decks usually give good results if they are connected direct to the Line Input socket of a computer. Record decks are more difficult, since they provide output levels that are too low to drive the Line Input. Another problem is that they require equalisation. In order to give the correct frequency response the signal must be given a reduction in treble and some bass boost.

Fig.2.31 There are typically three audio connectors on a PC

One way of handling things is to use a preamplifier between the record deck and the Line Input socket of the computer. There are programs designed specifically for producing audio files from vinyl records, and some of these are supplied complete with a suitable preamplifier. In most cases though, it has to be bought separately. Some preamplifiers now use a USB port and do not require the computer's soundcard at all. Yet another variation is for the record deck to be connected direct to an audio input of the computer, with the software providing the equalisation via some digital signal processing (DSP). Before buying anything you have to make quite sure that you know what you are getting, and that the hardware and software is fully compatible.

Where the hi-fi system has an auxiliary (Aux) output it is usually possible to dispense with a separate preamplifier. To make the connections from the hi-fi system to the computer usually requires a lead having a stereo 3.5 millimetre stereo plug at the computer end, and two phono plugs (Figure 2.30) at the hi-fi end. A lead of the same type is also suitable for

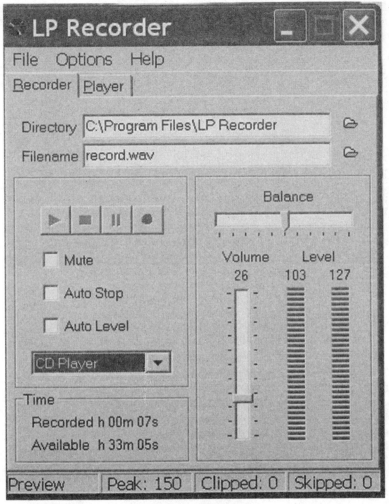

Fig.2.32 LP Recorder is straightforward to use

connecting most cassette decks to a computer. Incidentally, the 3.5 millimetre jack plug can be connected to the headphone output of an MP3 player and the phono plugs can be connected to a spare input on the amplifier. The player can then be used with the hi-fi system. There is usually a line of three audio sockets at the rear of a PC (Figure 2.31),

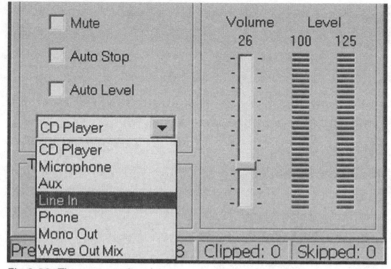

Fig.2.33 The correct signal source must be selected

with possibly another set of two or three if the computer supports some sort of surround sound system. The Line Input socket is colour coded light blue, so it should be easy enough to identify.

Windows does actually have a built-in sound recording facility, but it is not really adequate for making high quality digital recordings. If you obtain a preamplifier and recording software package, the supplied program should be able to handle high quality recording. In fact it will probably have an impressive range of features. When buying the recording software separately you have a vast choice. While a top of the range recording program will be very capable, it is unlikely to be easy to use. Initially it is probably best to opt for something relatively basic.

Figure 2.32 shows the LP Recorder program, which is very easy to use. It has tape recorder style controls for record, stop, etc., plus a recording level control. There is the option of using an automatic recording level facility. This ensures that the recording level is not set so high that distortion occurs on loud passages, but it can reduce the dynamic range of the signal. In other words, the loud bits are less loud than they should be, or the quiet bits are not as quiet as they should be, or a combination of the two. Results are generally better if the recording level is set

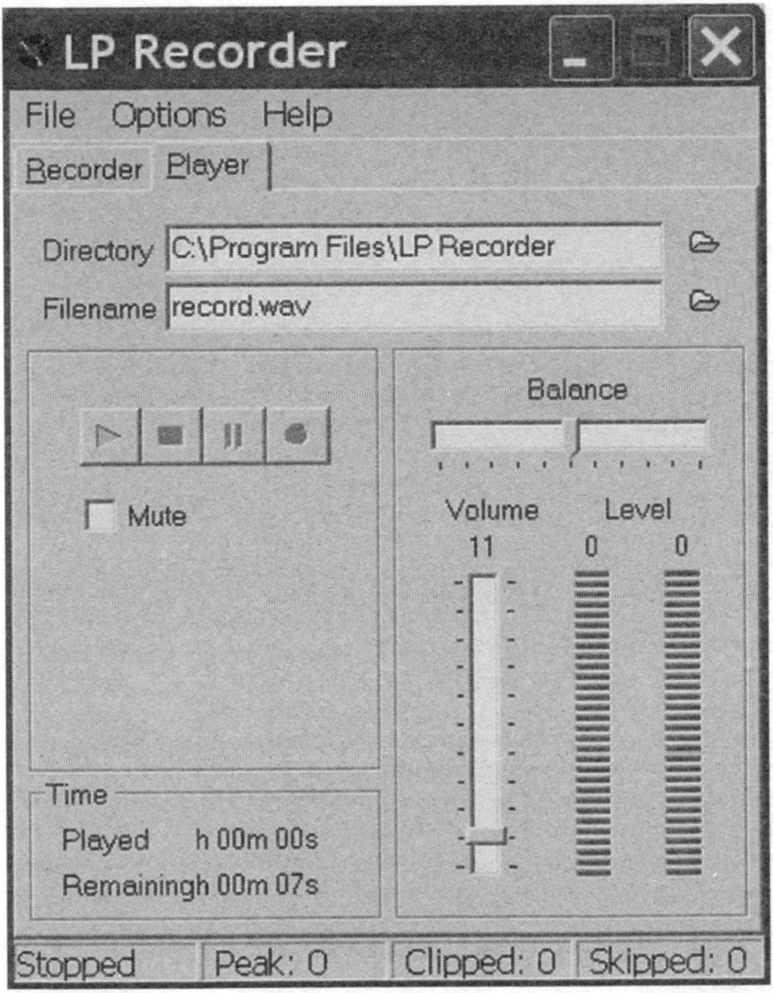

Fig.2.34 LP Recorder has a separate playback mode

manually, but only if you take the time to do some experiments so that it can be set accurately.

There is an auto-stop facility as well. This stops the recording when there is a very low signal level for a preset period of time. A feature of this type does not work well with types of music that have long quiet

Fig.2.35 *Cleaning Lab 2005 has a comprehensive range of facilities*

periods, because the recording is likely to be stopped during one of these periods. It can work quite well with music of a type that tends to be continuously loud. The gaps between tracks then stand out like the proverbial "sore thumb" and are easily detected by the system.

When first using a recording program it is quite normal to find that you are recording silence. The usual cause of the problem is that the wrong signal source has been selected. LP Recorder has a menu (Figure 2.33) that enables the correct signal source to be selected, which in most cases will be the Line Input. There is also a player mode (Figure 2.34) that enables recorded tracks to be played. The WAV files produced by this program can be played using practically any media player program and they are easily converted to MP3 and WMA files.

A program such as LP Recorder can do a very good job, but there are programs that offer a much greater range of facilities. As one would expect, the "all singing – all dancing" recorder programs are much more expensive and will take much longer to master. Magix Audio Cleaning Lab 2005 (Figure 2.35) has a comprehensive range of facilities for recording from various sources and editing the recorded tracks. It can also "clean" recordings to remove or reduce "hiss", "pops", etc. Some amazing results can be obtained from old recordings using modern digital processing, but do not expect to produce true CD quality results from old and worn recordings. Do expect to spend a fair amount of time learning to get the best results from a program such as this.

Points to remember

Not all recordings are still within copyright, but the vast majority are covered by some form of copyright. Downloading or distributing material that is still in copyright is illegal. Much of the material on offer via "free" music sites and via peer-to-peer services is still within copyright. Downloading and using this music is illegal.

Beware of sites that offer unlimited "legal" downloads for just one upfront fee. These are either straightforward scam sites or they are simply providing access to peer-to-peer networks that are freely accessible by anyone.

Some sites do offer free and genuinely legal downloads. The music on offer is either from independent artists and bands trying to gain exposure via the Internet, or the copyright in the material has lapsed. Music of many types is available, but as one would probably expect, the quality of this free music is not always particularly good. This is not to say that there are no good music and performances on offer. Some of these artists and bands will presumably go on to mega-stardom.

Downloading files other than from sites of well-established and respected companies has to be regarded as a slightly risky business. Downloading files via peer-to-peer services has to be regarded as very risky, since a significant percentage of the files on offer contain viruses, Trojans, etc. Only download material in this way if your PC is fully protected by antivirus software, a firewall, and a program specifically for dealing with spyware, adware, etc.

Downloading dozens of files via a dial-up connection is likely to take a very long time. Being realistic about it, it is probably more practical to buy the CDs rather than spend days downloading hundreds of megabytes of data. The situation is different with a broadband connection where it typically takes about 20 minutes to download a full CD in WMA or MP3 format.

Files in some form of protected format can not usually be converted to a different file format, and it might not be possible to burn them onto CDs either. Consequently, many of these files are not compatible with portable players, and can not be converted into a compatible format. Portable players that can handle WMA files will not necessarily be able to play any that are protected by DRM.

If you are in doubt about the restrictions on a protected file, right-click on its entry in the Now Playing List in WMP 10 and select properties from the pop-up menu. Select the License tab in the Properties window and any licensing restrictions will be listed.

WMP 10 and
playing files

Free player

If you have an iPod or MP3 player you can, of course, use this for listening to music while using your PC. Using a media player program installed on the PC is an equally valid approach though, and is probably the one that most people prefer. It is certainly the cheaper option if you have a portable MP3 player and feed it with non-rechargeable batteries. Most of these players will run for many hours on a single AA or AAA battery, but the running costs can build up over a period of time. Even if your player is powered by a rechargeable battery, it makes sense to use a player program running on your PC at times when you will be using the computer anyway. Doing so will help to extend the battery life of a well-used player, and it will also provide opportunities to get the battery fully charged again.

There is no shortage of media players for PCs. Most of these fully live up to the "media" part of the name, and are capable of playing video as well as audio files. As this book is strictly about digital audio we will not consider the video capabilities of any of the media players mentioned in this chapter. It is possible to buy media player programs for use with PCs, and many people do so. However, paying for player software is optional, and most PC users settle for the various free players that are available.

Any modern version of Windows comes complete with Microsoft's Media Player program, and it is part of a default installation of Windows. Therefore, this program should already be installed on your PC unless you have opted for some form of minimalist or custom installation. The Windows Media Player is updated quite frequently, and at the time of writing this it has reached version 10. It is certainly worthwhile obtaining and installing the latest version. Many programs seem to undergo annual updates that give little real improvement from one version to the next.

Some actually seem to become less usable with each "improvement". This is not really true of the Windows Media Player program, which has improved significantly over the years. The range of facilities it provides is probably much greater than most users realise.

As the latest version is always made available as a free download from the Microsoft site (www.microsoft.com), getting an update should be easy provided you have an Internet connection. Using "windows media player download" as the search string in Google or another major search engine should quickly locate the download page on the Microsoft site. Alternatively, use the built-in update facility of Windows to locate and install the latest version.

There are alternatives available if you are not happy with the Windows Media Player for some reason. MP3 players are often supplied with some free software. While it is by no means certain that this software will include a player program for Windows, it often does. A media player is often supplied with PCs as part of the support software for its soundcard or integrated audio system. The same is true of the video card or integrated video system. A program of this type might also be included with any CD/DVD burning software you have. My last PC came complete with four different media player programs.

iPod users

If your music player is an iPod you will presumably opt to use the iTunes program supplied with the player. Although you need this program in order to upload music files to the iPod, you could use a different player when listening to music on your PC. However, unless there is a good "down to earth" reason for doing so, it is probably best to use iTunes as your player program. The iTunes program undergoes frequent minor updates, so it is probably best to use the latest version from the Apple web site (www.apple.com) rather than install the version supplied with the player. If you install the program supplied with the player it will probably download the latest version and update itself. You can save time by "cutting to the chase" and installing the latest version right from the start.

Note that you do not have to be an iPod owner in order to use the iTunes program as a media player. It is a program that is clearly of more use to iPod users than anyone else, but it can be used to organise a collection of music files and play them on a PC. It is not just a file organiser and an upload utility for an iPod. Whether it represents the best choice for a non-iPod user is another matter. To a large extent this is a matter of personal preference. Depending on the type of Internet connection you use, it costs either little or nothing to download the program and try it. With most PC users being inundated with free and bundled media players, why does anyone pay for one? In general they do not. The freebies are mostly so good that relatively few people seriously consider buying a program of this type. It is only worth buying media player software if the various free programs are found to be inadequate in some way. This is unlikely unless you need to play files that are in one of the rarer formats, or some advanced feature is needed. Bear in mind that there are various plug-ins available for programs such as the Windows Media Player and the Nero CD/DVD burring program. This add-on software, some of which is available for nothing, enables these programs to handle additional file formats or provides additional functions. It is probably best to look for a suitable plug-in before giving up on your existing software and buying a new program.

Overhead

An important point to bear in mind when using any media player on a PC is that there is an overhead when using this type of software. In other words, using a player program uses the PC's resources, and it is likely to use up a significant amount of memory. It could also consume a fair percentage of the processor's time. The effect of this is to slow down other programs that you have running at the same time as the player program.

How much will a player program slow down your PC? This is very much a "how long is a piece of string?" type of question. It depends in part on the particular player program in use and how it is being used. Probably the main factor is the speed of the PC you are using. A PC having a few gigabytes of memory and the latest dual-core processor is not going to feel the strain when running a player program. You should be able to carry on computing normally, with no obvious change in performance.

The situation is very different when using an old PC having a slow processor and a very limited amount of memory. In an extreme case the PC might not have a high enough specification in order to run some modern player programs. However, most media players are not very demanding in this respect, especially if the program will only be used with audio files. Playing videos generally requires much more memory and computing power. Although an older or budget PC might play audio

Fig.3.1 WMP 10 in its normal mode but with no media files loaded

files perfectly well when no other software is in operation, there could be problems if other software is used at the same rime. The most likely problem is everything running very slowly, but it is also possible that there would be poor reliability with frequent crashes.

Bear in mind that PCs tend to have a substantial number of processes running in the background. Some of these are essential parts of the operating system, while others are associated with application programs installed by the user. These processes can be part of something like a firewall or antivirus program that has to monitor the PC's activity. Other processes are used by all-manner of programs, and in many cases have no obvious function. Large numbers of background processes tend to slow down any PC, but they can seriously degrade the performance of a PC that has a relatively modest specification.

If a PC is clearly struggling to run the normal application programs while also running a media player, it is possible that some "tuning" of the system will improve matters. Disabling unnecessary background processes, for example, might free sufficient resources to get everything working

Fig.3.2 There are six tabs below the menu bar

well. However, there is no guarantee that this will provide a sufficient improvement, you might find that "computer bloat" results in things slowing down again over a period of time. It is probably better to use a separate iPod/MP3 player unless your PC has sufficient resources to properly handle an audio player operating in the background.

WMP 10

The built-in Windows Media Player (WMP) program is by far the most widely used player at present, and it is the only one we will consider in detail here. Note that the examples featured here are based on WMP version 10, and that some facilities are different on other versions. In fact a few of the features covered here are absent on some earlier versions. Where possible, it is definitely advisable to use the latest version of this program.

There are various ways in which WMP 10 can be used, but at its most basic level it is merely necessary to load some music files and get it to play them. Figure 3.1 shows WMP 10 running on a PC, but with no media loaded. The large panel on the left that occupies most of the window is where any video content is displayed. In an audio context it is sometimes of no consequence, but it is occasionally used to show selected files. It can also be used by the program to indicate how well a task is progressing. Last and possibly least, there is the option of using a visualisation, which is basically just a display that changes in sympathy with the music. This feature is accessed via the Visualisations option is in the View menu, and it is covered in more detail later in this chapter.

There is the usual menu bar towards the top left-hand corner of the screen, and beneath this there are six tabs (Figure 3.2). In order to use the program as a simple player it is the Now Playing tab that should be

Fig.3.3 The Open option launches the usual file browser

selected. The required music files are selected by first choosing Open
from the File menu, which will open the usual file browser (Figure 3.3).
By default the program will filter any files of a type that it can not handle,
but it will show any files in a standard audio format such as MP3, WAV, or
WMA. What you consider to be a standard audio format and what WMP

Fig.3.4 The Any Files option will show the less common file types

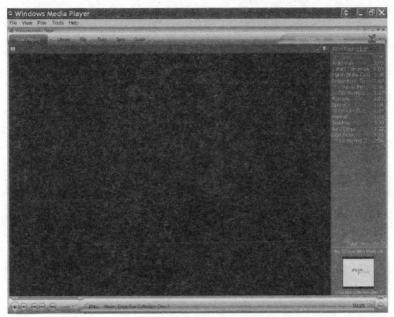

Fig.3.5 The loaded files are listed in the right-hand column

10 accepts as a standard format could be different. It is not equipped to handle the less popular but quite common formats such as FLAC and OGG Vorbis, although support for these can be provided by plug-ins. However, even if WMP 10 has been equipped with the necessary plug-in for one of these formats, by default it will not show the relevant file types in the file browser. In order to show these file types it is necessary to select the Any Files (*.*) option in the Files of type menu (Figure 3.4).

It is possible to open more than one file at a time. When you need to open several files they are selected using the normal Windows methods. To select a block of files you can left-click the entry for the first file, and then left-click the entry for the last file in the block while holding down the Shift key. In order to pick individual files it is just a matter of left-clicking each one while pressing the Control key. A selected file can be deselected by left-clicking its entry while holding down the Control key. Having selected the required file or files, operate the Open button.

The selected file or files will be listed in the right-hand panel of the player's window (Figure 3.5). In media player terminology this is a "play list". It is still a play list if it only contains one item, but a play list more usually contains a dozen or more items, which could be spread across several folders on the computer's hard disc drive. Play lists will be considered in more detail later in this chapter. When media files are loaded into WMP 10 it immediately starts playing the first item in the play list. Having finished the first item in the list, it will automatically move on to the next one, and work its way through the list until everything has been played. The program then stops and awaits further input from the user.

Repeat

It is possible to have the program play files using an alternative method. If you select the Repeat option from the Play menu, everything operates as before until the end of the final file is reached. As one would probably expect, the Repeat function then takes things back to the beginning and the entire list is played again. The list will be played indefinitely. The Repeat function can be toggled back to the "off" state by selecting it again from the Play menu. If you are unsure whether the Repeat function is in operation, activate the Play menu and look at the Repeat option. There will be a tick to the left of the word "Repeat" if this function is currently selected (Figure 3.6).

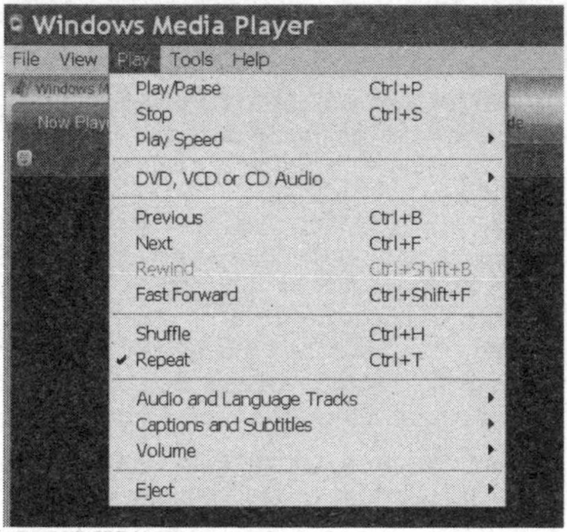

Fig.3.6 The Repeat function is currently
        selected

The Play menu also has a Shuffle option. This is much the same as the function of the same name that is often found on MP3 players. All the tracks in the play list will be played, but not in the normal sequence. Instead, the tracks are played in a random order. This helps to keep things interesting for those that find using the normal sequence a bit boring and predictable. Note that you can use the Repeat and Shuffle options together. Using them both at once results in the tracks being played randomly until the player is stopped manually.

Controls

The player has the usual set of manual controls in the bottom left-hand corner of the window (Figure 3.7). Working from left to right, the first control is the Play/Pause button that is used to stop and start the player. The Stop button is the next one, and this can only be used to stop the player. This button is greyed-out once it has been operated, and the Play/Pause button has to be used to start the player again. Unlike the Play/Pause control, operating the Stop button takes things back to the beginning of the current track. If you are distracted and would like to start a

Fig.3.7 The usual player controls are present

track from the beginning, operating the Stop and Play/Pause buttons in that order is one way of doing it. Use the Play/Pause button if you need to halt the player temporarily, to answer the telephone perhaps, and then carry on where you left off.

The next two buttons respectively move things back to the beginning of the previous track or on to the beginning of the next track. Use the Previous button when you would like to play a track again, but make sure you let the next track start before you operate this button. Otherwise you will get the previous track rather than the one you just played. The main use for the Next button is to skip a track that you do not wish to hear. Again, do not be too "trigger-happy". Make sure that the track has started to play before you operate the Next button, or you will simply jump forward a few seconds to the beginning of the track you are trying to avoid.

The last button is the Mute type, and this simply switches off the audio output. You can use this, for example, to cut off the sound from the loudspeakers while you answer the telephone or talk to someone in the room. However, the player will continue operating in silence. When you operate the Mute button again to switch the sound back on, you will have missed whatever was playing while the program was silenced.

Operating the Play/Pause button will silence the player, but it will carry on where it left off when the Play/Pause button is operated again. In general, the Play/Pause button is the better option. It is not too difficult to remember what each of the five buttons actually does. However, placing the pointer over any of the buttons will result in the usual hint-text that will show its function.

Volume

There is a slider control to the right of the five buttons, and this is the Volume control. Simply drag it to the right in order to increase the volume, or to the left if lower volume is required. A lack of volume can be a problem, and this could simply be due to inadequacies or incompatibilities in the hardware. Hardware issues go beyond the scope of this book, but in most cases the cause of the problem is more straightforward and is nothing to do with the hardware. The most likely cause of little or no volume is that the sound settings are not correct. The main volume control is probably the most common cause of an inadequate sound level.

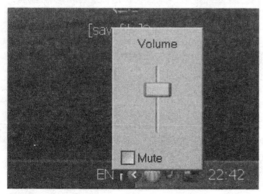

Fig.3.8 The taskbar volume control

A volume control is usually installed on the taskbar (the bar at the bottom of the Windows Desktop) when a sound system is installed in Windows. There is a row of buttons at the right end of the taskbar, and one of these should activate a pop-up volume control (Figure 3.8). However, the button for the volume control might be hidden with the taskbar in its normal state. Left-clicking the arrow at the left end of the row of buttons should reveal any buttons that are normally hidden. The icons on the buttons usually give little clue as to their functions, but placing the pointer over a button will produce some hint-text that shows its purpose.

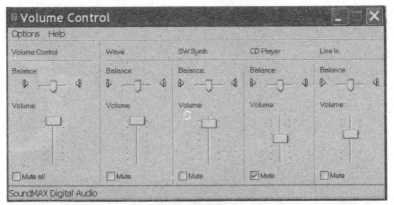

Fig.3.9 The full Volume Control window has basic mixing facilities

The master volume control on the taskbar sets the maximum level that can be output by audio application programs such as WMP 10. It will not be possible to get much volume from WMP 10, or any other program, if the master volume control is has a rather lowl setting. In general, it is best if this control is set at maximum. This enables high volume levels to be obtained from application programs, and the volume control of each program can be backed off when lower volumes are required. It is only worthwhile setting the master volume control below maximum in cases where distortion is apparent unless it is backed off somewhat.

Some PC audio systems have a mixer style control panel (Figure 3.9) rather than a simple volume control. In fact both features might be available, with a single click on the volume control button producing a single control, and a double-click bringing up the full control panel. The full panel might also be available from a pop-up menu if the button is right-clicked. Details of the audio controls should be included in your PC's instruction manual, but a little trial and error should soon determine whether a full control panel is available.

The exact features vary slightly from one audio control panel to another, but there will usually be a level and balance control for each signal source. There should also be an overall volume control, and it is important that this is not set well back at a level that gives an inadequate output level. Where a control panel and a simple volume control are both available, do not assume that adjusting one control will also alter the setting of the other. Often you have what are two master volume controls, and there will be a low maximum output level if either or both of them are well backed off.

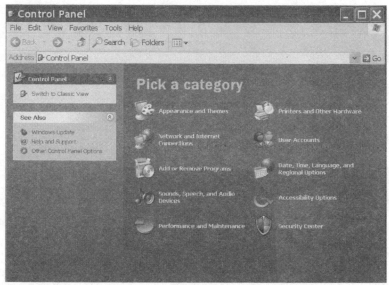

Fig.3.10 The normal version of the Windows XP Control Panel

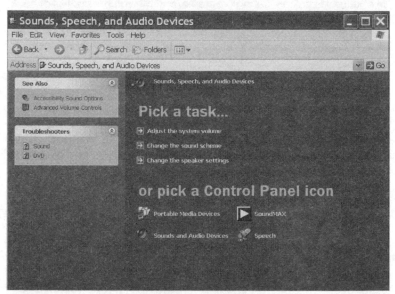

Fig.3.11 Activate the Sounds and Audio Devices link

Where this is the case it is also likely that the two mute controls will also operate independently. If there is no output at all from the player it is a good idea to check that the Mute checkbox for the master volume control or controls is not ticked. Ticking the Mute checkbox for an audio device effectively switches off that device. Muting a master volume control effectively switches all the audio devices that can produce an audio output, effectively silencing programs such as media players.

Default device

With no audio output at all, including an absence of the Windows start-up and closing down jingles, check that the audio hardware is all connected properly and installed in Windows correctly. It is also worth checking that the correct default audio output device is selected. With many PCs there is only one audio output device that can be used, but it is increasingly common for there to be two or three.

To check which piece of audio hardware is the default device, first go to the Start menu and select the Control Panel option. The normal version of the Windows Control Panel looks like Figure 3.10. You have the "classic view" if there are about two dozen icons in the main section of the Control Panel. Operating the Switch to Category View link near the top left-hand corner of the Window will change the Control Panel to look like Figure 3.10. With the right version of the window present, select the Sounds, Speech, and Audio Devices category, which will change the window to look like Figure 3.11. Activate the Sounds and Audio Devices link in the lower section of the Control Panel, and the Sounds and Audio Devices Properties window will then be launched (Figure 3.12).

This window has several categories with tabs at the top to permit the required section to be selected. It will probably default to the Volume section, where the master volume control and Mute checkbox will be found once again. Check that these are in order and then operate the Audio tab. This will change the window to look something like Figure 3.13. Here it is the Sound playback section that is of interest. The pop-down Default device menu will list anything from one to half a dozen or so devices. Some of the devices listed here might not be normal audio devices. For example, certain types of modem are basically audio cards plus some software to make them act as modems. A device of this type should not be selected as the default device.

Sometimes there are two or three entries for the real soundcard. This usually occurs where the sound system has two or three sets of outputs.

Fig.3.12 The Sounds and Audio Devices Properties window

Many PC sound systems now have normal front and rear audio connectors, plus one or two digital audio inputs and outputs. On the face of it, there is no point in having to select one set of outputs. All of them could be active simultaneously. In practice it seems to be quite normal for only one set of outputs to be active at any one time. Make sure that the appropriate audio connectors are set as the defaults.

Another potential cause of problems is where the PC is used with a USB headset for something like speech recognition or VoIP telephone conversations. A USB headset is installed as a separate audio system

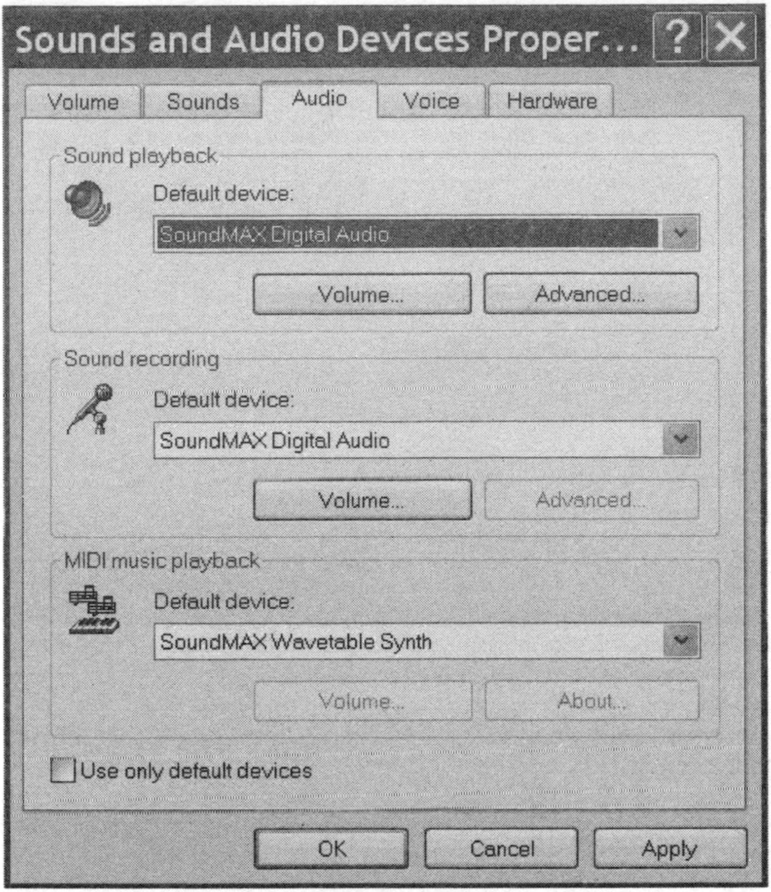

Fig.3.13 The Audio section of the Properties window

that is independent of the soundcard or integrated audio system. Accordingly, it will appear in the Default device menu as a separate item. If it is selected here, the output of WMP 10 or any other media player will be fed to the headset and not to the loudspeakers via the normal sound system.

Life can get a bit difficult if you need two different audio output devices. With luck, selecting the normal sound output device as the default will not prevent the relevant applications from using the USB headset. Unfortunately, it is often necessary to go into the Control Panel, etc., to

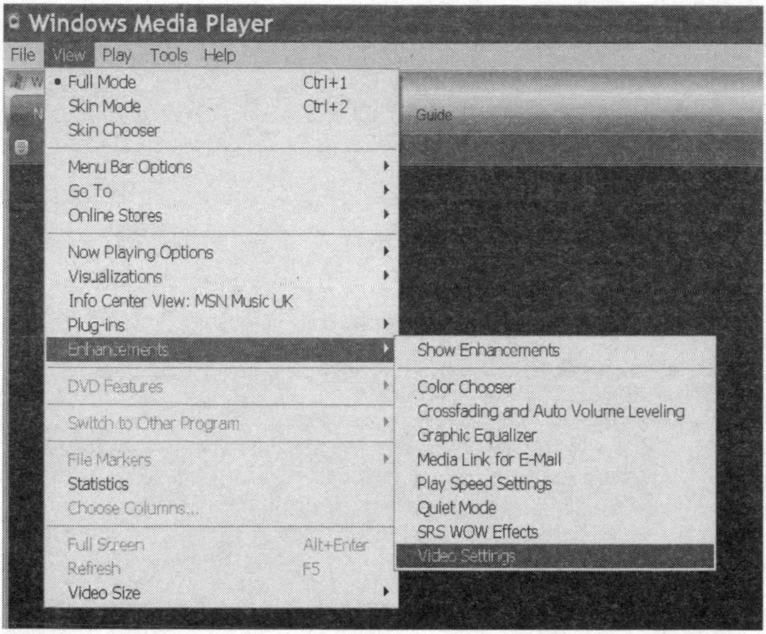

Fig.3.14 A number of facilities are available from the Enhancements
         submenu

select the appropriate output device when you change from one program
to another.

Enhancements

WMP 10 has some extra facilities that can be accessed via the
Enhancements submenu (Figure 3.14) of the View menu. Some of the
enhancements are not relevant to audio playback or are of limited value
to most users, but the Graphic Equaliser option is definitely well worth
trying. An additional set of controls are produced (Figure 3.15) when
this option is selected. The control at the extreme right end of this group
is an ordinary channel balance control.

The main bank of controls is for a 10-band graphic equaliser, and this is
much the same as the graphic equalisers found on some hi-fi systems.
It is a sort of highly versatile tone control. The WMP 10 graphic equaliser
has more controls than a typical equaliser on anything other than fairly

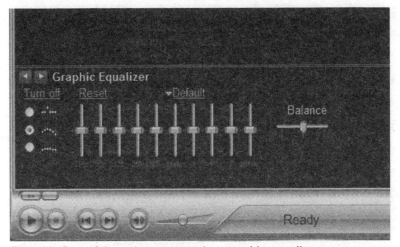

Fig.3.15 One of the enhancements is a graphic equaliser

upmarket audio equipment. With any device of this type the various bands are not perfectly defined, so adjusting one of the level controls has some effect on the adjacent bands. However, the WMP 10 graphic equaliser is quite good in this respect, and it is a very worthwhile facility that gives much better control over the sound than simple bass and treble tone controls. One slight drawback compared to the hardware "real thing" is that there is a slight delay between making an adjustment and the change being applied to the reproduced sound. This slows things down a little, but you soon get used to it.

For the benefit of those unfamiliar with graphic equalisers, the basic idea is to split the audio range into a number of bands. In this case there are 10 bands, with a separate level control for each one. The centre frequency of each band is shown beneath its level control. The lowest one is at 31 hertz, which is a very low (bass) frequency. Each control has a centre frequency that is about one octave higher than the control to its left, with the tenth control being centred on a frequency of about 16 kilohertz. This is a very high frequency that is only audible to people with reasonably good hearing.

By default the controls all start at a central setting so that no contouring of the sound is provided. By adjusting one of the controls you can boost or cut its range of frequencies relative to the other frequency bands. One reason for using a graphic equaliser is to produce a sound that you

Fig.3.16 Cutting the high frequencies can combat background "hiss"

find more pleasing than the "straight" sound. From the technical point of view the doctored sound might be less good than the "straight" version, but it is what sounds best to the listener that really counts, and not technical perfection.

Another reason for altering the sound is to compensate for inadequacies in the hardware or the signal source. For example, some older recordings contain a fair amount of background noise of one type or another. This is often in the form of predominantly high frequency sounds such as "crackles" and "hiss" types. As discussed in the final chapter of this book, there are now some sophisticated audio processing programs that can be used to counteract this type of problem. The WMP 10 graphic equaliser provides a simple alternative for those not wishing to go to the expense of a complex audio processing program.

Radio buttons

There are three radio buttons to the left of the level controls, and these govern how operating one control will affect those that are close to it. The level controls operate fully independently if the top button is operated. This is useful when extreme filtering is required, and dealing with "crackles" and "hiss" effectively often requires some uncompromising filtering. Something like the settings shown in Figure 3.16 should give quite good results, with the high frequency bands containing most of

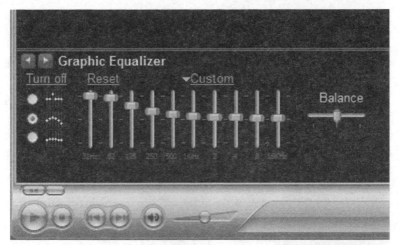

Fig.3.17 Only the slider on the extreme left has been adjusted

the noise severely attenuated. The bands that contain little noise are left unaffected. There is a large loss of treble content, but with older recordings the high frequency content is often a bit lacking anyway, so this loss of signal might not be very obvious.

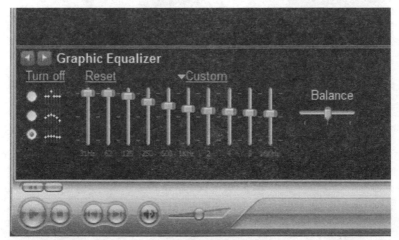

Fig.3.18 Again, only the extreme left-hand slider has been adjusted

A sudden jump from no filtering to a massive amount is not what is usually required when tailoring the frequency response for the best subjective sound. Relatively small jumps from one band of frequencies to another are normally used, so as to prevent the filtering from being too obvious.

Using the middle or bottom button makes it impossible to have large changes from one band to the next. Altering the setting of one of the level controls results in those on either side of it also being changed, albeit to a lesser degree. The difference between these two buttons is that using the middle one gives the level controls a degree of independence, whereas the bottom button binds them quite closely together.

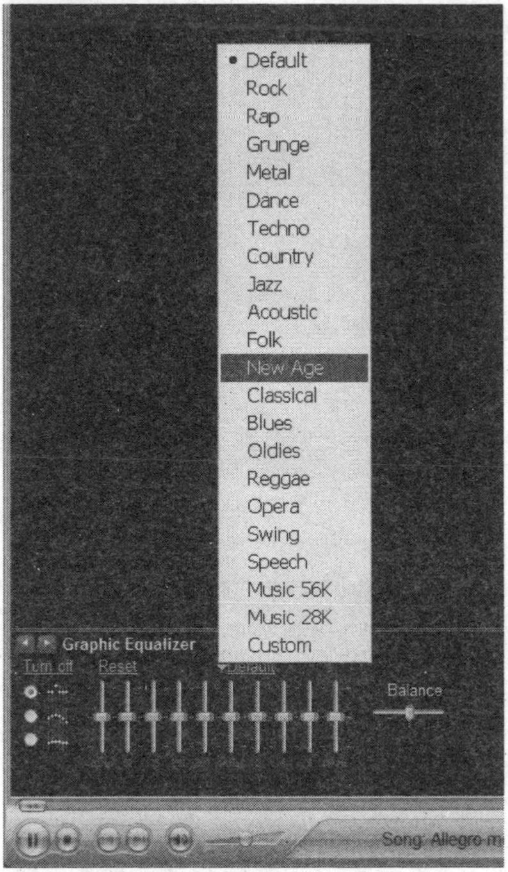

This is demonstrated by Figures 3.17 and 3.18. The bass output from the small loudspeakers normally used with PCs is often a bit lacking, as is the bass output from some types of headphones. It is easy to augment the bass slightly using a graphic equaliser, and it is even easier using the middle and lower buttons. In Figure 3.17 the middle button has been selected and the level control for the lowest frequency band has been set at maximum. This has resulted in the

Fig.3.19 A range of preset settings are available

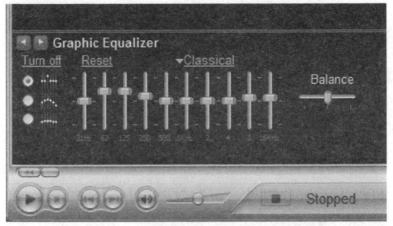

Fig.3.20 The preset control settings for classical music

nearby controls also being set for a certain amount of boost, although even the nearest of them is set for a slightly lower amount. In Figure 3.18 the lower button has been used, and it has produced more of the same. The second and third level controls have been set for nearly as much boost as the first one.

Using either of these settings gives the desired result, with a steady rise in the amount of bass that should (more or less) mirror the gradual reduction in the bass response of the loudspeakers or headphones. The linking of the level controls prevents any sudden and obvious steps in the frequency response. When using the bottom button the almost total lack of independence between adjacent controls can be rather limiting, and the middle button is probably better for most purposes.

A point worth bearing in mind is that large amounts of boost can result in the audio system becoming overloaded and large amounts of distortion being produced. This problem is most likely to occur when a high level of boost is applied to a wide range of frequencies. The problem can sometimes be cured by backing off the master volume control, but this does not work with all PC audio systems. In some cases this simply produces a quieter but still badly distorted signal. Moving all the level controls slightly downwards should always remove the distortion while leaving the relative frequency response much the same.

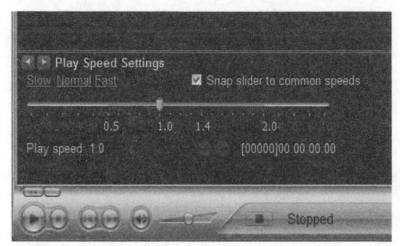

Fig.3.21 The playback speed can be varied

Preset equalisation

If you prefer not to fiddle with the level controls there is the alternative of using one of the preset settings. The menu for these (Figure 3.19) is activated by left-clicking the word "default", which is just above the level controls, or the triangle just to the left of this word. There are preset settings for various types of music, and the example of Figure 3.20 is for classical music. Of course, you can use any of these preset settings with any type of music. It is the way that things sound to you that counts, and nothing else.

There is also a setting for speech. This slightly reduces the highest and lowest frequencies, which often makes speech sound a bit clearer and easier to understand. There are also settings for music at the relatively low bit rates of 28 and 56 kilobits per second. Music at low bit rates tends to produce some odd effects with certain types of program material, and these settings are presumably designed to minimise any strange effects. It is likely that the audio quality will still leave something to be desired though.

When the level controls are adjusted manually, the last settings used become the Custom option. This is very useful because it provides an easy way of returning to a favourite set of adjustments. In order to return to "flat" settings it is just a matter of operating the Reset link just above the level controls, or selecting the Default option from the menu.

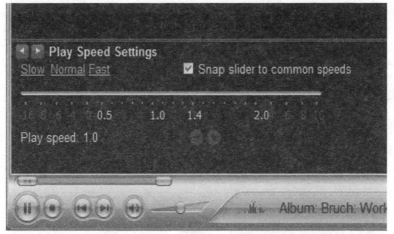

Fig.3.22 The speed control is inoperative with many program sources

The equaliser can be switched on and off using the Turn on/Turn off link. When the equaliser is switched off there is no tailoring of the frequency response. The equaliser panel remains in place, but the control knobs of the onscreen slider controls disappear and the equaliser is completely inoperative. Note that you can not remove the equaliser from the window by going to the View – Enhancements menu and selecting it again. It can only be removed from the WMP 10 window by left-clicking the cross in the top right-hand corner of the equalisers section of the window. Removing it from the screen does not switch it off, so any filtering in use will remain active if the equaliser panel is switched off. This is potentially useful, but you have to be careful not to leave unwanted filtering switched on.

Other facilities

There are other features available from the Enhancements submenu, although few of these are of use when playing audio files. The Play Speed Settings facility (Figure 3.21) enables the playback speed to be reduced or increased. Thanks to the wonders of digital technology, this does not work in quite the same way as altering the playback speed of a record deck or tape player. With these, increasing or decreasing the playback speed results in the pitch of all the notes being raised or lowered by a corresponding amount. Changing the speed setting of WMP 10 does not give these changes in pitch. Unfortunately, it does seem to produce a noticeable degradation of the audio quality, particularly when large changes in speed are used.

The speed can be adjusted via the large slider control. Only certain speeds will be available if the "Snap slider to common speeds" checkbox is ticked. A full range of speeds is available if this checkbox is not ticked. The three links near the top left-hand corner of the panel provide slow, normal, and fast speeds. The fast and slow speeds are respectively 1.4 and 0.5 times the normal speed. Note that the speed control is only available with certain types of media file. It is not usable when playing CDs for example, or even with some types of digital audio file. The speed control is available when playing MP3 and WMA files. When it is inoperative it looks like Figure 3.22, with the knob of the slider control missing so that it can not be adjusted. The Slow and Fast links remain in place, but operating them has no effect.

Quiet Mode

Selecting the Quiet Mode option produces the simple control panel shown in Figure 3.23. A problem when playing some types of music quietly is that either loud passages remain quite loud, or the quiet sections are so quiet that you can not actually hear them. It is impossible to find a volume setting that provides a happy medium where you can hear the quiet bits reasonably well but the loud sections are kept in check. This occurs with music that has a wide dynamic range. In other words, it occurs with music where the difference in the volume varies

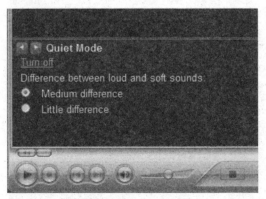

Fig.3.23 Quiet Mode has two settings

massively between the quietest and loudest passages. Classical music is probably the type that is most likely to give this problem, but it can occur with other musical genres.

The idea of the Quiet Mode is to reduce the difference between the highest and lowest volume levels so that you can hear the quiet bits without having the volume set high. It provides a form of what is termed audio compression. It is not a good idea to use compression unless music is being played at low volume levels. Reducing the dynamic range of music tends to give it less impact, making dramatic changes in volume decidedly unimpressive. Quiet Mode provides two levels of compression that are selected via the radio buttons. The Medium difference option gives the lesser degree of compression, and is the one that is probably best for most music sources. The Little difference option gives a large amount of compression, producing little change in the volume level. This is the option that is likely to give the best results only when playing music very quietly.

Unfortunately, at present this very useful feature does not work with most program sources. In fact it will only work with WMA files that have WMA 9 lossless encoding, or were encoded using the WMA 9 Professional codec. One would hope that it will be extended to cover a wider range of program sources in later version of the Windows Media Player.

Wow

The SRS Wow effects facility tends to be overlooked by most users, but it is one of the more interesting aspects of WMP 10. It utilizes technology from SRS Labs, and their web site (www.srslabs.com) provides a good description of this facility. It is really two facilities, with a separate slider control for each one (Figure 3.24). The control on the left is for the TruBass feature, which gives a form of bass boost. However, it does more than simply boost the very low frequencies, which can often be ineffective with small loudspeakers and some types of headphones. Large amounts of bass boost can result in some speakers failing to give convincing results even though they are being driven close to the point of destruction.

One of the ploys used is to boost certain harmonics of low notes in an attempt to fool the listener's hearing system into believing that the bass content is higher than it actually is. Just how convincing this type of thing really is in practice is a subjective matter, and probably depends on the capabilities of the sound system in use. It is certainly worth trying if your PC's audio system has something less than large hi-fi loudspeakers, which probably means the vast majority of systems.

Note that taking the TruBass control to the left of its central setting gives a reduction in the lowest bass frequencies. Although this might seem a bit pointless, there can be problems with "booming" from some

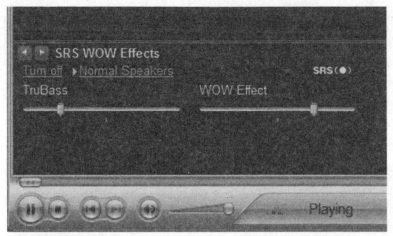

Fig.3.24 There are separate TruBass and WOW Effect controls

loudspeakers and headphones. In other words, for some reason the lowest bass frequencies are so strong that you tend to get a loud and continuous "booming" sound on some program material. The "booming" can be so loud that it is impossible to listen to the music properly. I have experienced this problem with certain combinations of headphones and PC sound systems. Using the TruBass control to "tame" the extreme bass response of the system will usually remove the "booming" while leaving a satisfying amount of bass signal.

The other control is for the Wow effect. The loudspeakers used with PCs are often positioned quite close together, and in some cases they are actually part of the monitor. This limits the separation to something in the region of 300 to 500 millimetres. Even where separate loudspeakers are used, space restrictions often result in the separation being no more than about one metre. Even given that the listener will be quite close to the loudspeakers, a larger amount of separation would be better.

The main purpose of the Wow effect is to extend the soundstage beyond the physical positions of the loudspeakers. This enables the listener to enjoy a bigger and better stereo effect without having to position the loudspeakers beyond the confines of the computer desk. Again, how well or otherwise this works is to some extent a subjective matter, and it probably depends to a significant extent on the particular equipment used, the program material, and the acoustics of the room. It is certainly worthwhile trying this facility if your PC's audio system has limited physical separation of the loudspeakers.

An interesting feature of the Wow effect is that it works with a monophonic sound source. The sound normally appears to originate midway between the two loudspeakers when playing a monophonic source through a stereo system. The situation is less satisfactory for users of stereo headphones, with the sound seeming to originate halfway between the two phones, or in the middle of the listener's head in other words! Some people are quite happy with this, but many users find it a bit disconcerting. Even if you do not find this effect off-putting, monophonic program material often tends to sound rather dull and lifeless when played through headphones.

Using the Wow effect with loudspeakers and a monophonic source broadens the soundstage, with the sound being spread from one loudspeaker to the other. It is not providing a true stereo effect since there is no proper positioning of voices or instruments within the soundstage. On the other hand, the spreading of the sound is quite convincing if you do not listen too carefully. I certainly find it preferable to "straight" monophonic reproduction.

When used with headphones the Wow effect again tends to broaden the soundstage, and make it less obviously focussed between the listener's ears. To my hearing at any rate, the effect obtained is often far better than the unprocessed version. It also seems to remove the problem with monophonic program material tending to sound dull and lifeless even though it is technically and artistically proficient.

Above the TruBass control there is a link that enables the processing to be toggled on and off. There is a single control for both effects, but it is still possible to have one without the other. Setting one of the slider controls at a central setting effectively switches off the corresponding effect. Note that setting the Wow effect control to the left of the mid setting results in a narrowing rather than a widening of the soundstage. A stereo signal is converted to a monophonic type if this control is set as far to the left as possible. There is another link, and this provides three versions of the effect. These are optimised for normal loudspeakers, large loudspeakers, and headphones.

Crossfading and levelling

The Crossfading and Audio Volume Levelling facilities can be very useful. When this enhancement is selected there are two links that enable them

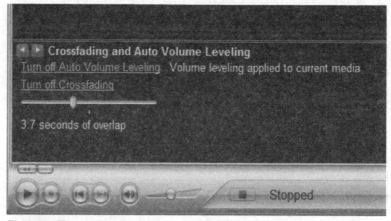

Fig.3.25 There are separate pieces of link-text that permit volume levelling and crossfading to be turned on and off

to be individually toggled on and off (Figure 3.25). There is a slider control for the crossfading effect, and this enables the crossfade time to be varied from zero to 10 seconds. Normally there is a short gap between tracks, but the tracks overlap when the crossfade facility is used. The crossfade time is the duration of this overlap. During this time the existing track is gradually faded out and the new track is gradually brought up to full volume. In audio terminology the new track is "faded up", which admittedly seems like a contradiction of terms.

The idea of crossfading is to give a smooth transition from one track to another with no break in the music. Because many tracks normally have quite a long fade out at the end, it can be necessary to use a fairly long crossfade time in order to get something approximating to a seamless transition from one track to another. There is otherwise a perceived gap between the tracks. Of course, crossfading is not appropriate for all types of music, and you might not like the effect at all, but it is there if you need it.

Volume levelling is designed to prevent jumps in the volume level when moving from one track to another. However, it requires the audio files to contain levelling data that WMP 10 can read. In practice this means that it will only work with certain Windows media files such as some WMA types, and with some MP3 files.

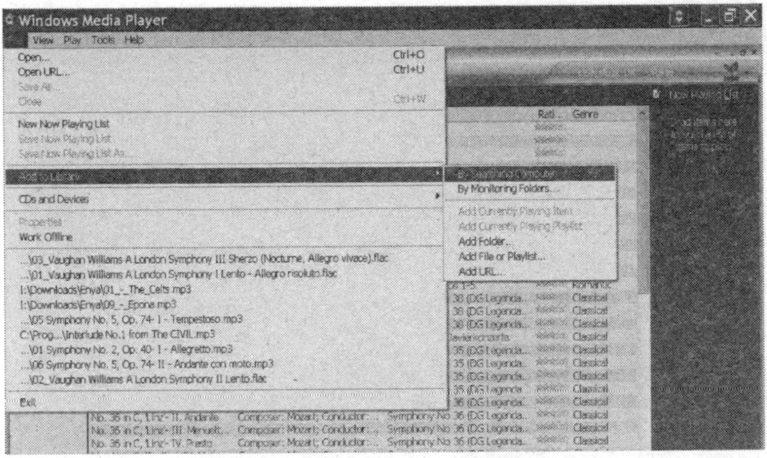

Fig.3.26 The computer can be scanned for media files

Play lists

The idea of a play list is to make it easy to select and play a collection of music files that you like to play together. Probably the most popular way of using play lists is to have a list for each album stored on the PC, but to also have additional lists for compilations of your favourite tracks. This makes it easy to select a complete album or a collection of favourite tracks, as and when required.

One way of making a play list is to go to the Now Playing section of the program and then choose the Open option from the File menu. The usual file browser then appears, and the required files are selected and loaded in the usual way. The loaded files are placed in the Now Playing play list. This method is fine in cases where the required files are in a single folder, but it becomes awkward to select the right files if they are scattered across several folders. Note that you can not load a few files into the Now Playing list and then use the File – Open option to add some more files to the list. The newly loaded files will replace the existing ones rather than being added to them.

An easier way of handling things is to use the WMP 10 library facility. The Library is really just a database that keeps track of the media files stored on your PC. When WMP 10 is run for the first time you are given the option of having the disc drives scanned for media files. Any

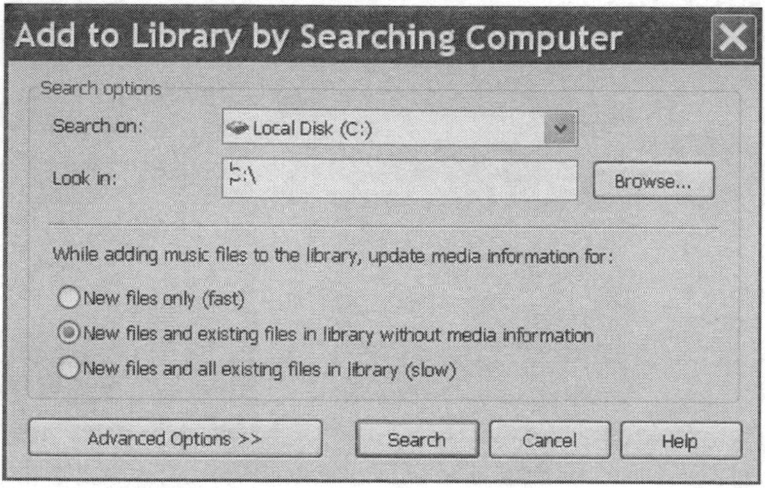

Fig.3.27 Here you select the disc drive to be scanned

recognised media files on these drives are added to the library if you accept this option. It is still possible to have the drives scanned even if you did not accept this option when WMP 10 was first run. This is just a matter of going to the File menu, selecting Add to Library, and then choosing By Searching Computer from the submenu (Figure 3.26).

The pop-up window of Figure 3.27 then appears, and here you select the disc drive to be scanned. There is also the option of choosing a particular folder using the Look in text box. You can either type in the path for the folder or use the Browse button and the file browser to locate and add the folder. It makes sense to point the program to the appropriate folder if all the files are stored in the same one. This avoids having the program waste time

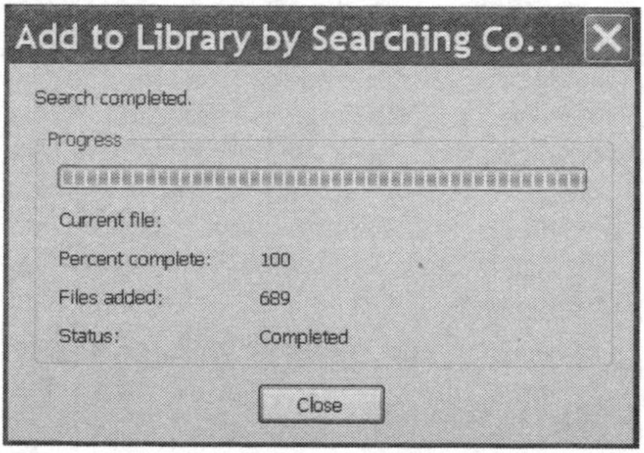

Fig.3.28 There is the usual bargraph

Monitor Folders   X

Add or remove folders you want to monitor for new, deleted, renamed, or moved media files. The library is
updated automatically to reflect changes.

Folders:

C:\Documents and Settings\All Users.WINDOWS\Documents\My Music
C:\Documents and Settings\All Users.WINDOWS\Documents\My Videos
C:\Documents and Settings\Robert.PENFOLD-8D5E445\My Documents\My Videos
C:\Temp

Add...

Remove

For best performance, avoid monitoring shared folders on a network, root folders, or a large
number of folders.

OK   Cancel

Fig.3.29 Folders that are currently being monitored are listed

searching numerous folders that do not contain any media files. Opt to
search the entire disc if the media files are in several folders. The search
process should still be reasonably short. Once the required settings are
in place, operate the Search button to get things underway. There is the
usual pop-up bargraph display which shows how things are progressing,
and once the search is finished this will indicate the number of files
detected (Figure 3.28).

There are three radio buttons that enable the thoroughness of the search
to be controlled. When having the disc scanned for the first time it is
best to use the middle or bottom buttons, both of which will provide
thorough scans of the disc. The top button is better when scanning the
drive to update an existing library.

Other means of adding to the library are provided by the Add to Library
submenu, such as directing the program to a folder where media files
are stored, or even selecting an individual file. Do not confuse the two
options that involve folders. The By Monitoring Folders option is used to
monitor a folder that is for storing downloaded or ripped media files.
Selecting this option produces the window of Figure 3.29, which shows
any folders that are already monitored. These are searched for new
media files each time WMP 10 is launched, and any new files that are
found are added to the library. A folder can be added to the list by
operating the Add button and using the pop-up browser (Figure 3.30) to
locate the appropriate folder. The browser is much like the normal
Windows file browser, but it only shows and handles folders.

Add Folder

Select a folder:

- 📁 Brahms Piano Concerto No 2 (Gilels
- ⊞ 📁 Brian Symphony No. 1 'The Gothic
- 📁 Charles Camille Saint-Saëns - Piano
- ⊞ 📁 Chopin - Piano concertos no. 1 & 2
- 📁 Dvorak - Cello Concerto - Jacquelin
- 📁 Dvorak - Symphony No 9 - Kertesz-
- 📁 Elgar Cello Concerto (Jacqueline du

Folder: Downloads

[Make New Folder] [OK] [Cancel]

Fig.3.30 This browser is used to add a folder

Add Folder

The same browser is produced if the Add Folder option is selected. This does not produce any monitoring of the selected folder, but instead immediately adds its contents to the Library. The Add File or Play List option produces the standard Windows file browser so that a media file or several files can be selected and added to the library.

Having produced the library by one means or another, something like Figure 3.31 should be produced when WMP 10's Library tab is operated. There will probably be a few unfamiliar files listed if you opted to have the whole of drive C scanned. These are things such as the WAV files

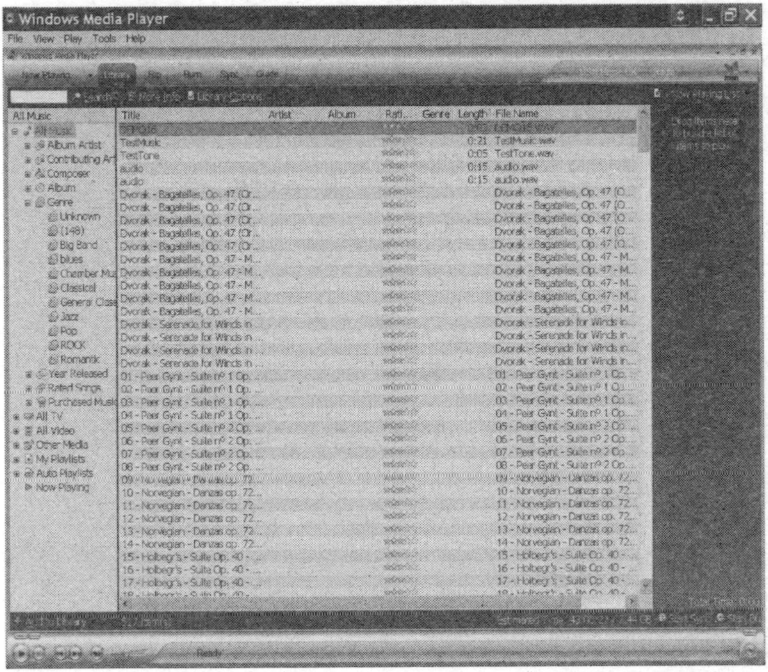

Fig.3.31 A large list of files has been added to the WMP 10 library

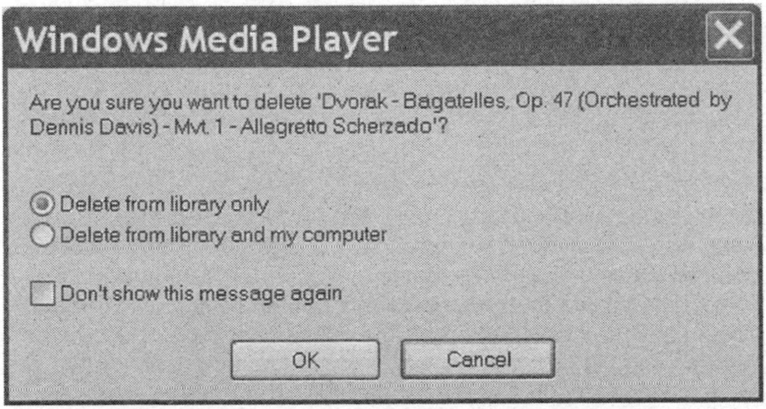

Fig.3.32 The item can be removed from the library or removed and
         deleted from the disc

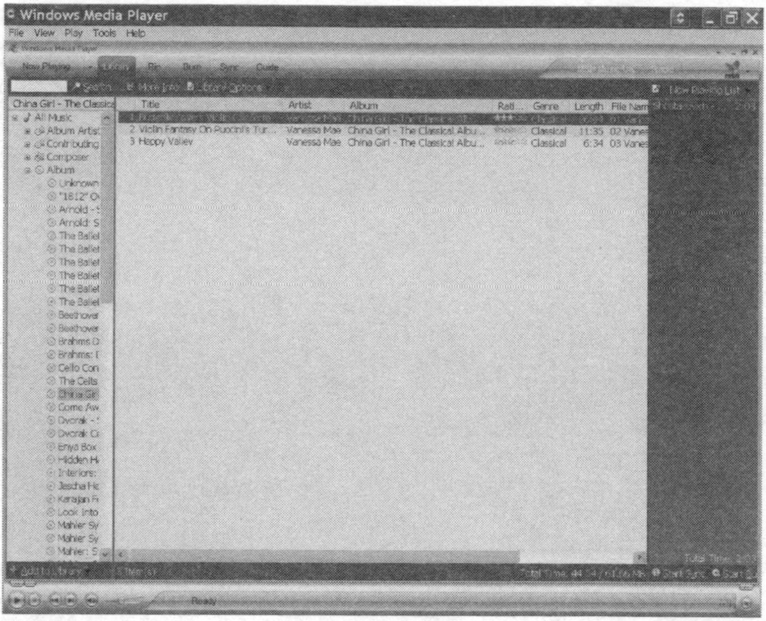

Fig.3.33 Selecting a category results in only files from that category being listed

used by Windows for its various sound effects (the start-up jingle, etc.). Any unwanted file can be removed by right-clicking its entry in the list and selecting Delete from the pop-up menu. This produces a pop-up window (Figure 3.32) where you can opt to remove the item from the Library, or to remove it from the Library and delete the file as well. You should obviously refrain from deleting any file that might be a system file or a support file for an application program. Only delete a file if you know exactly what it is and you are sure that it is no longer needed.

By default the All Music view is selected, and the entire contents of the Library will be shown in the main panel of the window. The usual vertical scrollbar will be present if the library contains a large number of files. It is possible to view a more restricted range of files by selecting one of the categories and subcategories in the left-hand section of the window (Figure 3.33). Sometimes there will be files that have been sorted into inappropriate categories, such as pop music that appears in the Jazz or Big Band section. Some parts of each entry can be edited by right-clicking them and selecting Edit from the pop-up menu. If you change

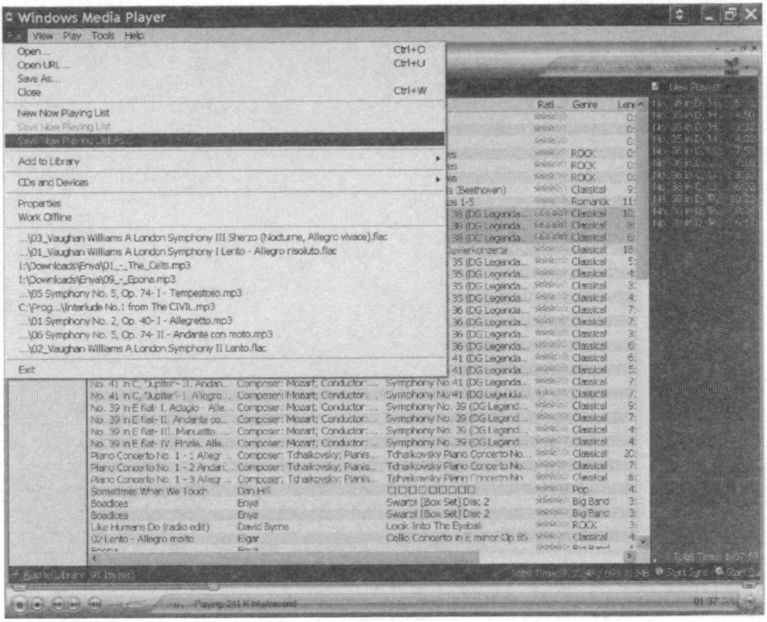

Fig.3.34 The play list can be saved to disc

(say) "Big Band" to read "Pop", the relevant file will be moved from the Big Band category to the Pop category.

An alternative is to select the offending file and drag it to the appropriate category in the right-hand panel of the window. This produces a small pop-up window where there is the option of moving the file from one genre to the other. Having selected this option, operate the Yes button in the pop-up window and the file will be transferred to the new category. This method also works with groups of files, so it is the better method if you need to shift several files from one category to another. It will usually be necessary to do a fair amount of editing in order to get the library organised just the way you like it.

With the library in place it is then very easy to produce a play list. All you have to do is find each file in the Library and drag it into the right-hand panel of the window. Make sure that it says Now Playing List at the top of this panel. If it does not, operate the button at the top of the panel and select Now Playing list from the pop-down menu. The usual methods can be used to select multiple files so that they can be dragged to the

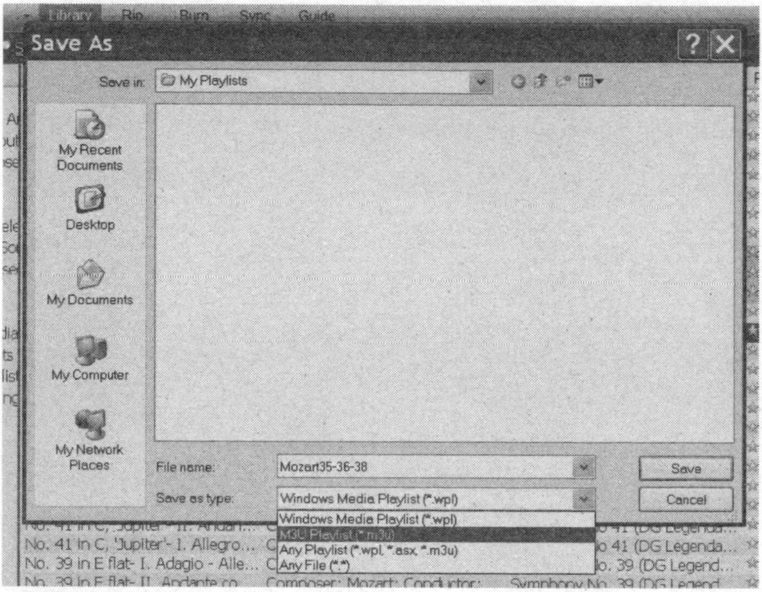

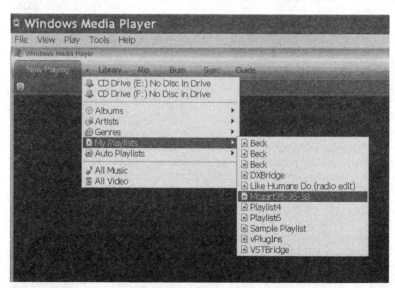

Fig.3.35 The play list is named and a file type is selected

Fig.3.36 The required play list is selected

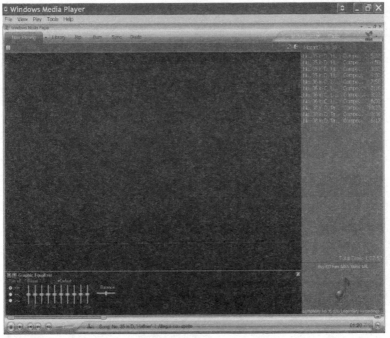

*Fig.3.37 The files selected by the play list are listed in the column
down the right-hand side of the window*

new play list en masse. Entries in the play list can be moved by simply
dragging them to a new position. If you change your mind and would
like to remove an item from the list, right-click its entry and select the
Remove from List option.

Having put together a play list it can be saved to disc by selecting Save
Now Playing List As from the File menu (Figure 3.34). This produces the
file browser of Figure 3.35 where the play list can be given a suitable
name. The menu at the bottom of this window enables the play list to be
saved in various formats. The WPL type is a Windows media play list,
which is the default type used by WMP 10. If you might need to share
play lists with other people it might be better to select the M3U type
instead. M3U is by far the most widely used form of play list, and
practically all media player programs are compatible with this format.
An M3U play list is a simple text file that can be viewed and edited using
a text editor such as the Notepad program supplied with Windows.

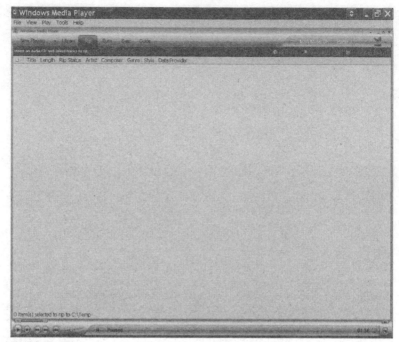

Fig.3.38 Operating the Rip tab produces a largely blank window

In order to load a play list, operate the Now Playing tab, followed by the small triangular button just to the right of this tab. From the pop-down menu select the My Play lists option followed by the required play list from the submenu that appears (Figure 3.36). The play list should then be displayed in the right-hand panel of the window (Figure 3.37), and the first track in the list will be played.

MP3 and WMA

Operating the Rip tab produces the rather blank looking window of Figure 3.38. Ripping is the process of taking music from a CD and converting it into a media file. This is not necessary in order to play an audio CD on a PC, since WMP 10 is capable of playing audio CDs. It might be set up to automatically play an audio CD that is placed in a CD-ROM drive. If not, it is just a matter of selecting the DVD, VCD, or CD Audio option from the Play menu, and then selecting the appropriate drive from the submenu

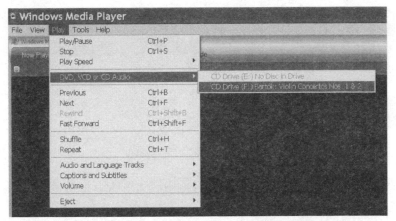

Fig.3.39 *Where there is more than one CD/DVD drive, the correct drive can be selected*

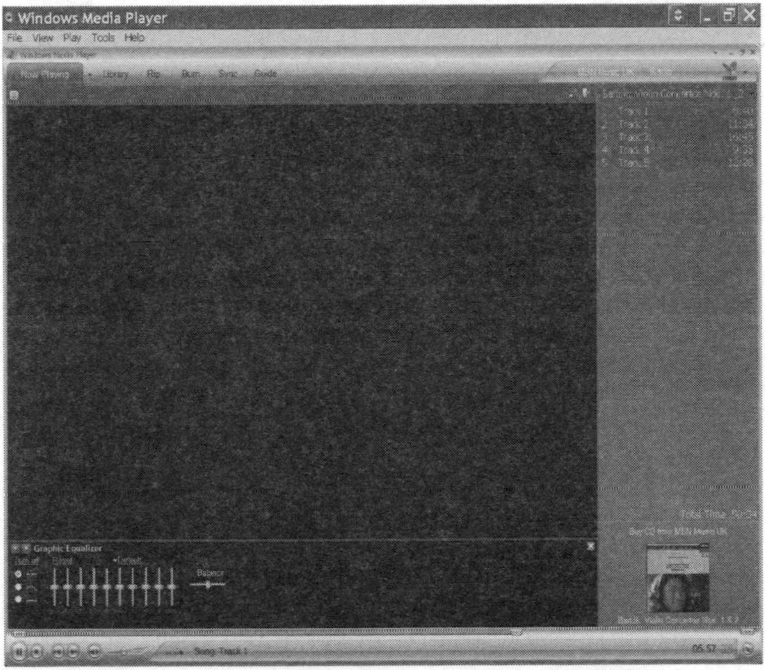

Fig.3.40 *The tracks on the CD appear in the Now Playing list*

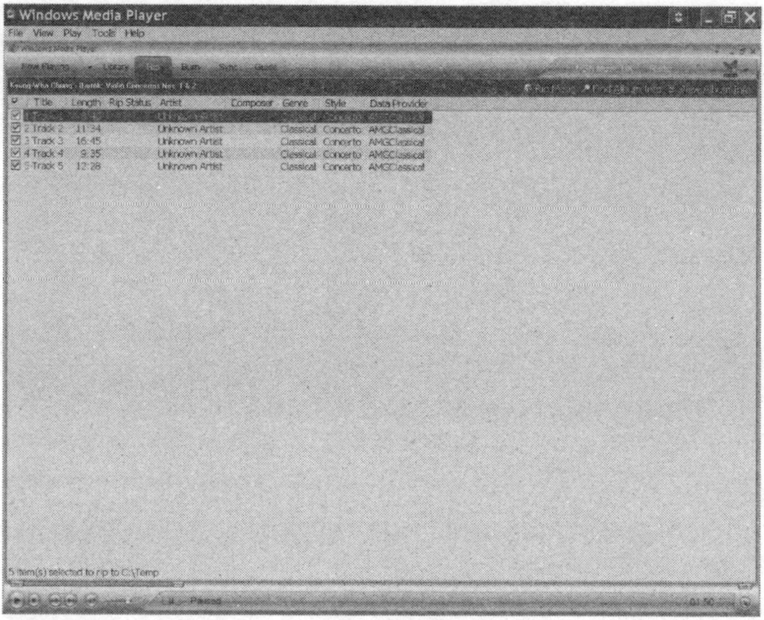

Fig.3.41 The tracks on the CD are listed in the main panel

(Figure 3.39). The tracks on the CD will then appear in the Now Playing list, and the front cover artwork will probably be displayed beneath the list (Figure 3.40).

I suppose there is potentially some added convenience in ripping CDs and playing the audio files stored on the hard disc drive instead of playing the CDs themselves. There are drawbacks as well, such as the time taken to rip the CDs and the fact that the resultant audio files will take up space on the computer's hard disc drive. The normal reason for ripping CDs is so that the audio files produced can be uploaded to an MP3 player. There is a real problem with WMP 9 and earlier versions in that they can only produce WMA files from CDs, and it can not produce MP3 files. This is not the case with WMP 10, which can produce MP3 files with bit rates of 128, 192, 256, and 320 kilobits per second. This is not to say that you should opt for MP3 and ignore the WMA format.

These days it seems to be the norm for MP3 players to handle WMA files as well. However, the ability to play WMA files is by no means universal. My upmarket MP3 player is capable of handling MP3, WMA, and WAV

Fig.3.42 Operate the Rip Music button to start the process

files, but my budget player can only play MP3 files. The instruction manual for your player or player should give details of which file formats it can handle. If in doubt, produce a WMA file, transfer it to the player, and see if it can play it.

Although MP3 is synonymous with media players and is the first choice of most users, there is an advantage in using WMA in cases where it is an option. WMA tends to produce smaller files for a given level of audio quality, so it enables more files to be stored on an MP3 player. This type of thing is very subjective, but some users consider that using WMA instead of MP3 effectively doubles the storage capacity of their players.

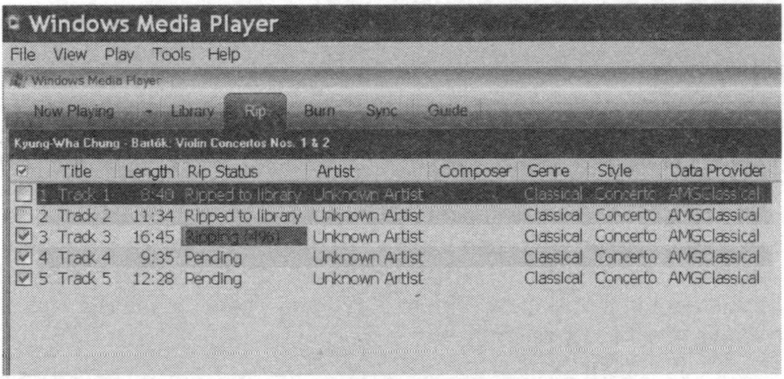

☑	Title	Length	Rip Status	Artist	Composer	Genre	Style	Data Provider
☐	1 Track 1	8:40	Ripped to library	Unknown Artist		Classical	Concerto	AMGClassical
☐	2 Track 2	11:34	Ripped to library	Unknown Artist		Classical	Concerto	AMGClassical
☑	3 Track 3	16:45	Ripping (49%)	Unknown Artist		Classical	Concerto	AMGClassical
☑	4 Track 4	9:35	Pending	Unknown Artist		Classical	Concerto	AMGClassical
☑	5 Track 5	12:28	Pending	Unknown Artist		Classical	Concerto	AMGClassical

Fig.3.43 The program shows how things are progressing

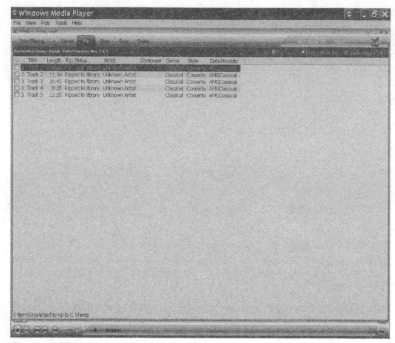

Fig.3.44 *The ripping process has been completed successfully*

Using WMA certainly enables a significantly higher number of audio files
to be accommodated in a given amount of storage space.

Ripping

In order to rip a CD the WMP 10 Rip tab should be active and the CD
should be placed in the CD-ROM drive. A list of the tracks on the CD will
then appear in the main panel of the WMP 10 window, as in the example
of Figure 3.41. There is a checkbox to the left of each track's entry, and
all the checkboxes are ticked initially. Remove the ticks for any tracks
that you do not wish to rip. There are three buttons near the top right-
hand corner of the window (Figure 3.42), and operating the Rip Music
button starts the ripping process.

The program will then start reading and ripping the selected tracks and
it will show its progress (Figure 3.43). To rip a full CD will take a few

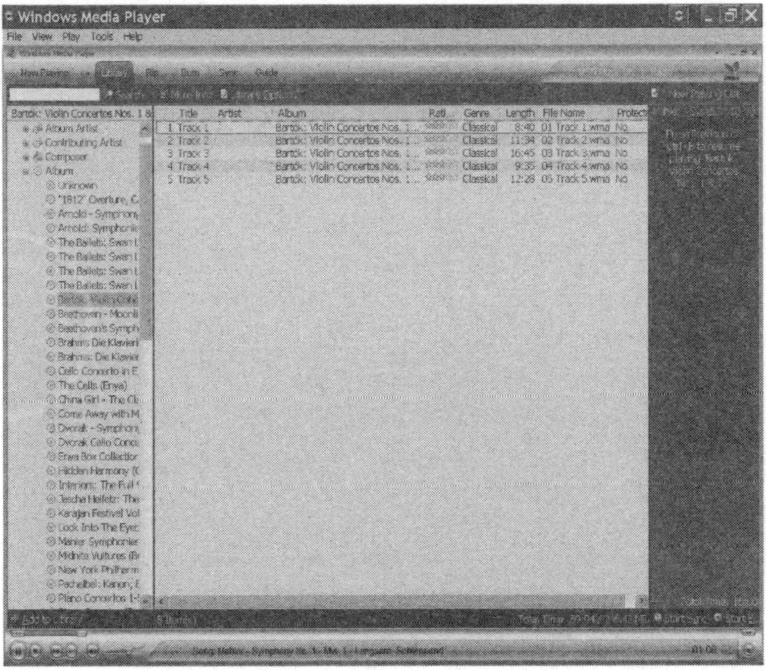

Fig.3.45 The ripped tracks have been placed in the library

minutes. The exact time taken depends on the total length of the tracks, the speed of the CD-ROM drive, and the speed of the PC, but it should only take a fraction of the time it would take to play the tracks. Eventually the process will finish (Figure 3.44) and the tracks will be placed in the Library (Figure 3.45).

The tracks are stored on the hard disc drive in the default directory, which is usually the My Music subfolder of your Documents folder. You can choose a different folder by selecting Options from the Tools menu, which produces the Options window (Figure 3.46). The Options window has numerous sections, with the usual tab arrangement at the top so that the required section can be selected. In this case the Rip Music tab should be operated, which switches the window to look like Figure 3.47. Operate the Change button to select a new folder for storing ripped music files. This produces the folder version of the Windows file browser.

This section of the Options window is also used to set the format for the ripped audio files. There are three WMA options available from the Format

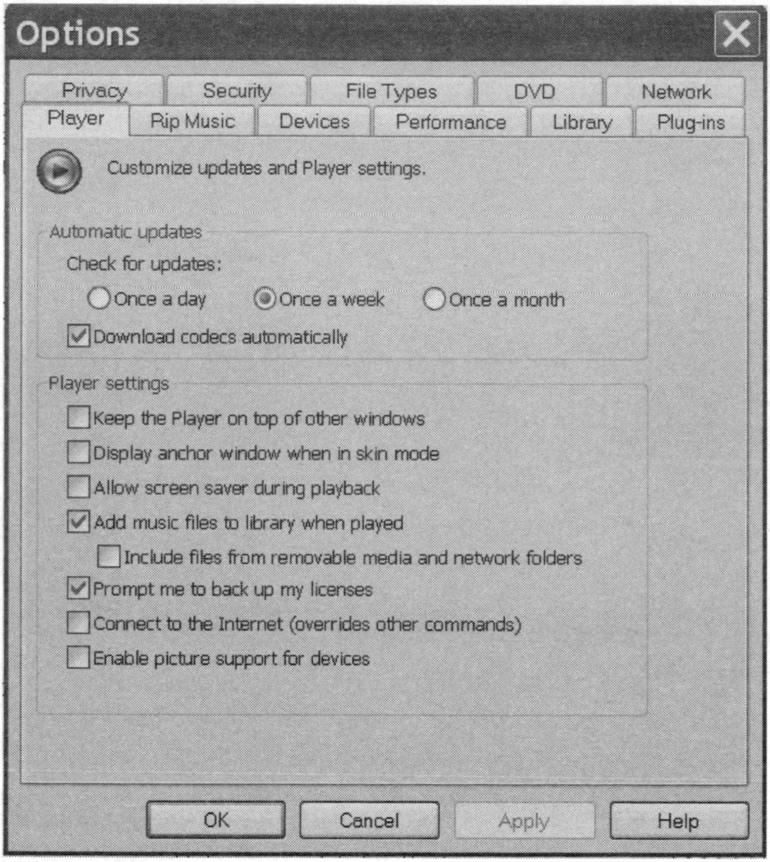

Fig.3.46 The Player section of the Options window

menu plus an MP3 option (Figure 3.48). The lossless version of WMA retains the full quality of the source material, but provides relatively little file compression and might give compatibility problems with some devices. The standard and variable bit rate versions of WMA are more appropriate for portable players. The standard version is the one that provides the best compatibility with portable players and other player software.

The Audio quality slider control is not active when WMA lossless audio is selected, since there is no loss of quality with this format. It does become

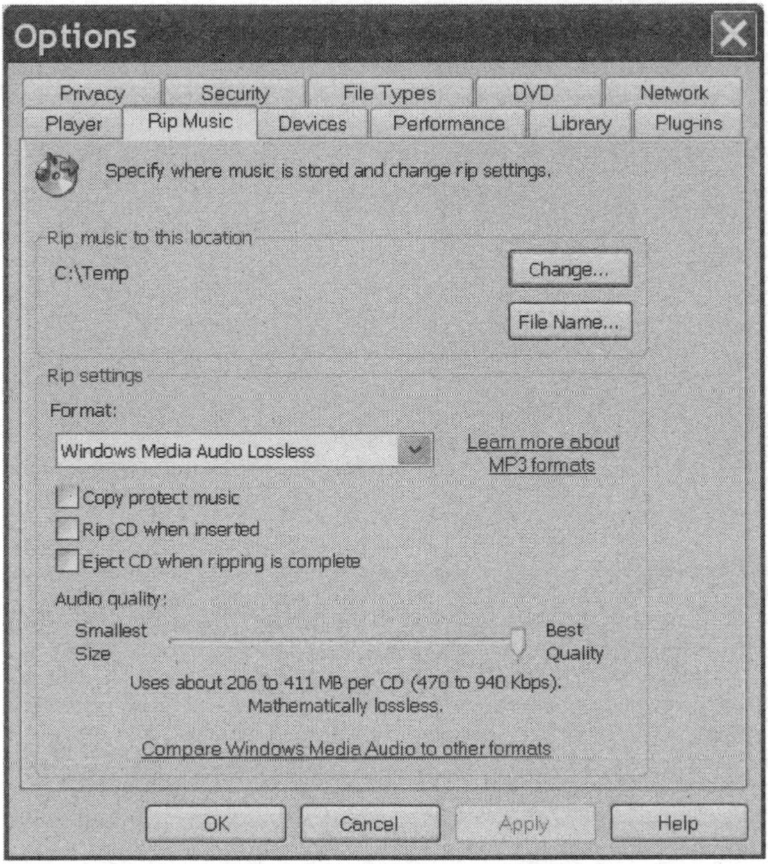

Fig.3.47 The Rip Music section of the Options window

active when the other three formats are selected. Figure 3.49 shows the control with MP3 encoding selected. In addition to showing the selected bit rate, an estimation of the total file size for a typical CD is also indicated. With MP3 music files it is not a good idea to use a bit rate of less than 128 kilobits per second, but this is academic here because no lower rate is offered by WMP 10. Higher rates give better quality, but some MP3 players can not handle the highest rates of 256 and 320 kilobits per second. It is best to try some experiments to determine which bit rates and formats your player supports, and to find the lowest bit rate that provides what you deem to be acceptable quality.

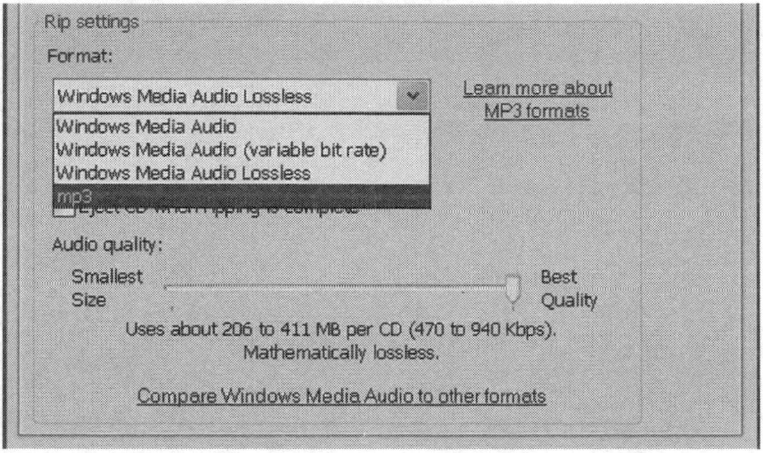

Fig.3.48 Three versions of WMA plus an MP3 option are available

Burning

In a digital audio context, "burning" is the process of copying files onto a CDR or CD-RW disc. It is important to realise that there are two very different types of audio CD. One type is the usual audio CD that will work properly in any CD player. The other is really a computer data disc where the data consists of audio files such as MP3 or WMA types. At one time there was little point in putting a data disc into any CD player, since it would not have the wherewithal to play the files on the disc. Indeed, it would not have the ability to properly read the disc, and would probably be unable to make anything of it at all.

These days the situation is rather different, and some CD players do have the ability to read data discs that contain music files. However, this feature is by no means universal even on new players, and very few can accommodate anything other than MP3 files. Also, players that can handle MP3 files will not necessarily be able to handle files that have a bit rate of more than about 256 kilobits per second, or a variable bit rate. The ever-popular bit rate of 128 kilobits per second is the safest option, and gives the widest possible compatibility.

There is a big advantage in using MP3 files if your players can handle this format. Using MP3 it is possible to fit onto a single CD-ROM what would otherwise require several normal audio CDs. The amount of audio

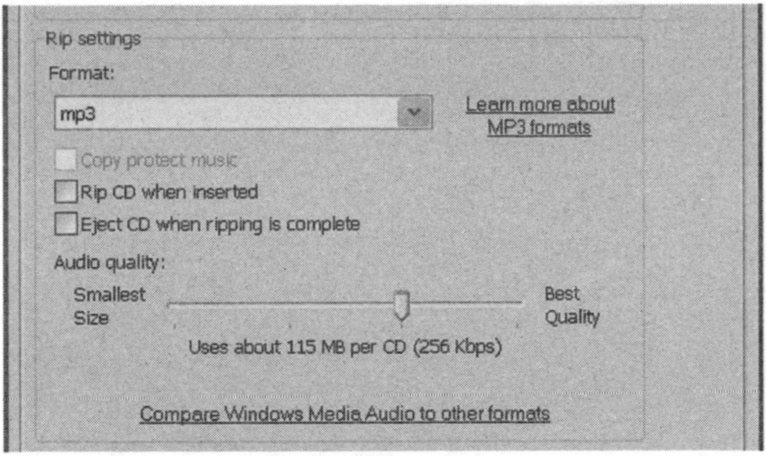

Fig.3.49 *The slider is used to control the bit rate*

that can be placed on a CD-ROM in MP3 format depends on the bit rate used, but with reasonable quality you could probably fit the contents of 10 typical CDs onto one CD-ROM. The big drawback is that a disc of MP3 files can only be used with some CD players, although it should be usable with any modern computer. A normal audio CD gives the widest compatibility, as it should be playable on any CD player or computer. Note though, that some CD players do not work well with CDR discs, and relatively few work well with CD-RW discs.

The fact that a player is not claimed to have CDR compatibility does not necessarily mean that it will not play ordinary audio discs recorded onto CDR discs. It just means that the manufacturer is not making any promises in this respect. Many players seem to be capable of handling CDR discs, but some discs give good compatibility with ordinary players while others are largely unplayable. Practical experience suggests that the CDRs which have strongly coloured coatings are less good for audio use than those that are very pale with an almost silver coloured surface. CDRs specifically for audio use are produced, and these should give the best compatibility with audio players. Unfortunately, they tend to be significantly more expensive than ordinary data discs. It is unlikely that a CD-RW disc will be usable in a player that is not specifically designed for use with this type of disc.

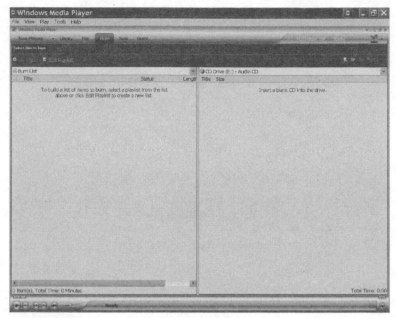

Fig.3.50 The CD burning mode of WMP 10

Burn list

To write MP3 or other audio files onto a CDR disc you need a CD burning program such as one of the popular programs from the Ahead Nero range. Most drives and PCs are supplied with Nero CD Burning ROM or a similar program, so it is unlikely that you will need to buy any burning software. You simply copy the music files to the disc in the same way that files are normally copied and burned to a data disc. Burning a normal audio CD is more complex because the source files must be converted into data of the correct format for the CD, and everything then has to be burned onto the CD using the standard audio CD format. Many CD burning programs can do this, but it is also a feature of WMP 10

In order to burn tracks onto a CD you must first make a burn list containing the required tracks in the order that they must be placed on the CD. One way of doing this is to first operate the Burn tab to take WMP 10 into the burning mode (Figure 3.50). Then left-click the Edit Play list button to produce the pop-up window of Figure 3.51. The left-hand section of this

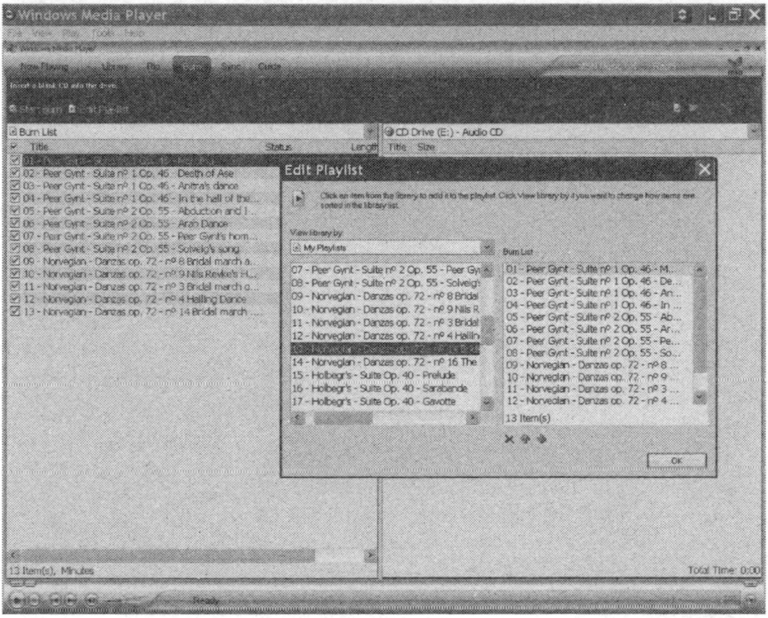

Fig.3.51 Play lists can be edited

window contains a sort of condensed version of the WMP 10 Library. The main sections can be expanded to show their contents, and left-clicking an entry for a file results in it being added to the list on the right. It is also added to the burn list in the main window.

The burn list is gradually built up by selecting each file for the new CD. If you change your mind, a file can be removed from the list by selecting it in the right-hand panel and operating the button marked with a red cross. The files will placed on the CD in the same order as they appear in the list. A file can be moved up in the list by selecting it in the right-hand panel and left-clicking the button that has an arrow pointing upwards. Essentially the same method is used to move a file down one place, but the button with the arrow pointing downwards is used instead. Operate the OK button when the list is just as you require it. Actually, it is probably best to select the required files and then do any "fine tuning" back in the main window. In order to move a file to a new position in the list it is just a matter of dragging it into position. An entry can be deleted by right-clicking it and selecting Remove Entry from the pop-up menu.

Fig.3.52 Select Burn List from the menu

An alternative way of making a burn list is to switch to the Library view, left-click the button at the top of the list column, and then select the Burn List (Figure 3.52). You then create the list in much the same way that a play list is produced. Find the required tracks in the main window and then drag them to the list in the right-hand column. With a very large number of items in the library it can be difficult to find the items you require even if the library is well organised.

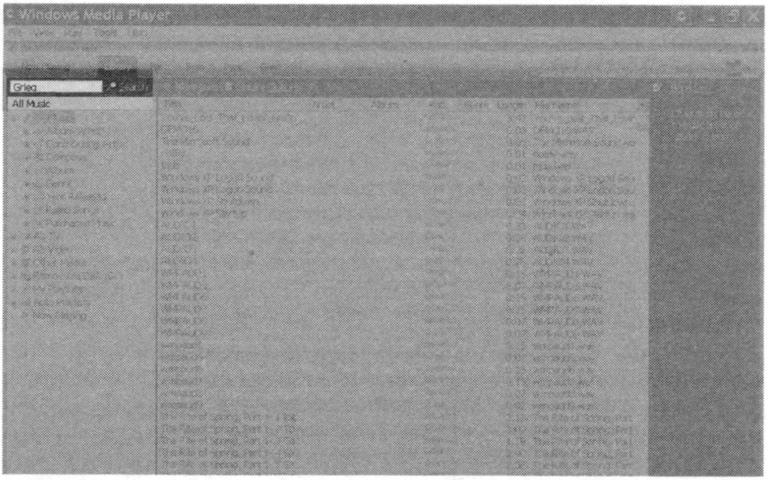

Fig.3.53 There is a search facility that makes it easy to find any track

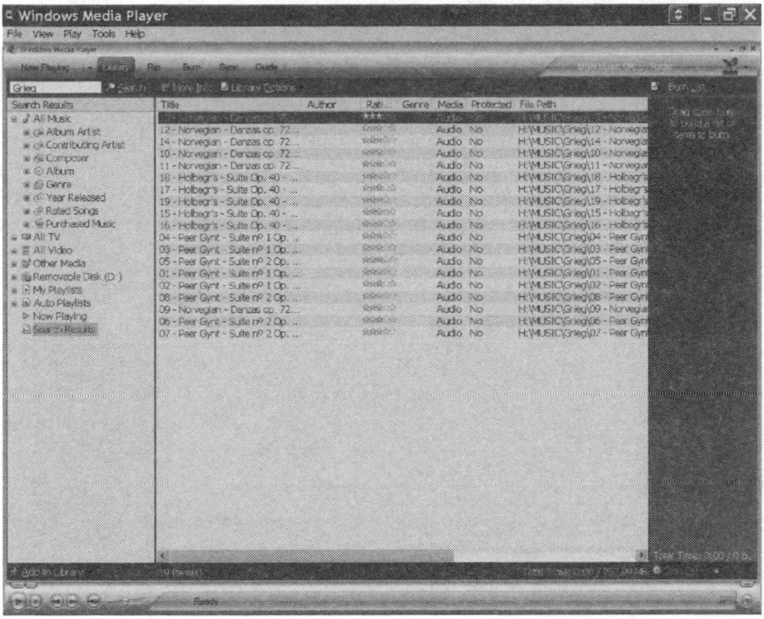

Fig.3.54 The search has produced a list of matching results

Often the easiest way of locating items is to type a suitable search term into the textbox near the top left-hand corner of the window (Figure 3.53). Operating the Search button with then produce a list of matching results (Figure 3.54). The required tracks are dragged into the play list (Figure 3.55), and they will then appear in the burn list back at the Burn section of the program (Figure 3.56). If necessary, the tracks are dragged into the appropriate order, and the list is then ready to be burned to a CD.

There are other ways of producing the burn list. For example, you can produce a Now Playing list in the usual way, and then select the items that you wish to place in the burn list. Next, right-click one of the selected items and select Add to ... Burn List from the pop-up menu (Fig.3.57). All the selected items will then be added to the burn list. If the required items are already in a play list, in the Burn section of the program operate the Edit Play list button. The play list should be listed in the left-hand section of the Edit Play list window, where its contents can be accessed in the normal way.

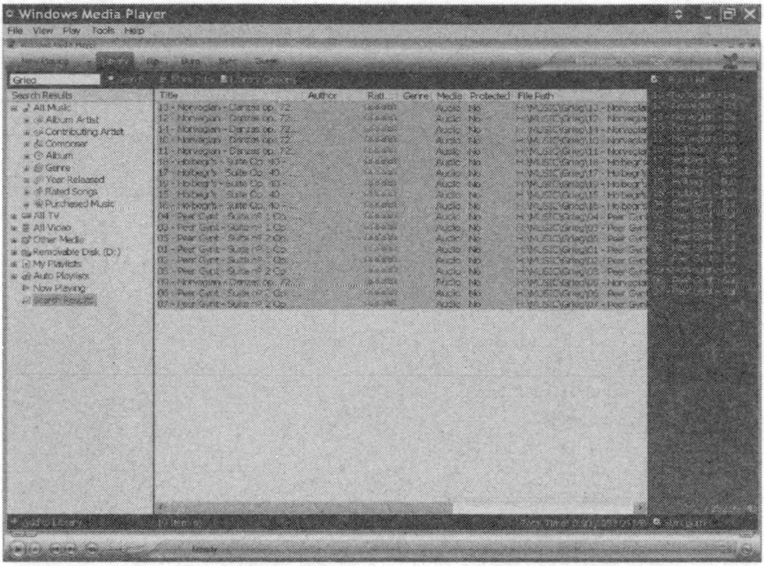

Fig.3.55　The required tracks have been dragged to the play list

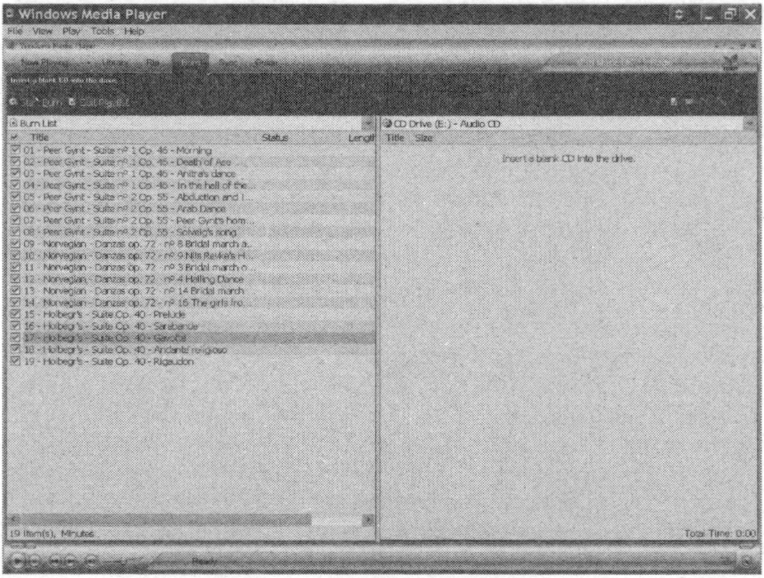

Fig.3.56　The selected tracks also appear in the burn list

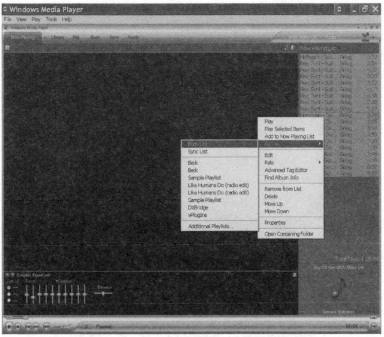

Fig.3.57 The Now Playing list can be added to the burn list

Start burning

Once the burn list is complete, the next step is to place a blank CDR or
CD-RW disc into the drive that you use for writing CDs. This should
remove the message in the right-hand section of the screen where it
says "Insert a blank CD into the drive". If this message does not disappear
after a few seconds the most likely cause of the problem is that you have
two CD/DVD writers and the wrong one is selected. The correct drive
can be selected by left-clicking the bar just above the right-hand panel
and selecting it in the drop-down menu (Figure 3.58). The message
should then change to read "There are no items on the CD". If all is well,
the left-hand section of the window should give the duration and file size
of each track, and the status for each one should be given as Ready
(Figure 3.59). Warning messages should be produced if there is a
problem, such as too much material to fit the CD. Do not try to go ahead
with the burn process until any problems have been rectified.

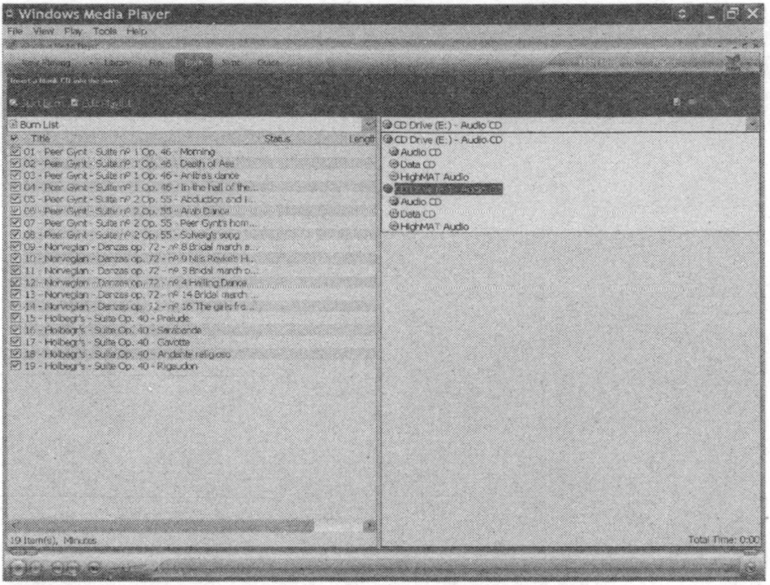

Fig.3.58 If necessary, select the appropriate CD/DVD drive

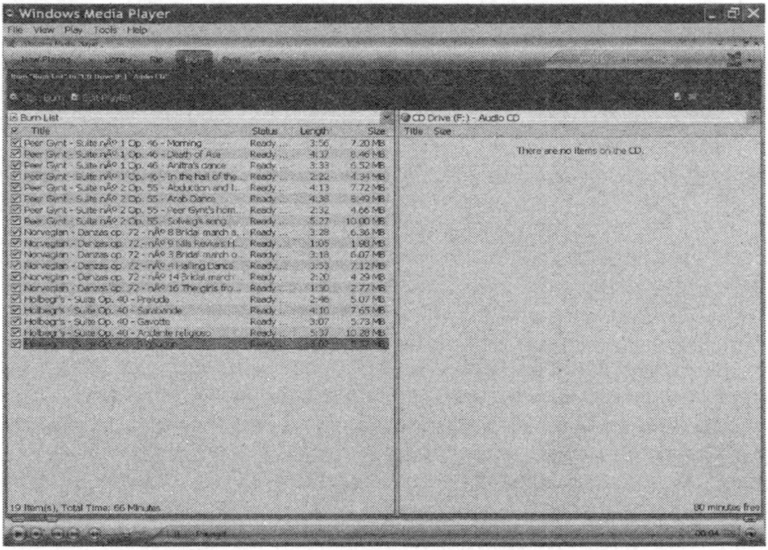

Fig.3.59 The status of each track should be given as "Ready"

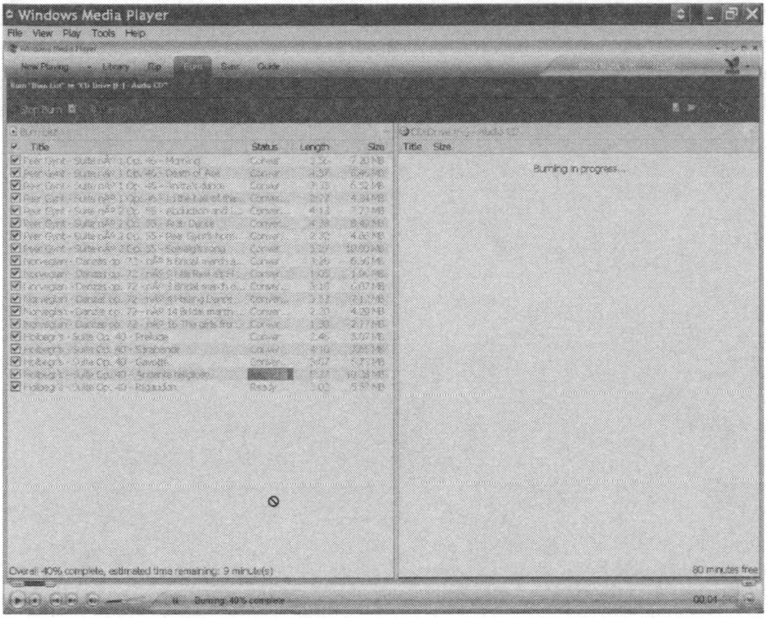

Fig.3.60 *The left-hand panel shows how things are progressing*

Assuming everything is present and correct, the burn process is started by operating the Start Burn button. Although the message in the right-hand panel changes to "Burn in progress", what actually happens first is that the source files are converted into the data that will be written to the CD. The original files are left intact, and the new data is temporarily stored on the hard disc drive. The left-hand panel shows how far the conversion process has progressed (Figure 3.60). Once the conversion has been completed, the burning process begins, with the tracks being burned onto the CD one by one. Once again, the left-hand panel shows how things are progressing (Figure 3.61).

Burning CDs has never been as reliable as writing data to a hard disc drive or most other types of mass storage media. In this example the burning process was nearly finished when the error message of Figure 3.62 was produced. Unfortunately, if the burn is not completed successfully you are left with an unusable CD. There are several common causes for CDs failing to burn correctly, and it can simply be that the particular drive and media you are using lack good compatibility. This is

Windows Media Player
File View Play Tools Help
Title
Status
Length
Size
Burning in progress...
Overall 83% complete, estimated time remaining: 3 minute(s)
60 minutes free

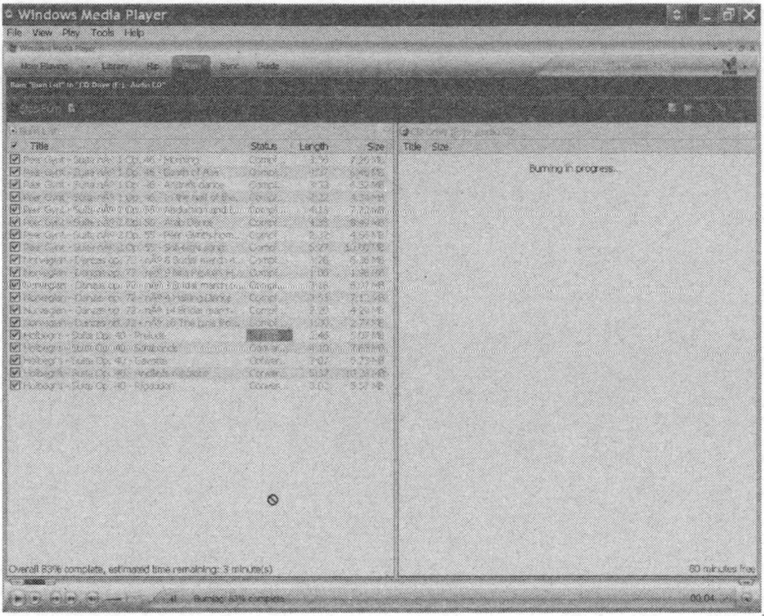

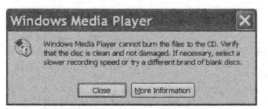

Fig.3.61 Again, the left-hand panel shows how things are progressing

less problematic than when the very fast (48x and 52x) CD writers first appeared, but it is an issue that has not completely disappeared.

Another possible cause of a CD burning failure is that the disc was damaged or that its surface was not clean enough. Minute scratches and particles of dust are unlikely to give problems, but anything more than this can bring things to an abrupt halt. If a CDR disc is dirty it should be cleaned prior to burning tracks onto it. There is no harm in using a disc that has scratches or other minor damage, but do not be surprised if the finished disc is unusable. Discs that are warped or significantly damage should not be used, as they could damage the CD writer.

Windows Media Player
Windows Media Player cannot burn the files to the CD. Verify that the disc is clean and not damaged. If necessary, select a slower recording speed or try a different brand of blank discs.
Close
More Information

Fig.3.62 The burn process has failed

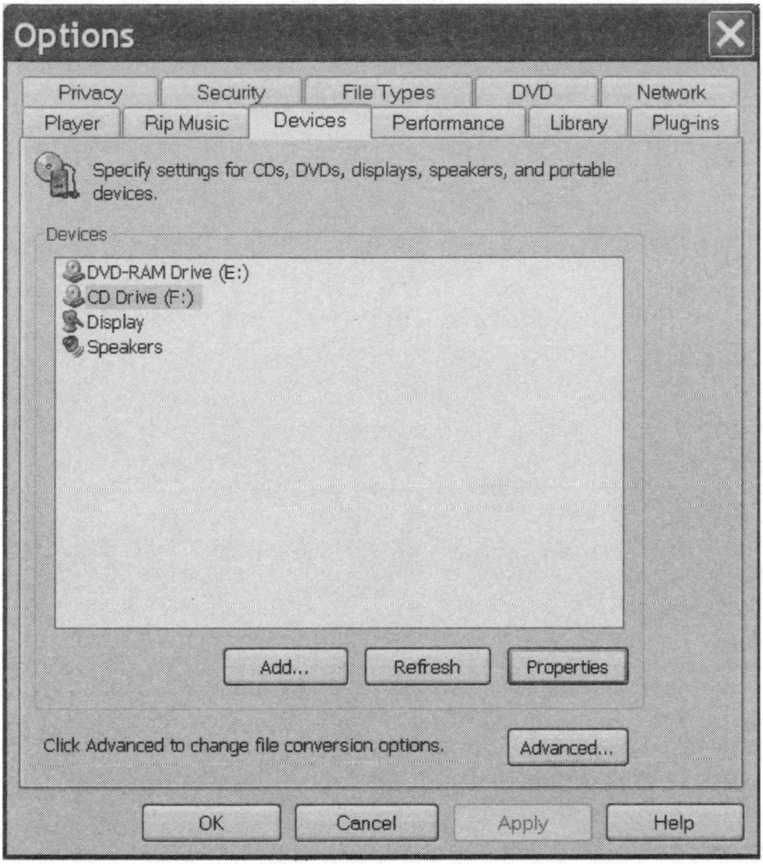

Fig.3.63 The Devices section of the Options window

Modern CD writers have various forms of burn-proof technology that are designed to avoid unusable discs if the computer momentarily "loses the plot" during the recording process. In the early days of CD writers it was essential to have no other applications running while any CD burning was in progress. If another program require too much of the computer's processing time it would not be possible for the burning software to continue burning continuously, and the disc would be ruined.

Things are much better these days due to PCs generally having much greater computing power and the drives having technology that can

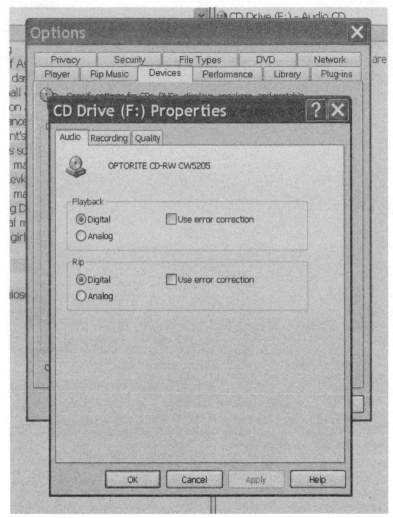

Fig.3.64 The Properties window for the selected drive

"gloss over" short breaks in the recording process. Even so, if the computer's workload is too high it is still possible that burning CDs will produce a significant failure rate. If burning sessions keep coming to an abrupt and unsuccessful conclusion, avoid having any other major computing tasks running while burning CDs to see if this helps.

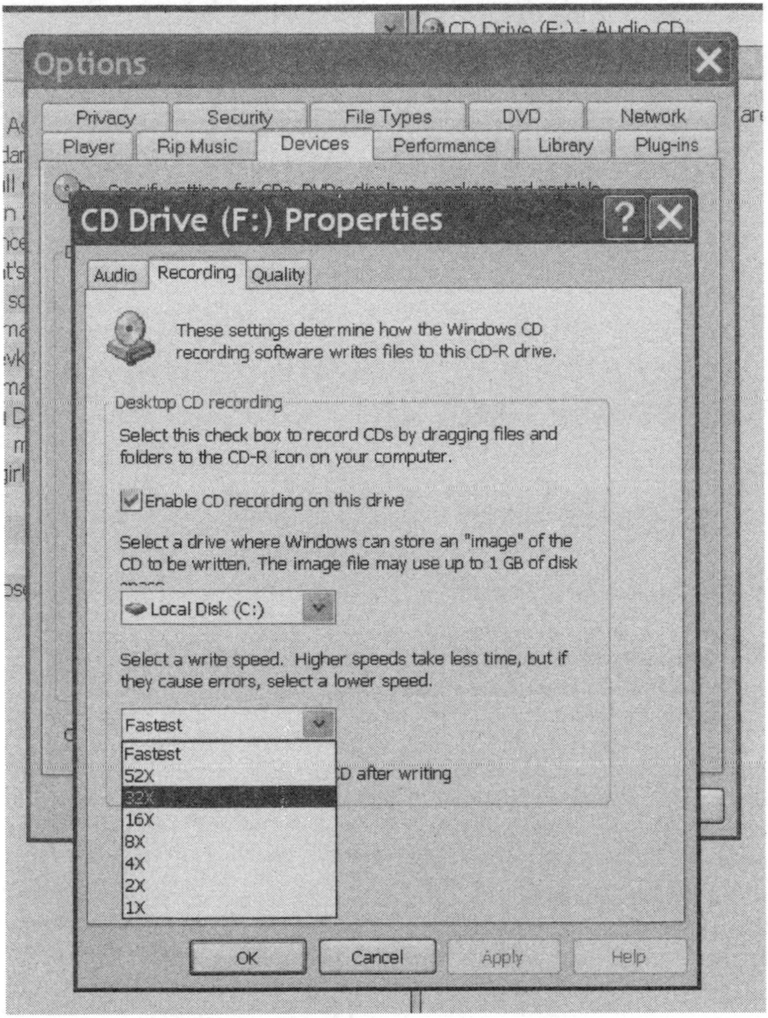

Fig.3.65 The menu offers a range of recording speeds

In this case the burning process had come to an end with the disc about 95 percent finished, which was happening quite often and when using various burning software. The problem could be due to the computer "running out of steam" before the disc was complete, or it could simply

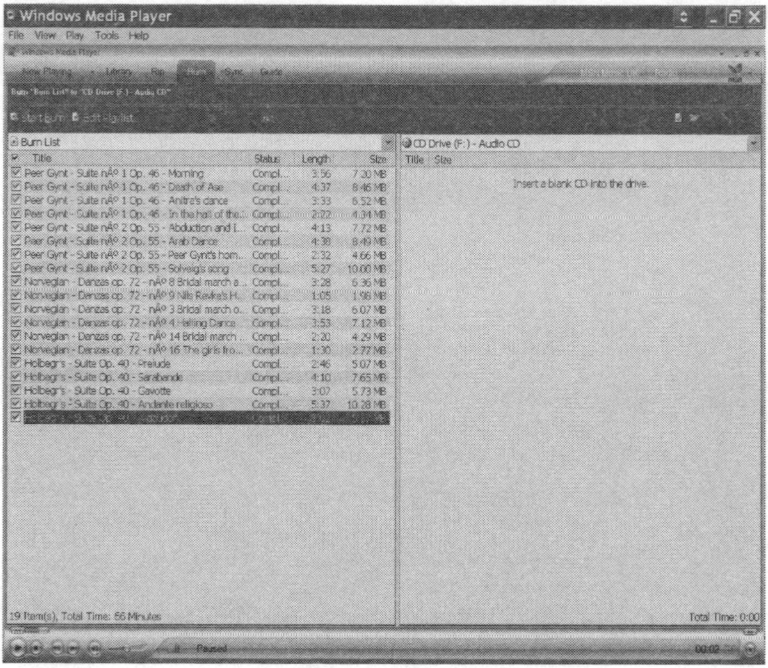

Fig.3.66 This time there is a successful conclusion

be due to the drive being what computer professionals term "cream-crackered". Either way, using a slightly slower burning speed will often help. In WMP 10 the burn speed is changed by going to the Options window (Tools – Options) and operating the Devices tab (Figure 3.63).

In the main panel select the device you are using for CD burning and then operate the Properties button. This launches the Properties window for the drive (Figure 3.64), and here the Recording tab should be left-clicked. The menu near the bottom of the window offers a range of recording speeds (Figure 3.65), and it is just a matter of choosing a setting that is one or two settings lower than the maximum. In this case I settled for a reduction in speed from 52x to 32x recording. Left-click the Apply and OK buttons to make the change take effect and to close the Properties window. Then operate the OK button of the Options window to close that one as well. Using a lower burning speed had the desired result, and a second attempt took the burning process through to a successful conclusion (Figure 3.66).

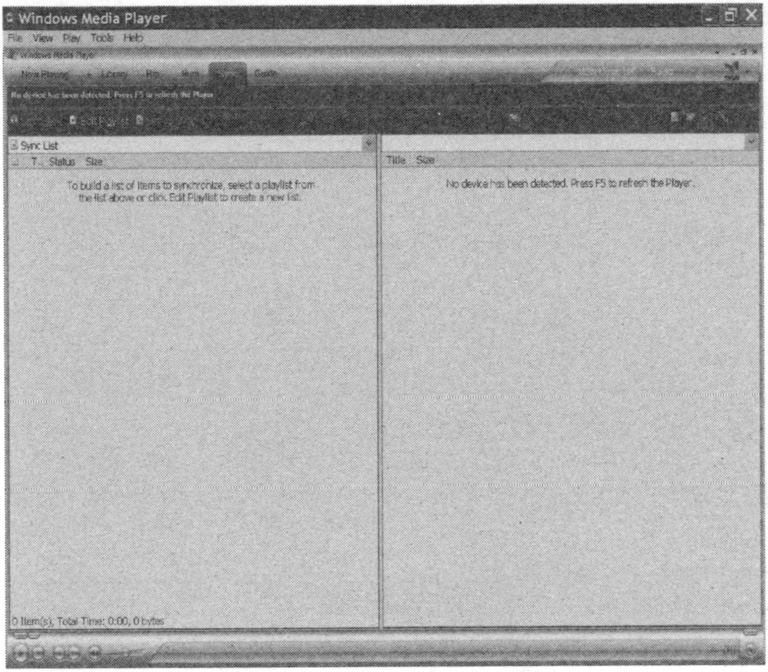

Fig.3.67 The Synchronisation section of the program

Synchronisation

Synchronisation is the process of maintaining identical file structures on two devices. In the current context it means keeping the music stored on a portable player the same as the music in the WMP 10 Library. WMP 10 has a synchronisation feature that is accessed by operating the Sync tab (Figure 3.67). Unfortunately, this feature is not usable with all portable players. The player must either be a Microsoft Multimedia Transport Protocol (MTP) type, or one that the computer regards as a mass storage device.

The chances of your player being MTP compatible are probably not very good, but a substantial percentage of MP3 players operate as a mass storage device when connected to a PC. In other words, the player is assigned a drive letter by the operating system, and it can then be accessed just like any other disc drive. In most cases you can use the player to store non-music files, effectively using it as an ordinary USB drive.

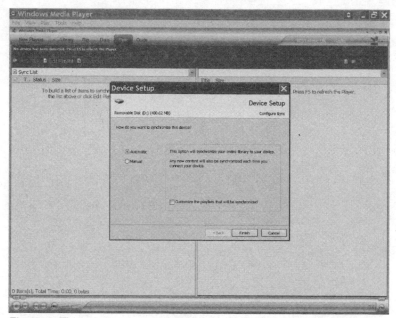

Fig.3.68 This window appears when the player has been detected

There is a slight complication here in that some players are assigned a drive letter, but simply copying music files to them does not have the desired effect. The player will only find and use music files if they are copied to the device in the appropriate fashion, which usually means that you have to use the software provided with the device. If your player is one that works properly when Windows Explorer is used to transfer files to it, and to delete any files that are no longer needed, then it should be possible to use the player with the WMP 10 synchronisation feature.

When the player is connected to the computer it will probably be detected by WMP 10, and the pop-up window of Figure 3.68 will appear when it is connected for the first time. Press the F5 function key if the player is not automatically detected, and WMP 10 will then search for it. The pop-up window gives the option of using manual or automatic synchronisation, and the automatic variety will be considered first. With automatic synchronisation the contents of the library will be uploaded to the player (Figure 3.69). The right-hand panel shows the files that have been uploaded to the player, and this will be all the files in the library when the uploading has been finished (Figure 3.70).

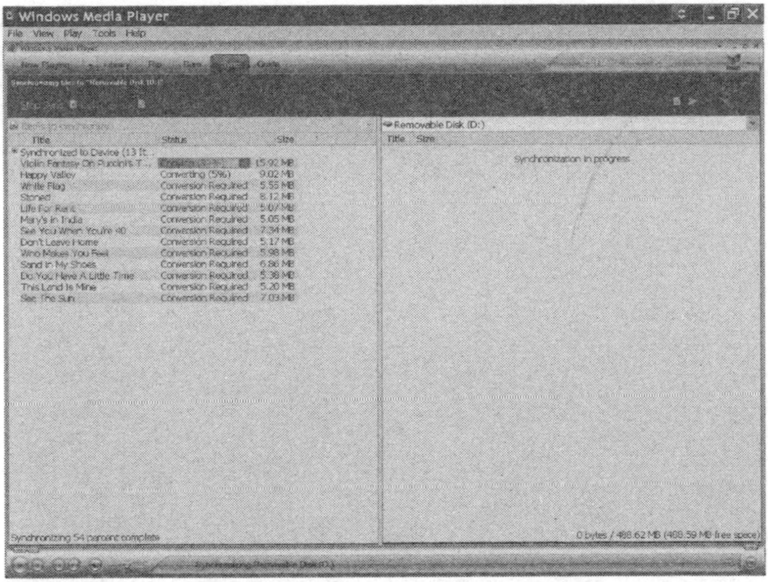

Fig.3.69 The contents of the library are being uploaded

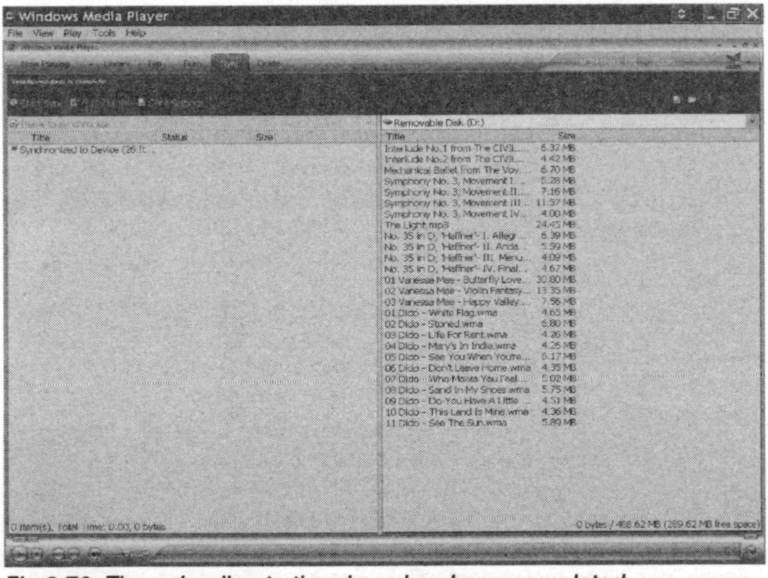

Fig.3.70 The uploading to the player has been completed

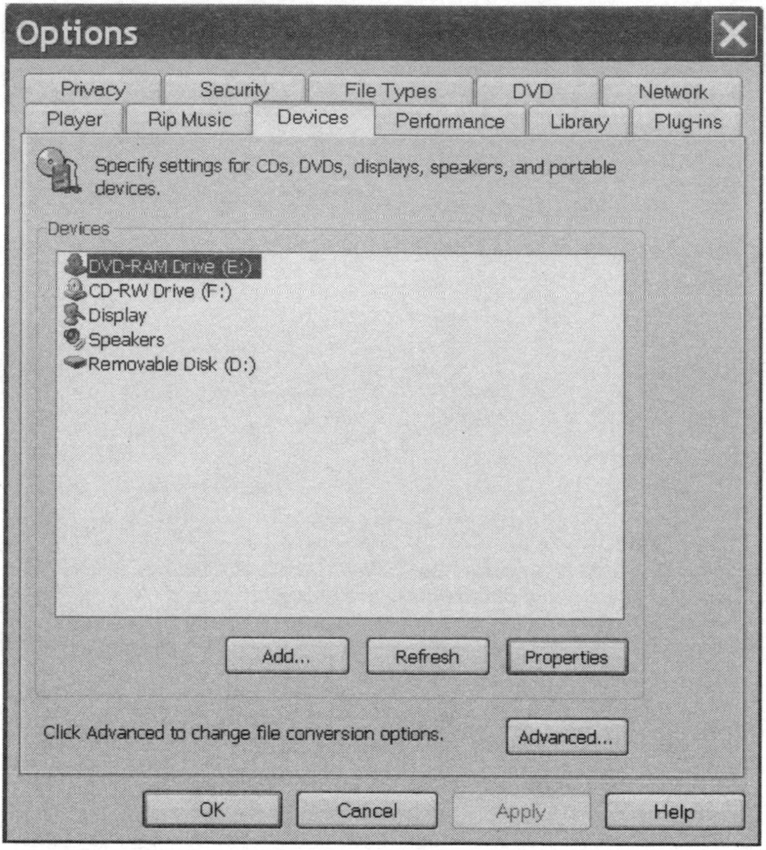

Fig.3.71 Select the appropriate device in the Options window

During the uploading process it is possible that the left-hand panel will indicate that some of the files are being converted, even if they are all MP3 types. By default, WMP 10 will try to ensure that the player is not fed with files that it will probably not be able to play. It will also try to keep files very compact so that as much music as possible can be uploaded to the player. Consequently, when left to "do its own thing" WMP 10 might decide to convert high bit rate files to a lower bit rate.

This is fine in principle, but it will not necessarily have the intended result in practice. Your player might have plenty of storage space and be well capable of playing high bit-rate files, variable bit rate types, or whatever.

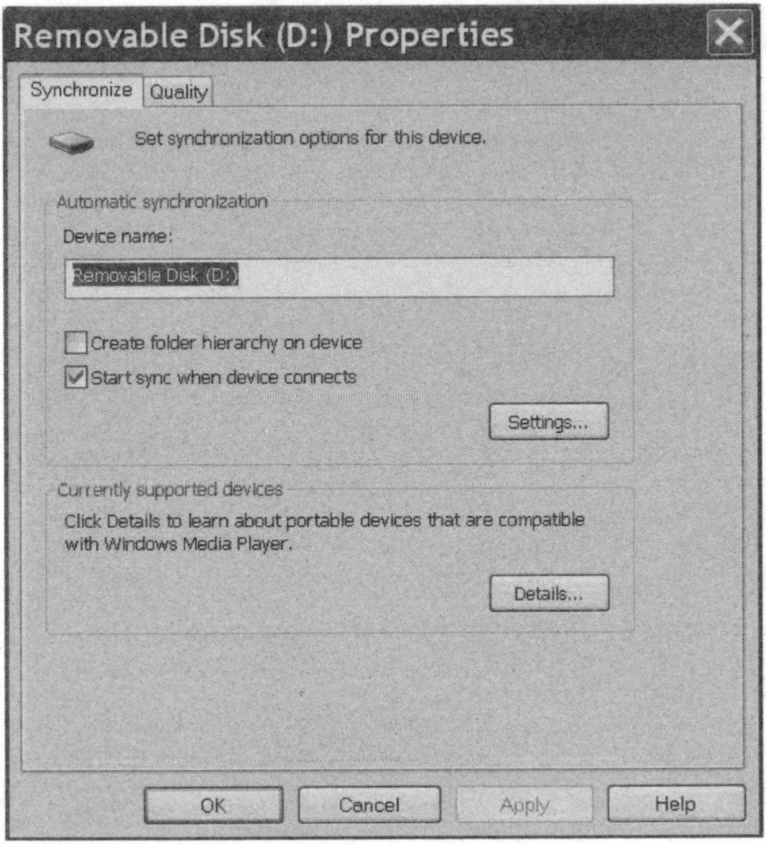

Fig.3.72 Remove the tick from the lower checkbox

The conversion could simply provide an unnecessary reduction in quality. A potentially worse problem is that WMP 10 might decide that a conversion from MP3 to WMA format is in order. This is a good idea with an MP3 player that supports the WMA format, since it has the potential to fit more music onto the player without any loss of audio quality. On the other hand, it is not much use if the player can not play WMA files.

In this example a number of files were converted to WMA format, but they were uploaded to a player that could only play MP3 files. Fortunately, it is possible to suppress the automatic converting of files, but it is then up to the user to ensure that the material uploaded to the player is

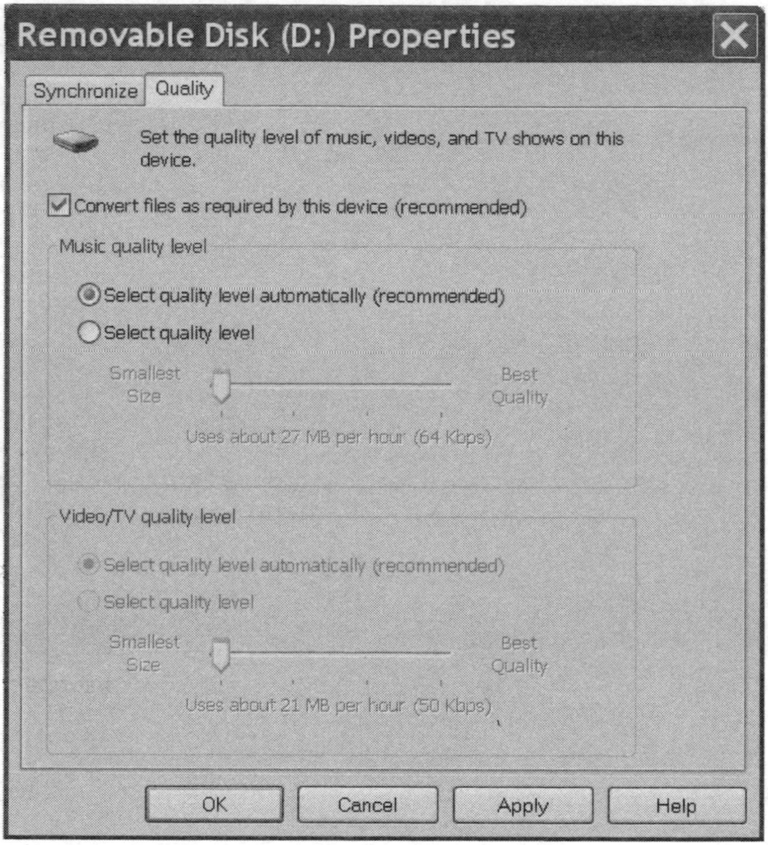

Fig.3.73 The Quality section of the Properties window

reasonably compact and in a form that it can handle. To prevent any file conversions, select Options from the Tools menu and then activate the Devices tab in the Options window (Figure 3.71). Select the appropriate device in the main panel and then operate the Properties button.

Quality

In the Properties window (Figure 3.72) there is a checkbox marked "Start sync when device connects", and this is ticked by default. Remove the tick from this box if would prefer to start synchronisation manually.

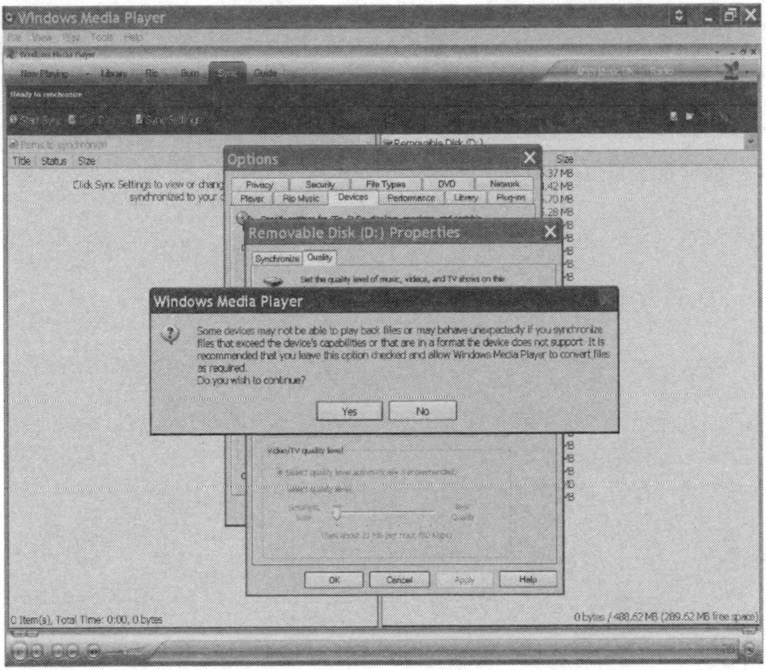

Fig.3.74 This warning message appears if you opt to block automatic file conversions

Operating the Quality tab switches the Properties window so that it looks like Figure 3.73. By default the audio quality is set automatically, but you can set the quality manually by operating the "Select quality level" radio button and adjusting the slider for the required WMA bit rate.

Remove the tick from the checkbox near the top of the window in order to completely block any automatic file conversions. This will produce the warning message of Figure 3.74, but you are clearly better off handling things manually if the automatic conversions are producing files that your player can not handle. Operate the Yes button to go ahead and block automatic file conversions. Then operate the Apply and OK buttons to close the Properties window, and then the OK button to close the Options window. Having deleted all the files from the player I tried to synchronise it to WMP 10 again, and Figure 3.75 shows the result. This time it has just uploaded the files to the player with no conversions, and the player worked fine with the unprocessed files.

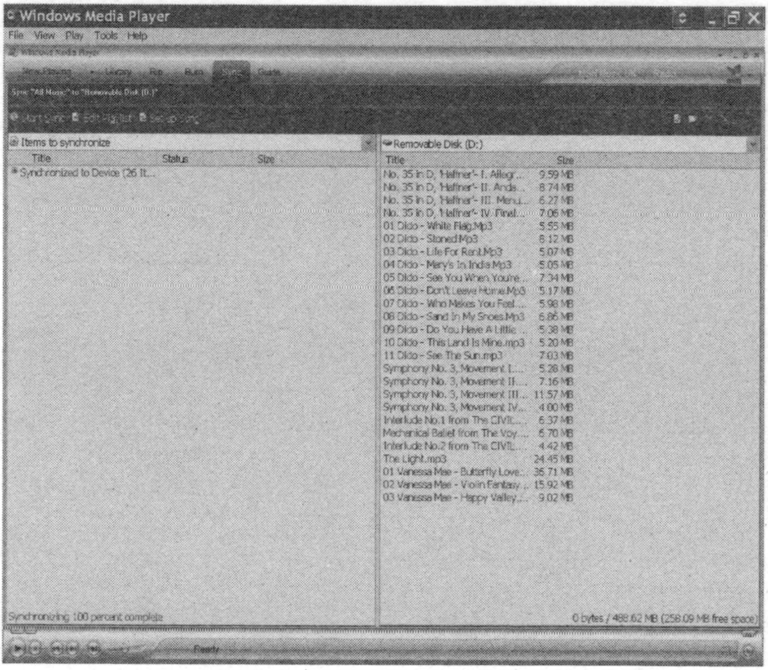

Fig.3.75 The files have been uploaded without any conversions being
applied

If changes are made to the library it is a simple matter to synchronise the
portable player to the new version of the library. In the Sync section of
WMP 10, operate the Sync List button and then select All Music from the
drop-down menu (Figure 3.76). All music is effectively the contents of
the library, so this should be everything you wish to upload to the portable
player. This loads the relevant entries into the left-hand panel of the
window, but by default none of the entries will be selected. In order to
select everything it is just a matter of left-clicking the checkbox at the
top, scrolling down to the bottom of the list if necessary, and then holding
down the Shift key while ticking the checkbox at the bottom. This will
result in the checkboxes being ticked (Figure 3.77).

With automatic detection it is then just a matter of connecting the player
and waiting for the newly added files to be uploaded to the player. In
order to avoid wasting time, WMP 10 will not upload any files that are
already stored in the player. Any music that has been deleted from the
library will also be deleted from the player so that it is kept fully

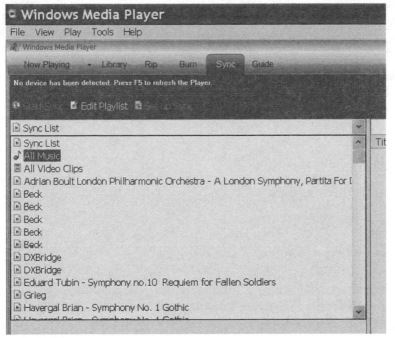

Fig.3.76 Select the All Music entry

synchronised with the library. The left-hand panel provides a summary of what it has done once the uploading has finished (Figure 3.78).

Note that you need to be careful when storing files other that audio types on the portable player. In general, WMP 10 will not delete any non-media files that it finds on the portable device. It will assume that these are files which are being stored separately from the audio types, and that you wish to leave them in place. The program will probably produce a pop-up message to this effect. You must delete any files of this type manually, using Windows Explorer perhaps.

It is important to keep in mind that WMP 10 can handle more than just audio files. It can play and display a wide range of media files including videos and even small graphic images. This opens up the possibility of WMP 10 detecting non-audio media files stored on the player and deleting them as part of the synchronisation process. Handling things manually is a safer option if you might need to store non-audio media files on the player.

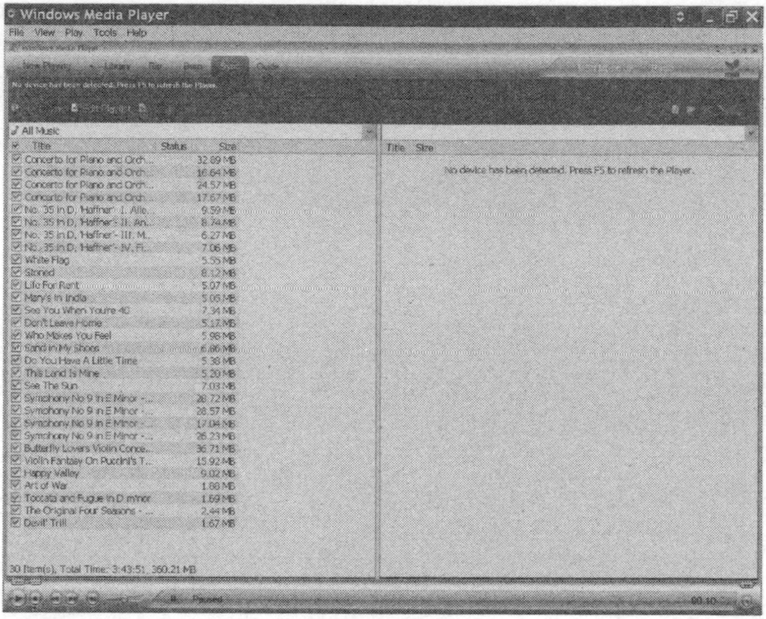

Fig.3.77 All the selection checkboxes have been ticked

Alternatives

The synchronisation offers plenty of alternatives from fully manual to totally automatic operation. When using the automatic method it is not necessary to upload every new track in the library. If you leave a track's checkbox without a tick it will not be uploaded. Uploaded tracks can be deleted should you change your mind. Use the right-hand panel to select the tracks you wish to remove, right-click on one of them, and then select Delete from the pop-up window (Figure 3.79).

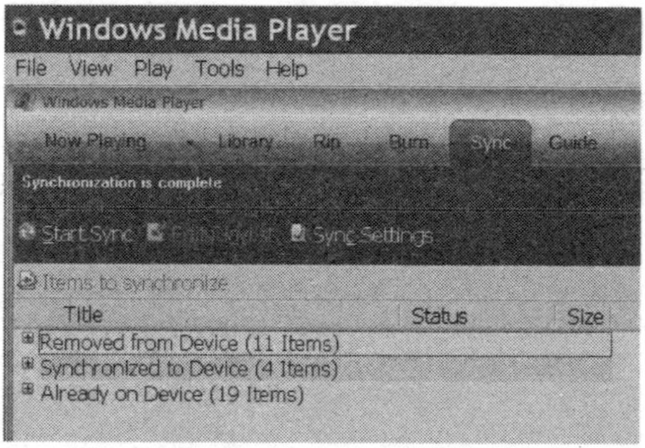

Fig.3.78 A summary is provided

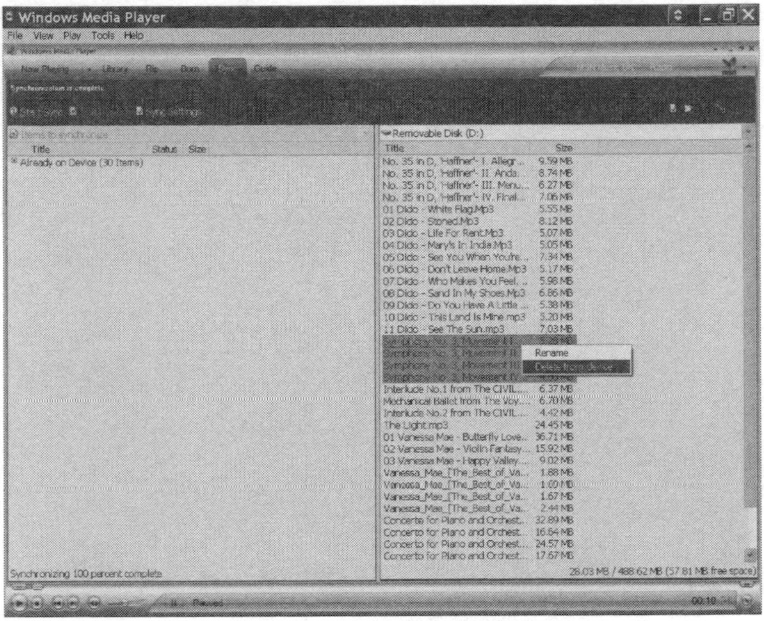

Fig.3.79 Tracks can be deleted from the player

In order to use the fully automatic approach it is necessary to have automatic detection enabled and to have no items listed in the left-hand panel of the Sync section of the program. Synchronisation will then start automatically when the player is connected (Figure 3.80), with the new tracks for uploading listed in the left-hand panel. The files present on the player are listed on the right-hand panel in the usual way once the uploading has been completed (Figure 3.81).

Note that the fully automatic method will only work if certain settings are correct. In order to check these settings, operate the Set up Sync button, and the pop-up window of Figure 3.82 will then appear. Make sure that the checkbox for All Music is ticked. It probably does not matter if some of the others checkboxes are ticked, but it is best to play safe and remove the ticks from any other boxes. The "Synchronise devices automatically" checkbox near the upper left-hand corner of the window must also be ticked.

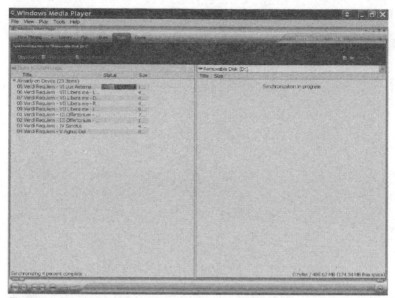

Fig.3.80 *Synchronisation has started automatically*

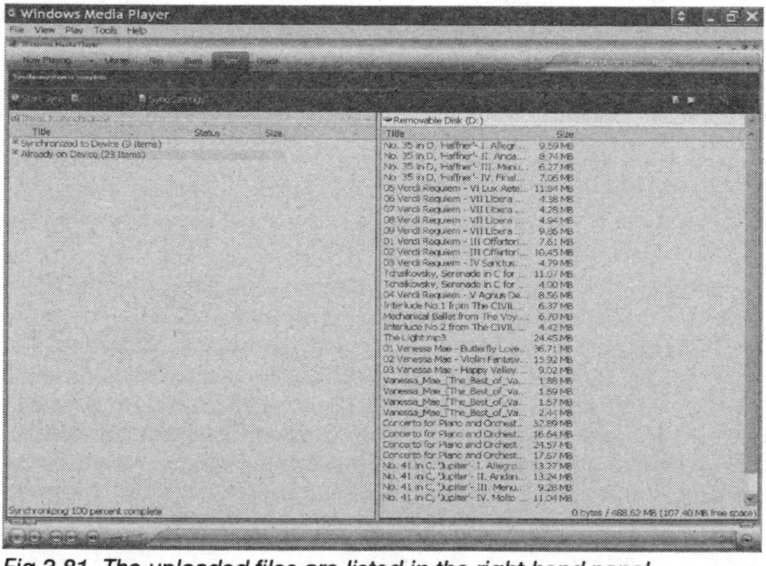

Fig.3.81 *The uploaded files are listed in the right-hand panel*

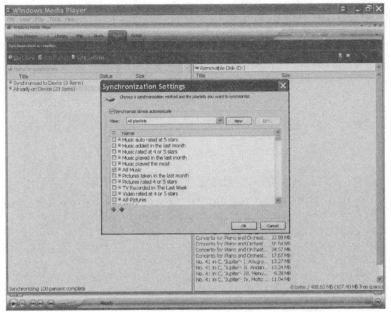

Fig.3.82 Make sure that the checkbox for All Music is ticked

Manual sync

The methods of synchronisation described so far assume that either the library is quite small or that the portable player has a large amount of storage capacity. A different approach is needed in cases where the library is large and the player has a capacity that is measured in megabytes rather than gigabytes. Simply dumping the entire library in the player is not possible because the size of the library is many times larger than the amount of memory in the player. With a setup of this type it is advisable to opt for manual synchronisation. You select the tracks that you wish to have on the player and tell WMP 10 to synchronise the player with the items on the list.

When WMP 10 detects a player of modest capacity it will almost certainly offer manual synchronisation as the default option (Figure 3.83). If you opt for automatic synchronisation and change your mind, it is easy to switch back to the manual variety. Operate the Set up Sync button and

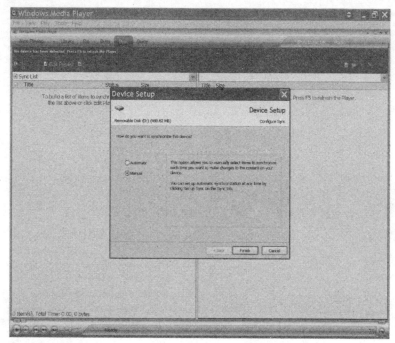

Fig.3.83 Manual synchronisation has been offered as the default

the clear the "Synchronise devices automatically" checkbox in the pop-up Synchronise Settings window. With manual operation you must provide WMP 10 with a list of items to synchronise with the player (the sync list), and then tell the program to perform the synchronisation.

The first task when making the sync list is to go to the Library section of the program and operate the button at the top of the right-hand column. Then select the Sync List option from the pop-out menu (Figure 3.84). The heading at the top of the column will then change to "Sync List", and the list can then be produced in the normal way with items being dragged from the main panel into the right-hand column. This should eventually produce a list something like the one shown in Figure 3.85.

Next the Sync tab is operated, and here the newly produced sync list should have been automatically transferred to the left-hand panel. No items in the list will be selected by default, so left-click the checkbox just

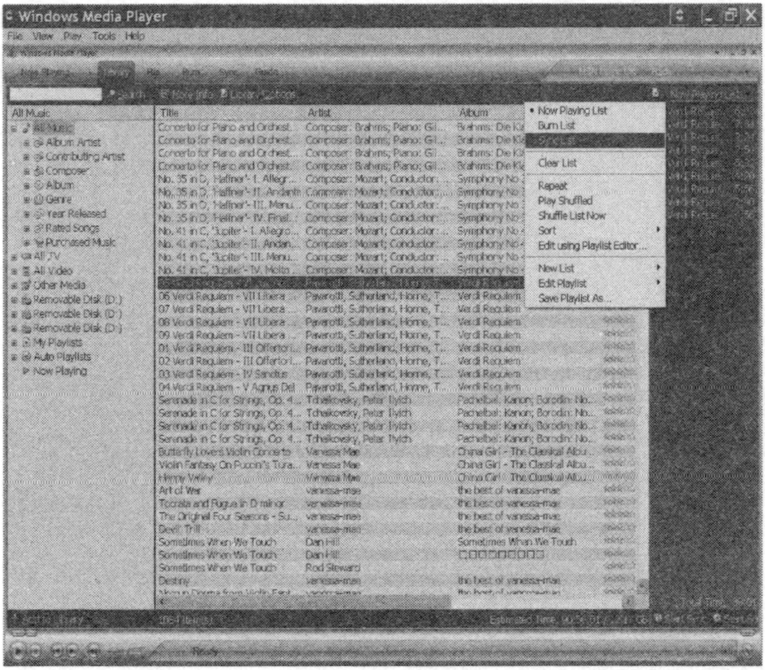

Fig.3.84 Select the Sync List option from the pop-out menu

above the left of the word "Title" in order to select everything in the list (Figure 3.86). Provided you are sure that everything in the list is present and correct, it is then just a matter of operating the Start Sync button and waiting for the process to be completed (Figure 3.87).

Note that the list must include everything that you wish to be included in the player's library of music, and not just any new items that need to be uploaded. WMP 10 will not waste time by uploading files that are already present in the player. It will only upload those that are not already present in the player. It will also delete music files stored in the player that are not in the new sync list, and it is for this reason that it is essential to have a complete list of tracks in the sync list.

This method works well if a substantially different set of tracks will be uploaded to the player each time the synchronisation facility is used. If there will only be a few minor changes it is better to have a play list that

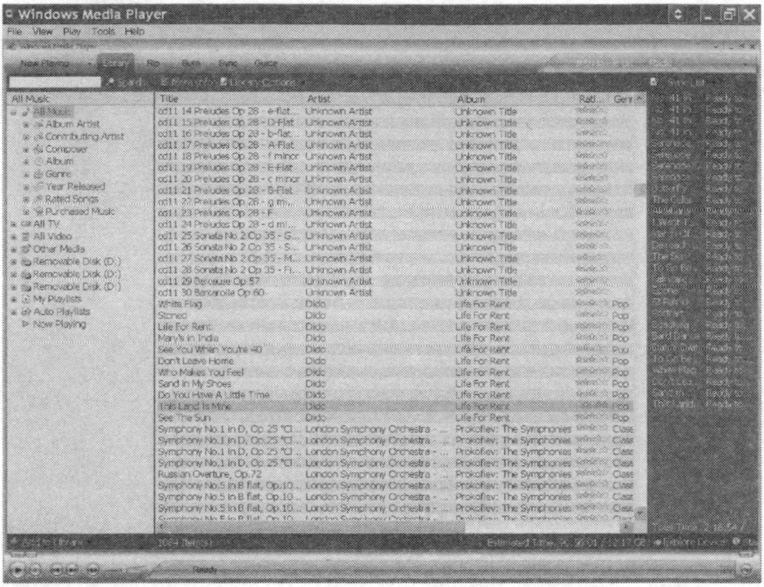

Fig.3.85 A sync list has been produced in the right-hand column

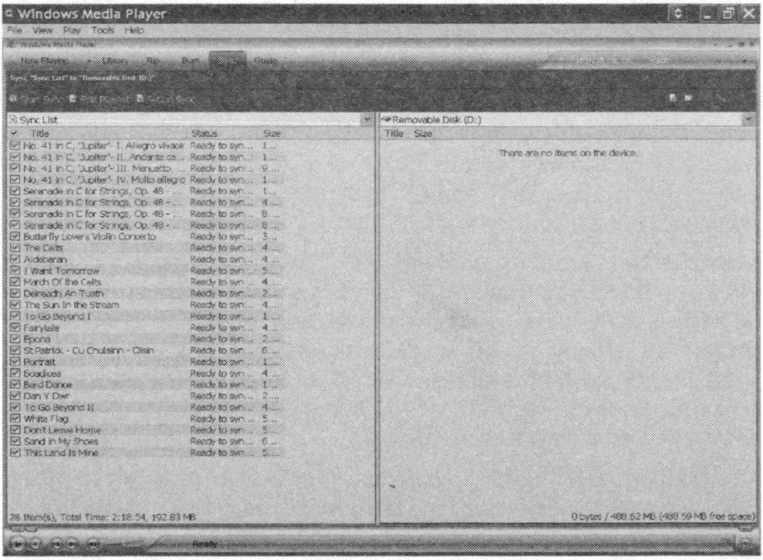

Fig.3.86 All the items in the list have been selected

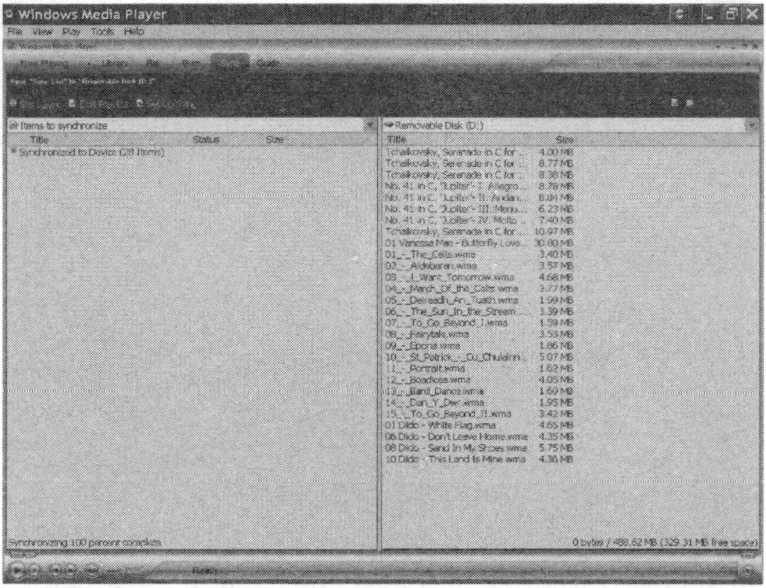

Fig.3.87 The files have all been uploaded to the player

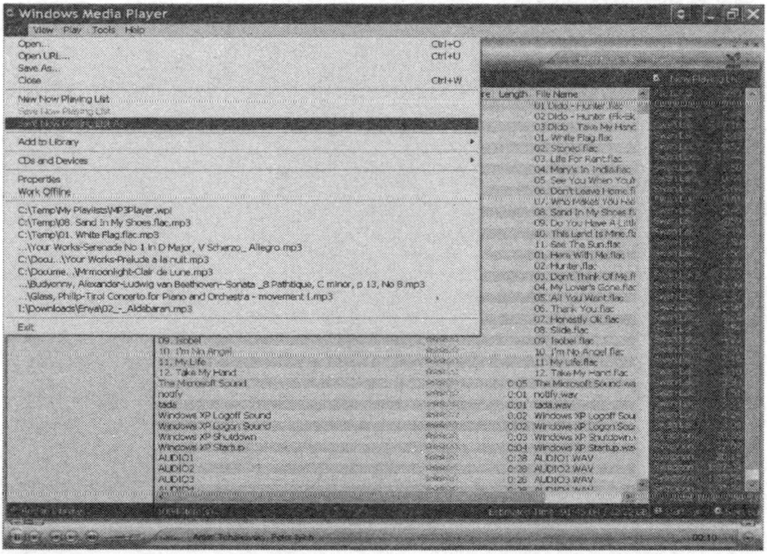

Fig.3.88 Select the Now Playing List As option from this menu

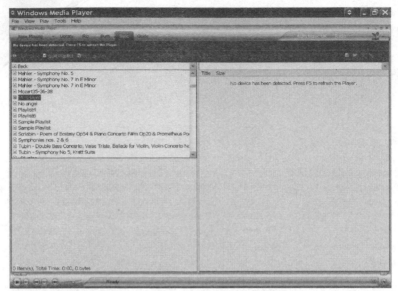

Fig.3.89 Select the appropriate list from the drop-down menu

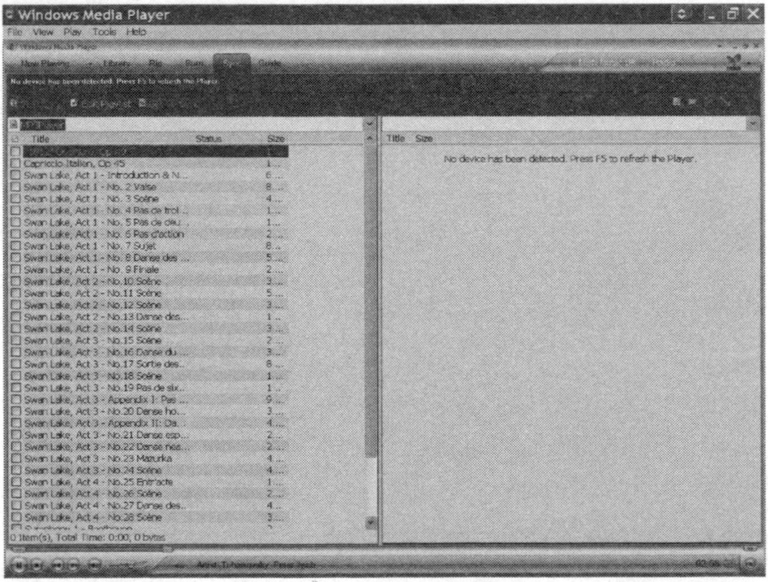

Fig.3.90 The selected list is loaded into the left-hand panel

can be edited and the synchronised with the player. This is just a matter of going to the Library section of the program and producing a Now Playing List in the normal way. The Save Now Playing List As option is then selected from the File menu (Figure 3.88), and the list is saved under a suitable name such as "MP3Player".

In the Sync section of the program, left-clicking the bar just above the left-hand pane produces a drop-down menu (Figure 3.89), and the appropriate list is selected from this. The list of items will appear in the left-hand panel (Figure 3.90), and the

Fig.3.91 Select Remove from List to remove the selected item

synchronisation process is then completed in the normal way. At some later time when you wish to update the player, go to the Library section of WMP 10 and use the Open option of the File menu to load the play list. New items can be added in the normal way. Unwanted items are deleted by right-clicking them and selecting Remove from List in the pop-up menu (Figure 3.91). The modified list is saved under its existing name by selecting the Save Now Playing List from the File menu, and it is then used to synchronise the player in the manner described previously.

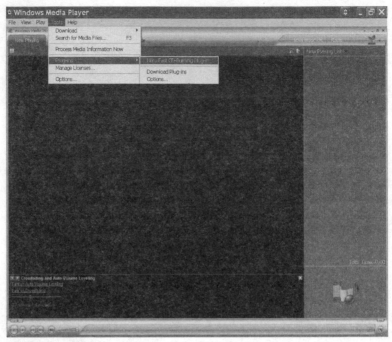

Fig.3.92 In this example there is just one installed plug-in listed

Plug-ins

As pointed out previously, there are various plug-ins available that provide enhancements to WMP 10. These provide such things as compatibility with a wider range of file types, additional signal processing and effects, etc. Some of these are not relevant when playing audio files, but a fair percentage of them are potentially useful when playing audio tracks. When investigating plug-ins you are likely to encounter the terms "rendering" and "DSP".

A plug-in that provides rendering simply enables the program to handle files of a type that it can not usually accommodate. Note that a rendering plug-in should enable WMP 10 to play files in the relevant format, but some facilities might not be supported by the plug-in. For example, it is unlikely to support burning the files to an ordinary audio CD, and some of the enhancements are likely to be non-operational or partially operational. DSP standards for digital signal processing. It means

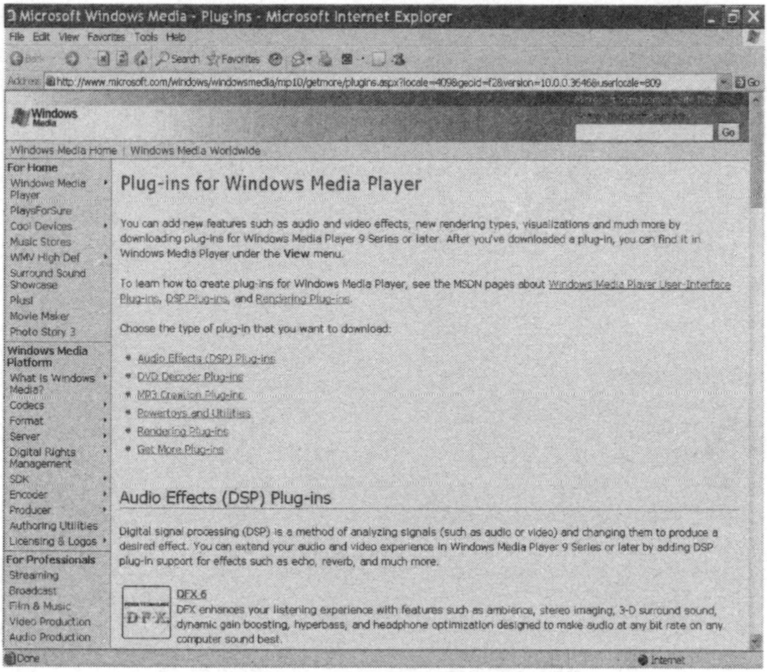

Fig.3.93 The Media Player plug-ins page of the Microsoft site

processing the digital data to doctor the sound in some way. DSP can be used to provide features such as reverberation and echo effects, tone controls, etc.

Selecting Plug-ins from the Tools menu gives a submenu (Figure 3.92) that includes a list of the installed plug-ins (if any) in the top section. Selecting one of the plug-ins toggles it on or off, as appropriate. There is a tick beside a plug-in's entry if it is operational. The Download Plug-ins option takes you to a page on the Microsoft web site (Figure 3.93) that provides brief details and sources for a range of WMP 10 plug-ins that you can buy. There are many other plug-ins and add-ons for WMP 10, though, so it is worth using a good search engine if you require a specific type of add-on. For example, if you need to play an OGG format file, using "Windows Media Player OGG" as the search string should provide links to plenty of pages that give advice on playing OGG files, and actual add-ons to provide the necessary decoding.

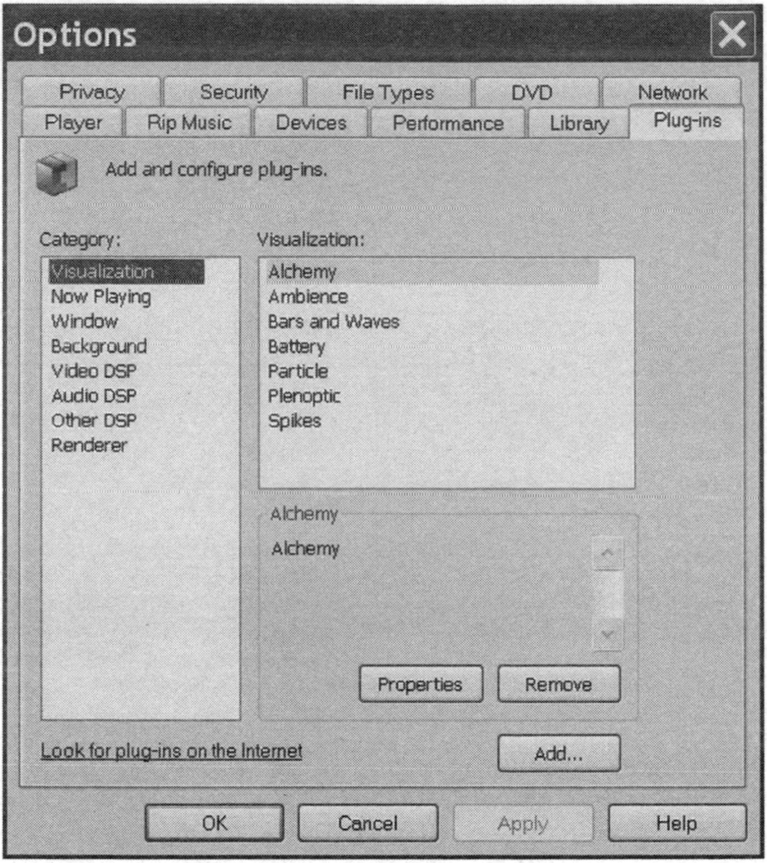

Fig.3.94 The Plug-ins section of the Options window

Choosing Options from the submenu produces the appropriate section of the WMP 10 Options window (Figure 3.94). Various plug-in categories are listed in the left-hand section of the window, and the installed plug-ins in that category are listed on the right. There will be more of them listed here than appear in the Plug-ins submenu. The extra plug-ins are native parts of WMP 10 such as the built-in visualisations. You can remove a plug-in by selecting it and operating the Remove button, but this does not work with those that are built into WMP 10. The Add button enables new plug-ins to be installed. Operating this button produces a file browser

Fig.3.95 WMP 10 with the default skin

that is used to locate and locate the plug-in's program file. Note that some plug-ins have their own installation program and that they are not installed via this route. Also note that some WMP 10 add-ons are not true plug-ins, and that they will not be listed in the Options window. Many rendering plug-ins fall into this category and will not be listed. Provided the add-on installs properly and runs, this is not really of any great practical importance.

Skins

Skins are not unique to WMP 10, or even to media players, but they are mainly associated with leisure programs, and media players in particular. The idea of skins is to enable the look of a program to be radically

changed so that instead of the standard Windows layout you have something that looks more stylish, jokey, or whatever. Although it looks very different, the program under the skin is exactly the same, and has the same features as the standard version. However, skins often provide a somewhat simplified user interface, so the full range of features might not be accessible unless you revert to the standard

Fig.3.96 The player is easily returned to Full mode

version of the program. Despite the simplified interface, there should still be everything you need in order to control the essential facilities of the program.

WMP 10 is supplied with a range of skins, and there are countless others available as downloads on the Internet. In order to use a skin it is necessary to switch WMP 10 from Full mode to the Skin mode. This is done by selecting Skin Mode from the View menu. Figure 3.95 shows the default skin. There are two buttons near the bottom right-hand corner,

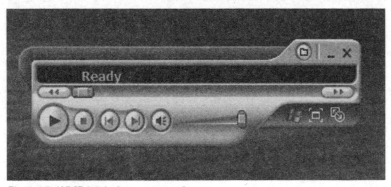

Fig.3.97 WMP 10 in its compact form

and the one on the right (Figure 3.96) is activated in order to return the program to Full mode. The other button reduces the program to its compact form (Figure 3.97), which just provides a basic set of controls. This is all that is normally needed for playing audio files.

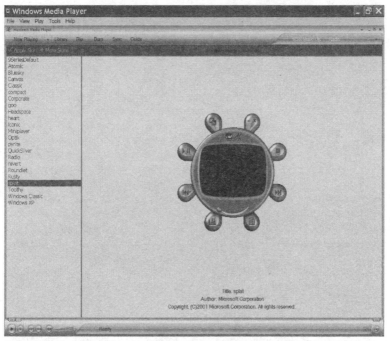

Fig.3.98 The Skin Chooser offers a range of built-in skins

To change to one of the other built-in skins the program must first be returned to Full mode. Selecting Skin Chooser from the View menu changes the window to look like Figure 3.98, where the available skins are listed down the left-hand side of the window. Left-clicking an entry results in its preview image being shown in the main section of the window. You can switch the program to one of the new skins by double-clicking its entry, or selecting its entry and activating the Apply Skin link. Figure 3.99 shows the player with one of the alternative skins. The more way-out skins tend to be something less than intuitive in use, but working out which control is which should not take too long.

If a greater range of skins is required, go to the Skin Chooser and operate the More Skins link. This takes the program to a page in the Microsoft web site (Figure 3.100) where more skins are listed, but this does, of course, require an active Internet connection. Any additional skins that are downloaded will usually be automatically added into the Skin Chooser's list so that they can be selected in the usual way.

Fig.3.99 WMP 10 with the Splat skin selected

It is often useful to have a media player visible while using other programs. One way of doing this is to simply size the various windows so that everything fits onto the screen properly. An alternative is to have the player appear on top of any other windows. Of course, this is not normally possible because launching any program in a full window will result in it appearing on top of the desktop and any other windows. Launching (say) a word processor will result in it covering the player's window. WMP 10 can be forced to appear on top of any other window by first selecting Options from the Tools menu, and then operating the Player tab. There are several checkboxes in the Player Settings section (Figure 3.101), and ticking the one at the top of this section (Keep the Player on top of

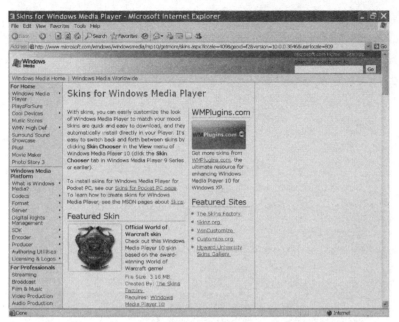

Fig.3.100 This page of the Microsoft web site provides access to a huge range of additional skins that are easily installed

other windows) will ensure that WMP 10 does not get buried underneath other windows. Figure 3.102 shows WMP 10 operating on top of a word processor program.

Visualisations

The Visualisations feature is accessed via the View menu, and there is a huge collection of them available as a standard part of a WMP 10 (Figure 3.103). The idea of the Visualisations feature is to provide animated graphics that change in response to the music being played. The effects vary considerably from one visualisation to another, but there are plenty of swirling and pseudo three-dimensional effects. Figure 3.104 shows a typical example (Ambience – Water).

The Visualisations can be fun, but bear in mind that they produce a significant increase in the loading of the PC. Generating the visual effects

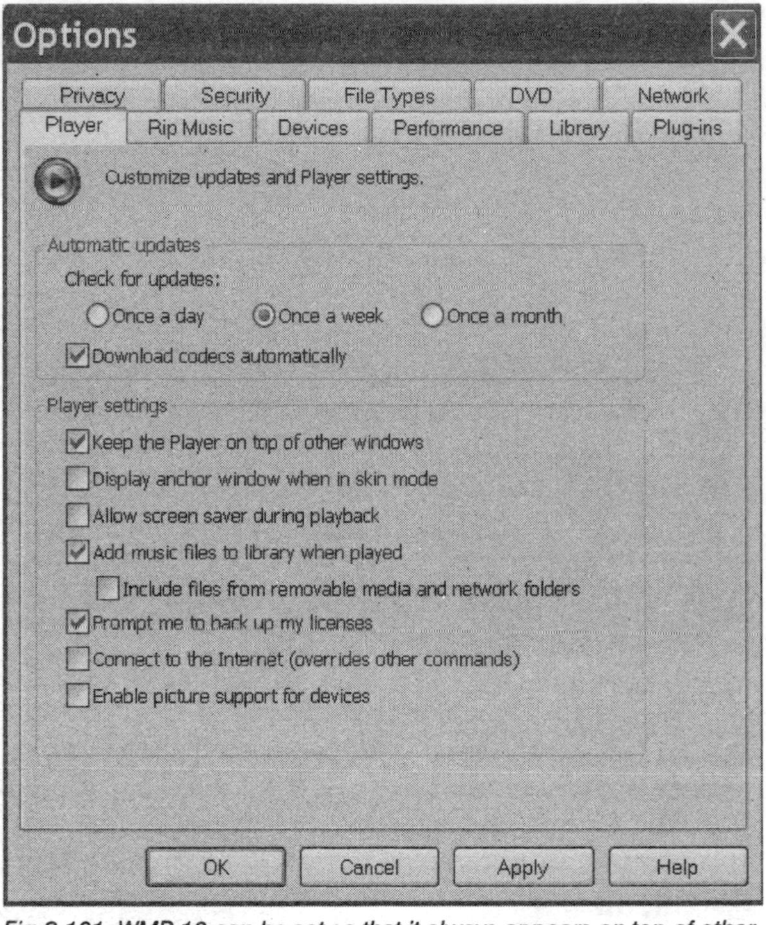

Fig.3.101 WMP 10 can be set so that it always appears on top of other programs

takes up additional resources such as memory and processing time. The more clever the effects and mathematics behind them, the greater the loading that is placed on the PC. This is unlikely to matter too much if you are using the latest "state of the art" PC, but it could result in a substantial reduction in speed with older and less well specified PCs.

Although there are plenty of visualisations supplied as standard with WMP 10, there are even more available on the Internet. The easy way to look

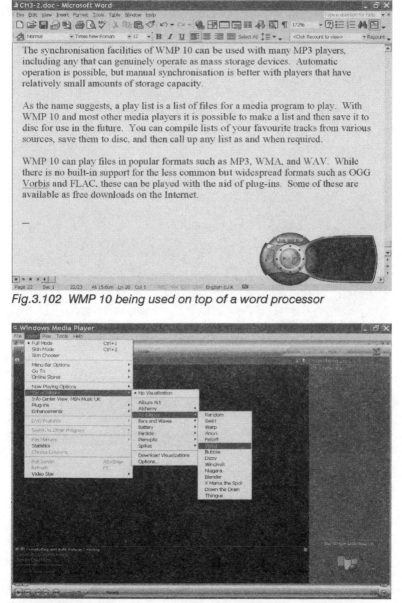

CH3-2.doc - Microsoft Word
File Edit View Insert Format Tools Table Window Help
Normal
Times New Roman
12
Select All
<Click Recount to view>
Recount
The synchronisation facilities of WMP 10 can be used with many MP3 players, including any that can genuinely operate as mass storage devices. Automatic operation is possible, but manual synchronisation is better with players that have relatively small amounts of storage capacity.
As the name suggests, a play list is a list of files for a media program to play. With WMP 10 and most other media players it is possible to make a list and then save it to disc for use in the future. You can compile lists of your favourite tracks from various sources, save them to disc, and then call up any list as and when required.
WMP 10 can play files in popular formats such as MP3, WMA, and WAV. While there is no built-in support for the less common but widespread formats such as OGG Vorbis and FLAC, these can be played with the aid of plug-ins. Some of these are available as free downloads on the Internet.
Page 22 Sec 1 22/23 At 15.6cm Ln 28 Col 1
English (U.K

Fig.3.102 WMP 10 being used on top of a word processor

Windows Media Player
File Play Tools Help
Full Mode Ctrl+1
Skin Mode Ctrl+2
Skin Chooser
Menu Bar Options
Go To
Online Stores
Now Playing Options
Info Center View: MSN Music UK
Plug-ins
Enhancements
Statistics
Video Size
No Visualization
Album Art
Alchemy
Bars and Waves
Battery
Particle
Plenoptic
Spikes
Download Visualizations
Options...
Random
Swirl
Warp
Anon
Falloff
Bubble
Dizzy
Windmill
Niagara
Blender
X Marks the Spot
Down the Drain
Thingus

Fig.3.103 WMP 10 comes complete with numerous visualisations

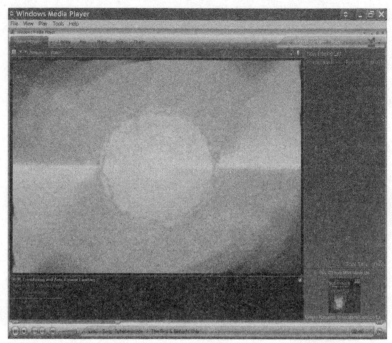

Fig.3.104 The Ambience - Water visualisation

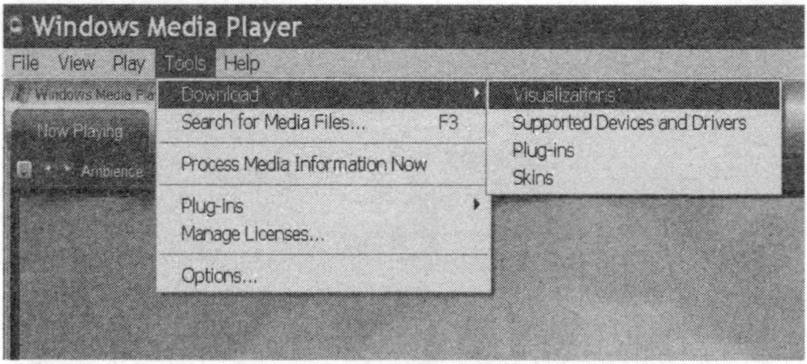

Fig.3.105 There is a built-in facility that makes it easy to search for more visualisations on the Internet

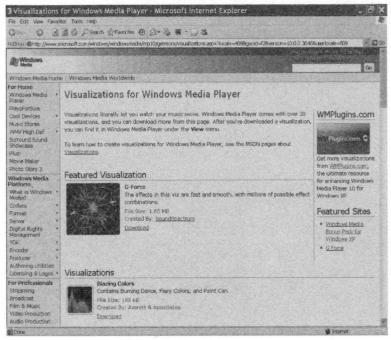

Fig.3.106 The visualisations page of the Microsoft web site

for them is to select Download from the Tools menu, and then Visualisations from the pop-up submenu (Figure 3.105). Assuming that there is an active Internet connection, this takes you to the appropriate page of the Microsoft web site (Figure 3.106). Here there are links to numerous sources of visualisations. These are not all free, but in most cases there is some sort of demo version or slightly simplified free version. I downloaded and installed the G-Force visualisation (Figure 3.107).

Of course, there are many visualisations on the Internet that are not featured on the Microsoft web site. Using a likely search string in any good search engine should produce large numbers of them. They can also be found on some of the popular software download sites. Visualisations are usually installed via a standard Windows installation procedure. They can not be uninstalled from within WMP 10. Some are supplied with an uninstaller program, but in most cases they must be uninstalled via the Windows Control Panel, just like a standard program (Figure 3.108). Note that you can not uninstall the visualisations that are

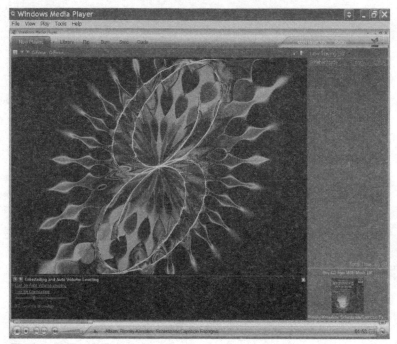

Fig.3.107 The G-Force visualisation

supplied as part of WMP 10. These are effectively part of the program and can not be removed separately from the rest of the program.

Other players

As should be apparent by now, WMP 10 is a well-specified program that can be expanded still further using various plug-ins and add-ons. It should be more than adequate for most purposes, but there are plenty of other media player programs available for those that need them. If WMP 10 proves to be inadequate in some respect and there are no add-ons that provide it with the feature you require, there will probably be another player that has the required feature. However, a player program that has the missing feature could prove to be a bit limited in other respects. You will probably still need WMP 10 from time to time.

Probably the most popular alternative to WMP 10 is Nullsoft's Winamp program (Figure 3.109), which is well-specified and almost certainly has

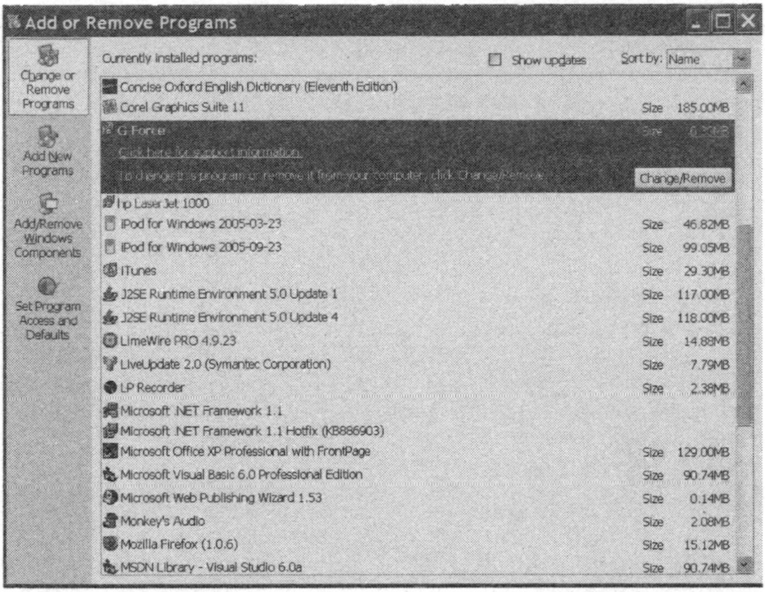

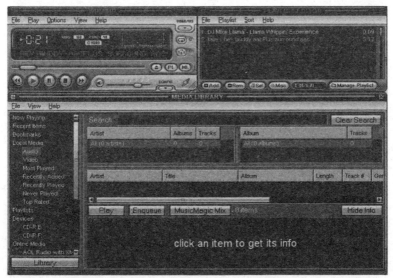

Fig.3.108 A visualisation is often uninstalled like a program

Fig.3.109 Winamp is probably the best known alternative to WMP 10 more third-party support than any other player apart from WMP 10. This is available as a free download, but you have to buy the Pro version in order to obtain the full feature set. Winamp can be downloaded from www.winamp.com, where further details can be found. Any good search engine should provide links to countless Winamp plug-ins.

Points to remember

Windows comes complete with a high quality media player, and media players are often supplied with the support software for CD writers, sound cards, and video cards. You can buy media player software, but one of the bundled programs is usually more than adequate. The Windows Media Player is very popular and the latest version (WMP 10) satisfies the requirements of most users.

Bear in mind that using a media program uses some of the computer's resources. Most media players are not very demanding when playing audio files, so any modern PC should be accommodate a media player plus other normal applications software such as web browsers and word processors. Older PCs might not be able to handle this sort of multitasking. With any PC a media player might not work properly when used alongside demanding programs such as some games.

Although some of the features in the Enhancements section of WMP 10 are only applicable to video playback, there are some features that are useful when playing audio files. The graphic equaliser is well worth investigating, as are the cross-fading and SRS Wow effects.

Provided it is within any copyright restrictions, WMP 10 can rip tracks from a CD to produce WMA or MP3 files that can be uploaded to a portable player. Note that earlier versions of the Windows Media Player can not produce MP3 files, but can produce the WMA variety. It is advisable to upgrade if you are not using the latest version of the Windows Media Player.

Audio files such as MP3 and WMA types can be copied to a CD, and they can be played on practically any PC. However, few CD players can handle a disc of this type. Most CD burning software can produce normal audio CDs from source files in formats such as MP3, WMA, and WAV. Bear in mind though, that compressed formats have to be decompressed in order to produce ordinary audio CDs. You would typically need 10 or so CDs to accommodate the contents of one disc of WMA or MP3 files.

3   WMP 10 and playing files

The synchronisation facilities of WMP 10 can be used with many MP3 players, including any that can genuinely operate as mass storage devices. Automatic operation is possible, but manual synchronisation is better with players that have relatively small amounts of storage capacity.

As the name suggests, a play list is a list of files for a media program to play. With WMP 10 and most other media players it is possible to make a list and then save it to disc for use in the future. You can compile lists of your favourite tracks from various sources, save them to disc, and then call up any list as and when required.

WMP 10 can play files in popular formats such as MP3, WMA, and WAV. While there is no built-in support for the less common but widespread formats such as OGG Vorbis and FLAC, these can be played with the aid of plug-ins. Some of these are available as free downloads on the Internet.

WMP 10 has a number of built-in skins that change the look of the program and the user-interface, but the program is otherwise unchanged. Further skins can be downloaded from the Internet. There is also a compact mode that provides a minimalist set of controls.

170

iTunes and
iPods

New concept

Although you could be forgiven for thinking that Apple invented the portable music player, this is not in fact the case. There were plenty of MP3 players in existence before Apple came up with their first iPod. Although it was not the first portable player, the iPod was a new concept. At the time it was launched most MP3 players had what was typically only about 32 or 64 MB of memory. Even when using a high degree of compression this was only sufficient to hold one or two CDs of music.

Rather than having Flash memory for storage, the original iPod used what was essentially a miniature version of a hard disc drive, as used in every PC. The capacity of the hard disc drive was not vast by normal hard disc standards, but it was very good for a drive of such small physical size. It certainly provided masses more storage space than the MP3 players of the same period. Rather than only being able to store one or two CDs on the player at any one time, you could probably put your entire music collection onto it. In effect, you could carry your entire CD collection and hi-fi system in your pocket!

Many predicted that the new iPod would stand no chance in the marketplace, primarily on grounds of cost. It was certainly not a cheap piece of equipment, but it was a "quality act". Even at its high initial price, many people were lured by the ability to take their entire music collection wherever they went. It soon became the "must have" gadget and sales rocketed. As is usually the case with high-tech products, prices have dropped over the years and compared with the original unit the current iPods are real bargains.

Of course, there is a downside to owning an iPod, and using one to maximum effect does involve a certain amount of work. You cannot simply take it out of the box and immediately play anything from your collection of music. It is necessary to take a certain amount of time to get everything set up and working properly, and that is primarily what this chapter is about. Unless you are prepared to put in a certain amount of effort initially, you will not get the most from your iPod. Although some people try to give the impression that uploading a large amount of music to an iPod can be achieved in a very short space of time, this is not really the case.

Admittedly, the upload process itself is quite short. A full CD can be uploaded to an iPod in a few seconds. It is getting the music ready to upload that tends to be time-consuming. The easy option is to get a specialist company to do the work for you, but with a large number of CDs this is likely to cost substantially more than the purchase price of the iPod. For most of us the do-it-yourself approach is the only practical option, but remember that you do not have to process and upload your entire music collection in one go. Adding a few CDs to your iPod as and when you would like to listen to them is a more practical way of handling things. In this way you can gradually and painlessly built up a large collection of music on your iPod.

Probably the biggest problem with the iPod is simply that it is new and unfamiliar. The results from some surveys suggest that a significant proportion of iPods are never used in earnest because their owners do not know how to use them. Apparently some iPods never even make it out of the box! It seems to be getting music into the gadget that is the main problem, rather than playing tracks once they are safely uploaded. Uploading music to an iPod is actually fairly straightforward once you understand the basic way in which the system operates.

Basic method

At the time of writing this we are into the fourth generation of iPods. There are now several different models to choose from. The method of organising and uploading music described here is applicable to any reasonably modern iPod, but it might not be applicable to older models. Although iPods are manufactured by Apple, they are fully compatible with both Mac computers and PCs running a modern version of the Windows operating system. These days the vast majority of computer owners have PCs, so the examples provided here will be based on a PC rather than a Mac computer.

It is important to realise from the outset that you do not actually organise your music on the iPod itself. The general scheme of things is to organise the music on your PC and to upload it to the iPod. If you wish to add or remove music from the library in your iPod you must first make the necessary changes to the library stored on your PC. These changes are then uploaded to the iPod, which is a process known as synchronisation. This is a well established way of handling things that is used with some other music players, and other gadgets such as backup devices for storing digital photographs.

There is a good and practical reason for handling things in this fashion. A modern PC has a large screen and a full typewriter style keyboard plus a mouse, which make it easy to deal with complex tasks and large amounts of data. Trying to handle everything using a small portable device would be very fiddly and probably impractical for many people. Anyway, a small portable player lacks the wherewithal to build and organise a music library, such as a means of reading audio CDs. Being realistic about matters, the only way of organising a large music collection efficiently is to use a computer, and to upload it to the iPod as a fait accompli.

Connections

In order to upload music from a PC to an iPod it is necessary to have a data link between the two. As yet, wireless connections are little used with portable music players, and are not used at all with iPods. The iPod has to be physically connected to the computer via either a FireWire interface or a USB type. FireWire is an interface that was designed to enable Mac computers to be used with digital video equipment, or anything else that required a high-speed connection.

USB was designed to enable PCs to be used with a wide variety of peripheral devices, but was relatively slow in its original version (USB 1.1). Modern PCs have USB 2.0 ports that are, in theory at any rate, even faster than Firewire ports. However, with a sustained flow of data it is likely that a Firewire connection is actually the faster of the two. In practice the maximum transfer rate might be limited by the computer or the peripheral gadget rather than the interface that links them.

Although USB was originally designed for PCs, and Firewire was primarily an interface for Mac computers, matters are less clear-cut these days. Many Mac computers are equipped with USB ports, and FireWire ports are not exactly a rarity on PCs. Practically any PC can be fitted with FireWire ports using an inexpensive expansion card. However, there is probably little point in PC owners using a Firewire port with their iPods when a spare USB port is available.

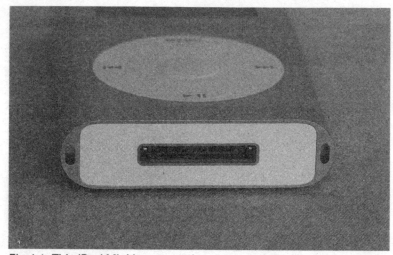

Fig.4.1 This iPod Mini has a port that can be used with a USB or FireWire port

I suppose one exception would be if the choice was between a USB 1.1 port and a Firewire type. Transferring data via a USB 1.1 port is likely to take half an hour or so per gigabyte, which means that is could take a few hours to upload a lot of music to an iPod via this route. Not all iPods are compatible with USB 1.1 ports, although you can sometimes get away with it provided you are not in a hurry. Firewire and USB 2.0 are many times faster and offer a more practical way of swapping large amounts of data.

Note that with most PCs you can use an expansion card to add USB 2.0 ports if the existing ports are of the USB 1.1 variety. Of course, if the USB ports on your PC are already in use but there is a spare Firewire port, it makes sense to use the spare port. This avoids the expense of fitting more USB ports or the hassle of having to keep plugging in and unplugging peripherals in an attempt to accommodate everything with the existing ports.

There is a single connector on the iPod for the connection to the computer (Figure 4.1). This combined USB/FireWire connector is not a standard USB or Firewire type, and has to be a "special" in order to accommodate both types of interface. An iPod comes complete with a lead or leads to make the connection to the computer. It is possible to have a sort of double combination cable that could accommodate USB or FireWire

Fig.4.2 The plug that connects to the iPod. The symbol is on the front side of the plug

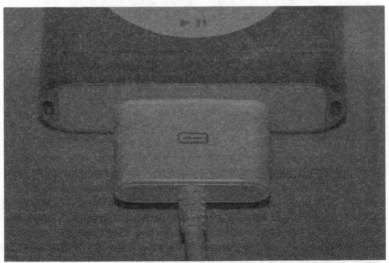

Fig.4.3 The connector locks in place when fitted to the iPod

ports, and I believe a cable of this type is available from Apple as an optional accessory.

Supplied cables

For the cables supplied with iPods, Apple has opted for separate cables for the two types of interface. This is probably the more practical way of handling things, but it means that you have to make sure that you buy an iPod which comes complete with the right cable for the interface you intend to use. Because the cable is non-standard at the iPod end, normal USB and Firewire cables are not suitable for use with an iPod.

Fig.4.4 The USB connector

The connector for the iPod (Figure 4.2) is essentially the same on both types of cable. It will only fit the right way round, which is with the side of the connector that is marked with a symbol at the front (Figure 4.3), and the plain side at the rear. This connector, unlike normal USB and Firewire types, locks in place. The sides of the connector must be squeezed slightly in order to pull it free of the iPod. Figures 4.4 and 4.5 respectively show the computer ends of iPod USB and FireWire cables.

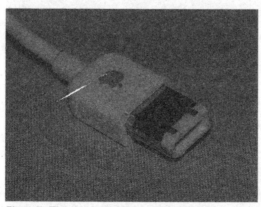

Fig.4.5 The 6-pin FireWire connector

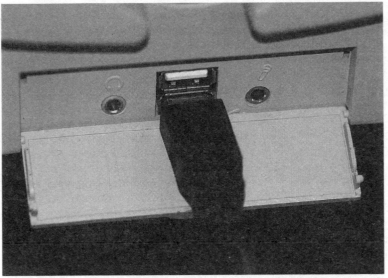

Fig.4.6 Many PCs have connectors on the front panel, including a couple of USB ports

A PC usually has a few USB ports at the rear, and if it uses colour coding of the ports, black is the colour to look for. A reasonably modern PC is almost certain to have at least a couple of USB ports at the front, although these are often hidden away behind a cover (Figure 4.6). These are usually much easier to access than the ports at the rear, and are intended for use with peripherals that will need to be connected to and disconnected from the PC fairly frequently. Whether your iPod falls into this category depends on how you use it, but it is likely that it will. If you use your iPod with a USB port at the rear of the PC it is probably best to leave the cable permanently connected to the PC. You can then connect the iPod to the PC without having to delve into the mass of cables and connectors at the rear of the computer.

Note that some iPods are supplied with a dock, and the general idea is to have the dock permanently connected to the computer. You fit the iPod into the dock when it is necessary to connect it to the computer. This is a sort of upmarket version of leaving the USB or Firewire cable connected to the PC so that it is easy to connect the iPod to the computer.

There are two versions of a FireWire interface, which are the standard and miniature varieties. A PC that has Firewire ports sometimes has both versions (Figure 4.7). There is no difference between the two as far

Fig.4.7 4-pin and 6-pin FireWire ports

as data transfers are concerned. Both types have the same connections and work at the same speed. The only difference, apart from the size of the connectors used, is that the standard type includes the ability to power the peripheral device. No supply lines are included on the miniature type.

Power

An iPod is usually supplied complete with a mains powered charger for the battery, but this is unnecessary most of the time. The battery can be recharged by connecting the iPod to the computer. This obviously requires it to be connected to a standard FireWire port that has power supply connections, and this is the only type that the supplied Firewire cable fits. There is the option of using some iPods with a 4-pin FireWire port via an adapter, but recharging the battery from the computer is not possible when a 4-pin FireWire port is used. Note that the battery in an iPod can not be changed by the user, and that it is not possible to install ordinary batteries such as AA cells. An iPod must be returned for servicing when the built-in rechargeable battery can no longer hold a charge properly.

A USB port includes supply lines that enable it to power small peripheral gadgets. You can therefore connect an iPod to a PC via a USB port and recharge it from the PC. There is a potential problem here in that the USB ports of simple hubs can only provide a limited amount of power. A simple hub provides (typically) four USB ports from a single USB port of the computer. The problem with this method of obtaining extra USB ports is that it each port can only draw its share of the power available from the USB port on the computer. Each port can therefore provide what is typically about one quarter of the normal amount of power available from a USB port.

This is all right with devices that do not draw power from the port, or with simple devices such as mice that draw very little power. Ports on simple hubs are not usable with gadgets that require significant amounts of power, which includes iPods. It is preferable to connect an iPod direct to a USB port of the PC, but using a port on a powered hub should be satisfactory. The hub's power supply unit should enable each of its ports to provide the full amount of current.

Do not overlook the practicalities of the situation when deciding how to use your iPod. Some iPods do not support USB operation with a Mac computer even though they can be used successfully with the USB port of a PC. The iPod Mini does support USB operation with both types of computer. Only USB operation is available from the two versions of the iPod Shuffle. Check that your intended way of using the iPod is a practical possibility before actually buying it. A different model could be better suited to your particular setup, or one or two accessories might be needed in order to get everything working correctly. In general, computer peripherals are more usable if things can be kept as simple and straightforward as possible, so try to avoid a setup that has more than its fair share of wires and adapters.

Charging

As normal for gadgets that have a rechargeable battery, iPods are supplied with the battery in an almost totally uncharged state. It is recommended that the battery should be charged for at least one hour before the iPod is used, and it takes about four hours for the battery to fully charge. There is no need to carefully charge the iPod for a certain amount of time, since it will automatically stop charging once the battery is "full".

The battery icon in the top right-hand corner of the screen is solid when the battery is fully charged, or nearly so, and it is just an outline when the battery is exhausted. Intermediate amounts of charge are indicated by a corresponding amount of filling in the battery icon. The icon continuously goes from "empty" to "full" to indicate that the battery is charging, and a "lightning bolt" is added to the icon. This ceases once the battery is fully charged, and the main part of the screen displays a message indicating that the unit is ready for use. You may get an outsize version of the icon when charging the battery from a charger or when initially charging it (Figure 4.8).

Depending on the particular model you have, the battery can be charged by connecting the iPod to the computer via a USB or FireWire port, or it can be charged from the mains powered charger. There is no power supply port on an iPod. It connects to the mains adapter via the USB or Firewire cable. Note that the iPod might not initialise properly if the battery has an extremely low charge and it is charged from a USB port. Charging it from the mains adapter should get it properly initialised and operating properly.

In the past it was necessary to make sure that rechargeable batteries were fully exhausted before you recharged them, and to make sure that they were then fully recharged. Anything other than full discharge/ recharge cycles resulted in the capacity of the batteries being reduced and their operating life being curtailed. This is still the case with some rechargeable batteries, but not the type used in iPods. Since an iPod battery is about 80 percent charged after one hour of charging, you can charge it for about this time rather than the full four hours if you are in a hurry.

With most rechargeable batteries, including the type used in the iPods, it is not a good idea to let the battery reach an extremely low level of charge.

Fig.4.8 You will probably be left in no doubt when the battery is charging

Most iPods use a small but significant amount of current when in the "off" state, since they are really in a sort of standby condition rather than genuinely switched off. This means that the battery could become totally discharged if an iPod is not used for a period of a few weeks. The normal advice is to remove the batteries from any gadget that you will not be using for a while. This is clearly not an option with the built-in battery of an iPod, but there is the alternative of recharging the battery every two weeks when an iPod is not in regular use.

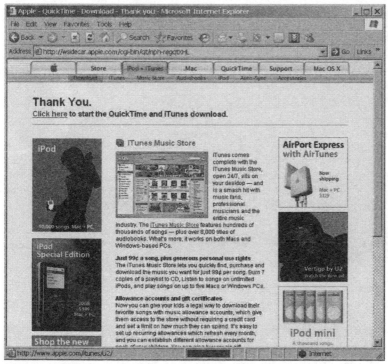

Fig.4.9 The download page for the iTunes program

iTunes

The program used to build and organise your library of music is called iTunes, which is also the name of Apple's music download service. It is supplied on the CD-ROM supplied with each iPod, but it is also available as a free download from the Apple web site (www.apple.com). The iTunes program seems to be updated quite frequently, so if you have a non-metered Internet connection it is probably best to download and use the latest version of the program. If you install the version on the CD-ROM it will probably download and update itself to the latest version as part of the installation process.

At about 22 megabytes the iTunes program is a substantial download. With a broadband connection it possible to download at least a few megabytes per minute, but with a dial-up connection the download rate

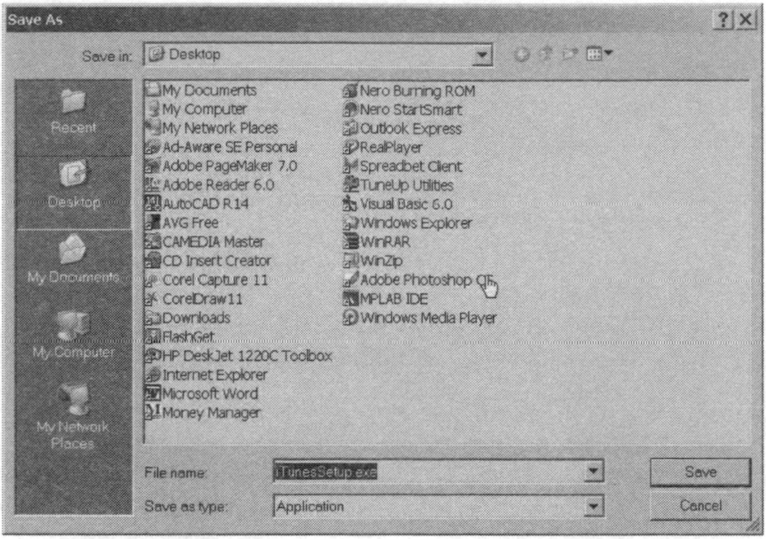

Fig.4.10 Select the destination for the downloaded file

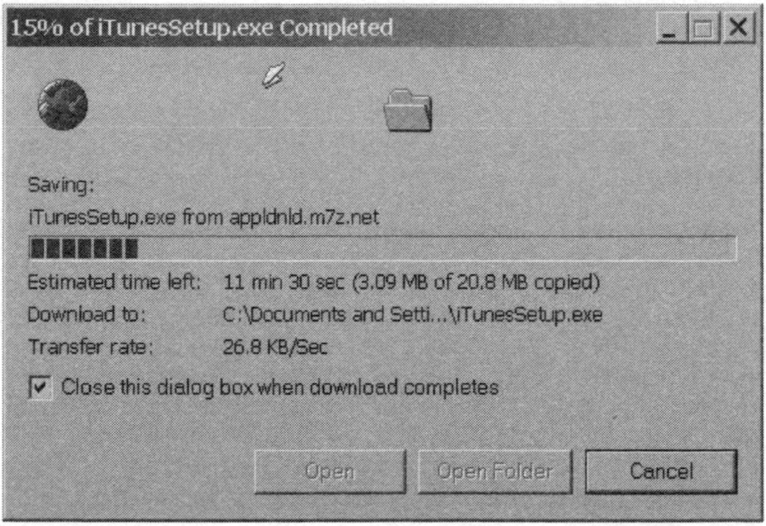

Fig.4.11 The usual bargraph shows how far the download has
progressed

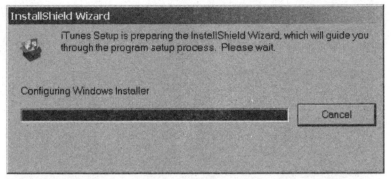

Fig.4.12 *This window appears during the initial setting up period*

is usually a few minutes per megabyte. A 22 megabyte download is likely to take over an hour, but it should eventually be completed successfully. However, you might prefer to settle for the version on the iPod's installation CD-ROM.

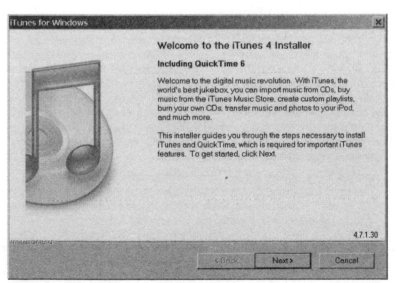

Fig.4.13 *This is just an information screen*

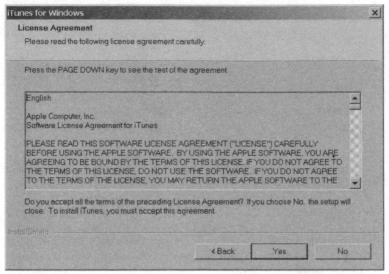

Fig.4.14 As usual, you have to agree to the licence conditions. The iTunes program can not be installed unless you do

The iTunes download page on the Apple website should be straightforward to locate (Figure 4.9), and left-clicking the download link will produce the usual Save As browser (Figure 4.10) so that you can choose a location for the iTunes Setup program. The Windows Desktop is a good choice, since it easy to locate and run the file. It is just a matter of double-clicking the new icon that appears on the Desktop once the file has finished downloading. If you decide to keep the program file it can be relocated to a suitable folder using the Windows Cut and Paste facilities. A small pop-up window (Figure 4.11) keeps you informed about how well the download progressing.

Once the file is downloaded and run, the small window of Figure 4.12 will be produced initially. It might take a while for the Setup program to decompress the downloaded data and get the installation routine ready to go, but eventually the welcome screen will appear (Figure 4.13). Operating the Next button moves things on to the inevitable licence agreement (Figure 4.14), and installation can only proceed if you operate the Yes button and agree to the licensing conditions.

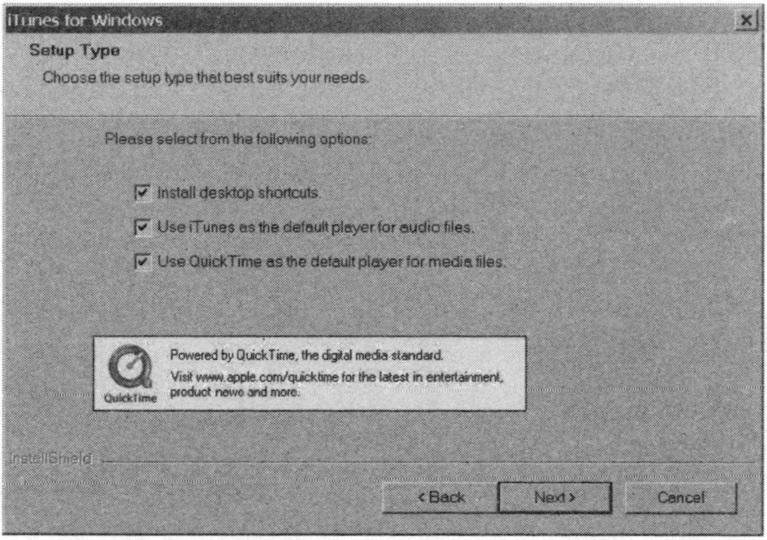

Fig.4.15 *This window gives three start-up options for the program*

Minimum specification

A screen with some basic information about the iTunes program appears next. This includes the minimum specification needed to run iTunes, but you should check the Apple web site for the current minimum requirement long before you reach this stage. ITunes is not a particularly demanding program, but it is probably beyond the capabilities of many of the older PCs that are still in regular use.

Moving on to the next screen (Figure 4.15), there are three options on offer. An entry in the Start-Programs menu is usually added automatically for any normal program. An icon on the Windows Desktop and (perhaps) one on the taskbar are sometimes added automatically, but these days they are more likely to be optional extras. In this case, ticking the top checkbox will result in a Desktop icon being installed. Whether this is a worthwhile addition is to some extent a matter of personal preference, and how much use you make of Desktop icons. In general it is worth having a Desktop icon for programs that you will use a fair amount, as it provides a quick and easy means of launching them. It is probably not worthwhile cluttering the Desktop with icons for programs that will be used only rarely, if at all.

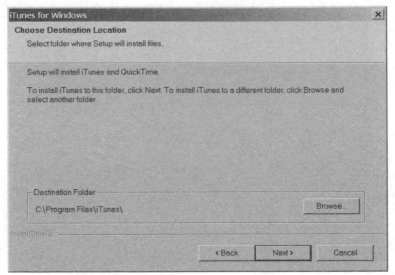

Fig.4.16 Unless there is a good readon for doing otherwise, install the
program in the default folder

Fig.4.17 This window is just an advertisement for the iTunes music
download service

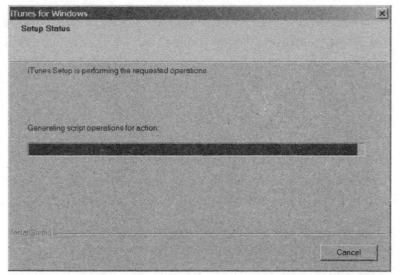

iTunes for Windows

Setup Status

iTunes Setup is performing the requested operations

Generating script operations for action:

InstallShield

Cancel

Fig.4.18 Another bargraph shows how far the installation process has progressed

The remaining two options enable iTunes to be used as the default audio player, and QuickTime to be used as the default program for playing media files. In this case the term "media files" presumably means any files that have some form of video content and not just sound. By choosing an iPod you are also making the decision to use iTunes for playing and organising your audio files. It therefore makes sense to use it as the default audio player, but you might prefer to keep some other player as the default for videos. Again, this is a matter of personal preference and the decision is yours.

At the next screen you are given the usual opportunity to change the folder that will be used to store the program itself and any support files (Figure 4.16). Unless there is a good reason to choose a different location, such as having too little space on the target drive, it best to settle for the default location. The next screen (Figure 4.17) is just an information screen (advertisement). Operating the Next button starts the installation process and moves things on to the screen of Figure 4.18. This has the customary bargraph to show how things are progressing. It will soon be replaced by the screen of Figure 4.19, which indicates that the program has been successfully installed. Operating the Finish button closes the window and completes the installation.

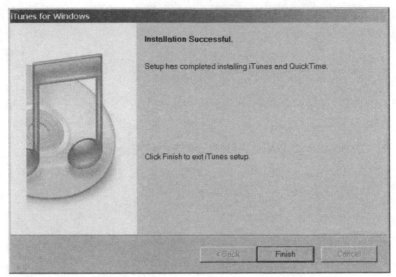

Fig.4.19 The program has been successfully installed

Getting started

Running a media player for the first time tends to involve a certain amount of preamble, and this is certainly the case with iTunes. First you have to answer Yes to accept the inevitable user agreement, and then the Welcome screen of Figure 4.20 appears. As this explains, it is necessary to answer some further questions in order to get the program configured correctly. A certain amount of configuration by the user is required in order to get a fair proportion of modern programs "up and running". This can be necessary to match the program to the particular hardware you are using, or simply to get it operating in the way that best suits your particular requirements.

In this example we are dealing with a program that is used for playing music, and it handles three types of audio file. Configuring the program ensures that it handles audio files in the way that best suits your requirements. Figure 4.21 shows the first of the configuration screens. AAC (advanced audio coding) files are in iTunes own format. MP3 is the most popular of the audio file formats, and it is the one that is most familiar to the "man or woman in the street". The iTunes program can play MP3 files, as can an iPod.

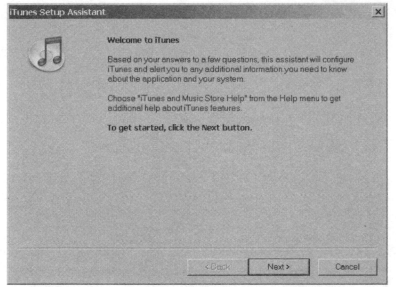

Fig.4.20 The Welcome screen explains that some setting up is needed

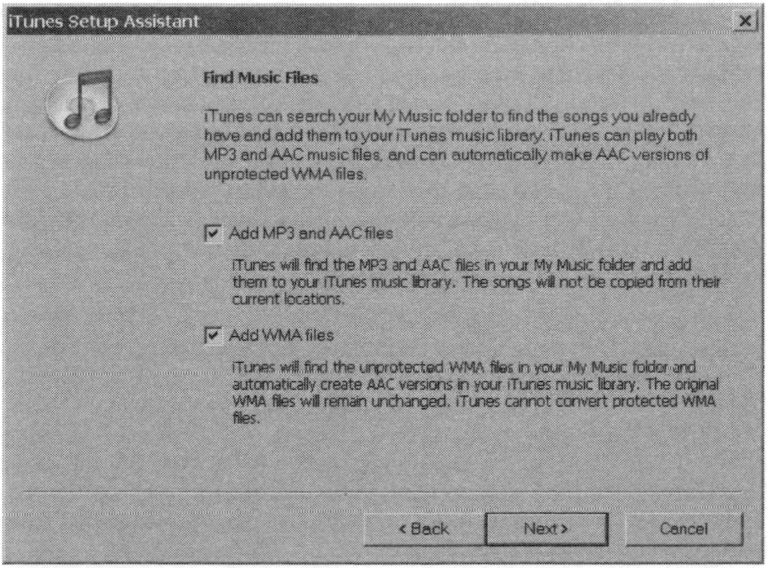

Fig.4.21 The program can search for files to add to the library

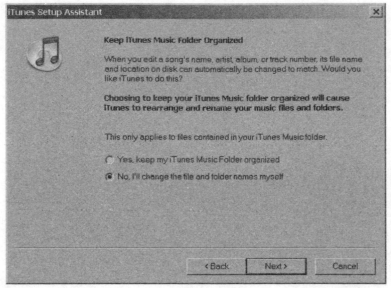

Fig.4.22 Your music library can be organised automatically or you can
do it yourself

WMA (Windows media audio) is Window's own audio format. While WMA is not as widely used as MP3, it is still very popular and preferred by many. Although iTunes can not play WMA files, it can automatically convert them to AAC format so that they are effectively made compatible with this program and iPods. Note though, that the protected WMA files sold by many download sites can not be converted to AAC format by the iTunes program. This makes them incompatible with the iTunes program and iPods. The protected AAC files sold from the iTunes site are equally incompatible with most MP3 players.

The screen of Figure 4.21 explains that unprotected WMA files can be converted by iTunes, and also points out that the program can search the My Music folder and add any MP3 or AAC files to your iTunes music library. When Windows is installed it automatically produces a folder called My Documents, and this is used to store your word processor files or other documents. During installation Windows also produces four subfolders in the My Documents folder. These are called My eBooks, My Pictures, My Music, and My Videos, and their names make their intended functions self-evident.

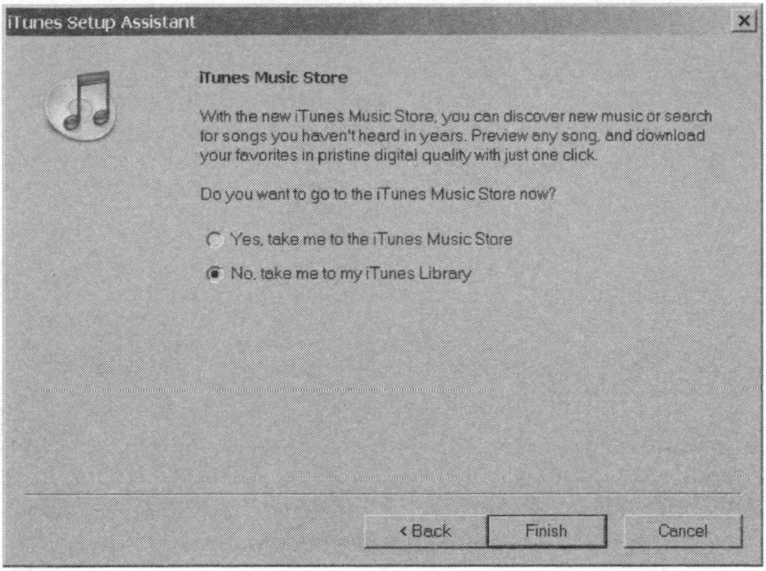

Fig.4.23 Operating the Finish button completes the setting up process

Ticking the upper checkbox will result in the iTunes program searching for AAC and MP3 files, and those that it finds will be added to the iTunes music library. Ticking the lower checkbox adds WMA files to the library, but they are converted into AAC format. Note that your original WMA files will be left intact and will not be altered in any way. The new AAC files are in addition to the originals and do not replace them. Of course, this means that some hard disc space will be consumed by the new files, which could be significant if you have large numbers of WMA files.

As pointed out previously, protected WMA files can not be converted. However, music files that you make yourself, by ripping tracks from a CD for example, do not usually have any form of copy protection. Any WMA files produced by ripping a CD will probably be convertible, although you might get better results ripping them straight to AAC format using iTunes. Files that are legitimately downloaded from the Internet are almost certain to have some form of copy protection. In some cases they can only be played on the PC that was used to download them, while in other cases you are given a bit more latitude. Conversion to another format is usually blocked as well, so the inability of iTunes to convert protected files is not a shortcoming of the program. It is a general restriction that applies to all media programs.

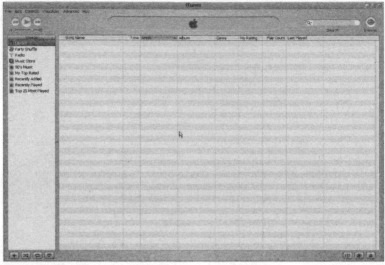

Fig.4.24 The iTunes program is "up and running"

Operating the Next button moves things on to the window of Figure 4.22. Here you use the radio buttons to either have iTunes organise your music files for you, or to do it yourself. Again, this is a matter of personal preference. Having the program organise things for you looks like the easy way of doing things. However, as a general rule it is better if you do this type of thing yourself. Relying on a program to organise things might work well or you might find that it simply confuses matters.

The next window (Figure 4.23) is just an advertisement that invites you to visit the iTunes online store. Operating the Finish button completes the setting up, and the program is launched (Figure 4.24). In Figure 4.25 I have added some files to the program's library and it is playing the first file.

Uploading

There has to be some music in the iTunes library before you can upload it to your iPod. We will therefore assume that the iTunes program found some music files during the installation process, or that you have added some music to the iTunes library. If your iTunes program is a music-free zone at this stage, follow the steps described in the next section of this

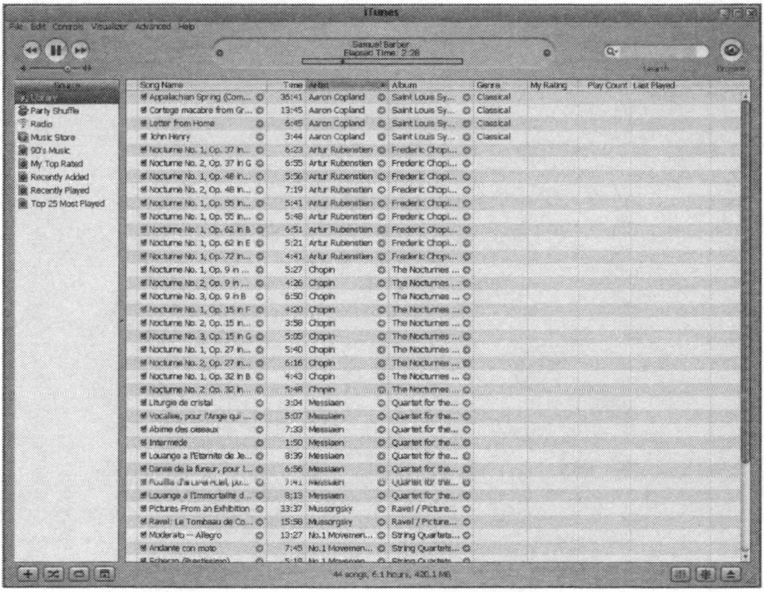

Fig.4.25 Some files have been added to the library and one of them is being played

book in order to load some music files to the library. Then upload the music to your iPod using the steps covered in this section.

Uploading is very simple, especially if automatic operation has been selected. When the iPod is connected to the PC it will be detected and it will be automatically synchronised with the iTunes library. There is a small amount of setting up to do when the iPod is connected to the computer for the first time. The iPod Assistant will be launched (Figure 4.26), and you have to provide a name for your iPod or accept the suggested name. The latter is presumably based on the Windows account name for the current user, since it seems to be something appropriate rather than something general such as "my iPod". Make sure that the checkbox is ticked if you would like the music stored on your iPod to be updated automatically.

The iTunes program will then run, and the music in the library will be uploaded to the iPod. A banner near the top of the iTunes window keeps you informed about the progress of the uploading (Figure 4.27). The time taken to complete the process will depend on the amount of music that has to be transferred to the iPod, but it should be a matter of minutes

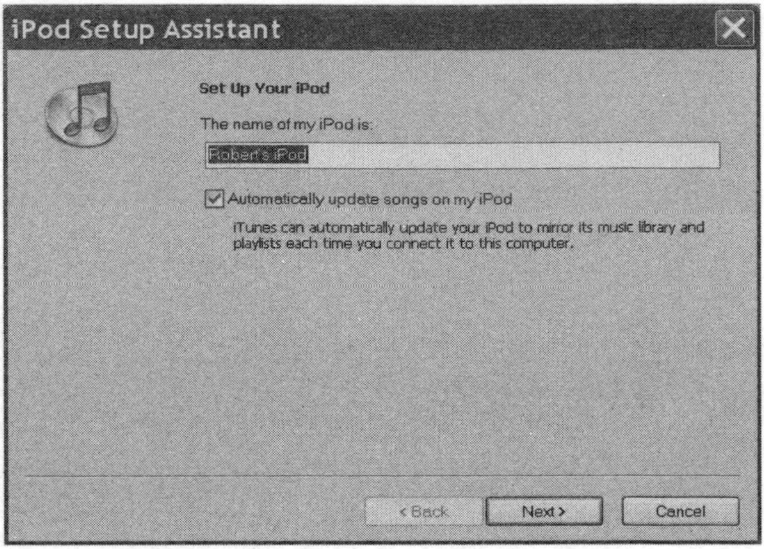

iPod Setup Assistant   ✕

Set Up Your iPod

The name of my iPod is:

Robert's iPod

☑ Automatically update songs on my iPod

iTunes can automatically update your iPod to mirror its music library and
playlists each time you connect it to this computer.

< Back   Next >   Cancel

Fig.4.26 Type a name for your iPod or accept the default

rather than hours. It will only take a few seconds with just a CD or two to
upload. The banner at the top of the window will indicate when the
uploading has finished, and it will also inform you that it is safe to
disconnect the iPod from the computer.

*Fig.4.27 An information panel keeps you informed about the progress
of the uploading*

Disconnecting

It is important not to disconnect the iPod from the PC when iTunes or the
screen of the iPod itself (Figure 4.28) displays a message stating that it
should not be disconnected. Doing so is unlikely to damage anything,
but it is best not to put this type of thing to the "acid test". Disconnecting

Fig.4.28 The iPod warns you if it must not be disconnected

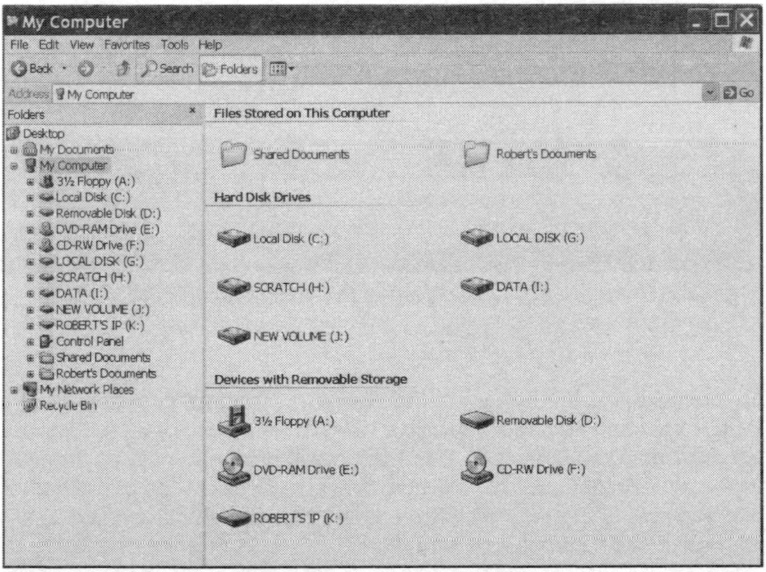

Figure 4.29 The iPod is integrated with the operating system as a disc drive (drive K in this case)

a peripheral device without first deactivating it in the operating system could make your computer operate in an unstable fashion. This is not to say that you always have to wait until iTunes and the iPod indicate that it is safe to disconnect the iPod. However, things must be done in the right manner.

You should definitely not disconnect the iPod while it is being synchronised with the iTunes library. When any synchronisation has been completed it is likely that the message telling you not to disconnect the iPod will continue to be shown. The reason for this is that the battery is being recharged from the computer, and not because there is any continuing communication between the computer and the iPod. As pointed out previously, you do not have to let the battery fully recharge before disconnecting and using an iPod. Before disconnecting the iPod you must first instruct Windows to remove it from the current hardware configuration. In other words, you are effectively telling Windows to let go of it.

As far as Windows is concerned, an iPod is not a music player. It is merged into the operating system as a mass storage device, which means that it is effectively a hard disc drive. This is not unreasonable, since to a large extent this is what an iPod actually is. If you use Windows Explorer to check the disc drives that are present when an iPod is connected to the PC and active you will find it listed amongst the other drives. In Figure 4.29 it is drive K, which is listed at the bottom of the window.

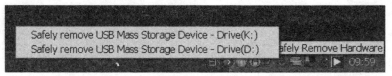

Fig.4.30 There are two USB drives in this example, and the iPod is drive K

In the taskbar at the bottom of the Windows Desktop there should be a button that can be used when you need to safely remove a USB mass storage device. Operating this button will produce a list of the USB mass storage devices that are currently connected to the computer. In the example of Figure 4.30 there are two of these devices. Drive D is a Compact Flash card reader and drive K is the iPod, which is actually an iPod Mini. In order to extricate one of the listed devices from the operating system it is merely necessary to left-click its entry in the list. There will then be a short delay while the operating system removes the device, after which there will be an onscreen message stating that the device can be physically disconnected from the system.

Adding music

While it is possible that iTunes will find all the music files on your PC during installation, it is likely that there will be music files in locations where it did not search. Also, you will probably wish to add downloaded or ripped files to the library from time to time. There are various ways of adding music to the iTunes library, and one of these is to simply direct it to the files or a folder that contains the files. In the File menu there are separate options for adding a file or folder (Figure 4.31).

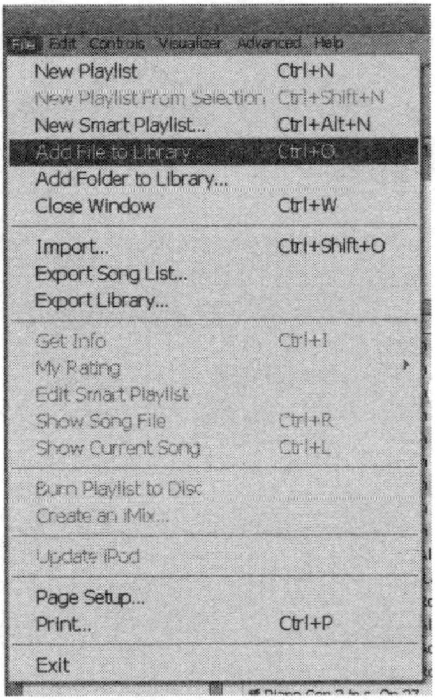

Choosing one of these launches the appropriate browser, and you then select the appropriate file or folder in the normal way. Note that it is actually possible to add more than one file using the Add File option, since the standard Windows methods of selecting files will work with the file browser. By default iTunes will not make a copy of any files or folders that are added to the library. Instead, the program has a database that tells it where to find the corresponding file for each piece of music in the library.

Fig.4.31 A file or a folder can be added

The practical importance of this is that things will go awry if you move or delete any of the files used by the iTunes without removing them from the library first. If you delete a music file used by iTunes, remove it from the library first. Of course, iTunes does have to store files for the library when you add to it by ripping CDs, download tracks from the iTunes online store, or convert WMA files to AAC format. You can find the location of the folder used to store these files by selecting Preferences from the

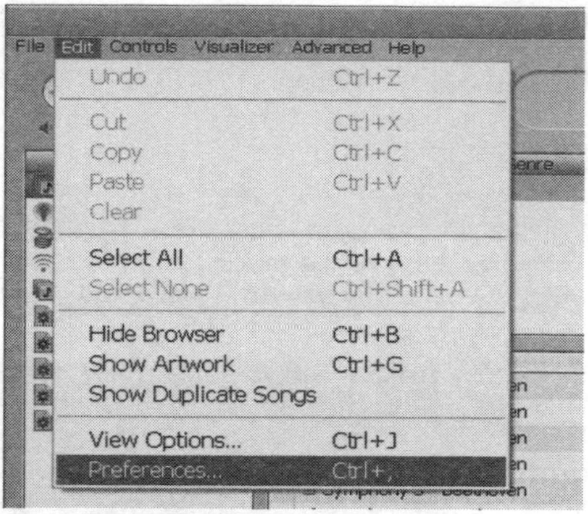

Edit menu (Figure 4.32). This launches the Preferences window, which will be set at the General page by default (Figure 4.33). In this case it is the Advanced section that is required, and operating the Advanced tab changes the window to look like Figure 4.34.

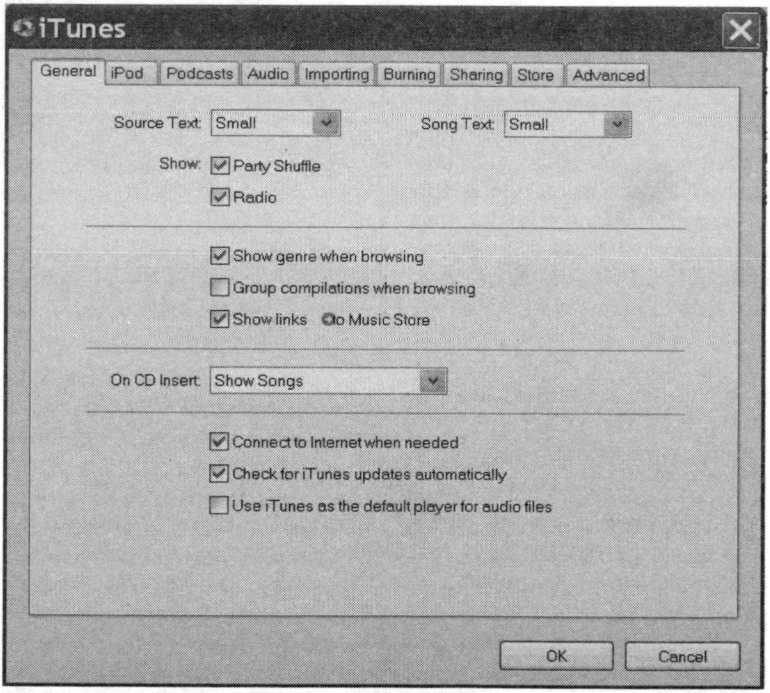

Fig.4.32 Select the Preferences option

Fig.4.33 The General section of the Preferences window

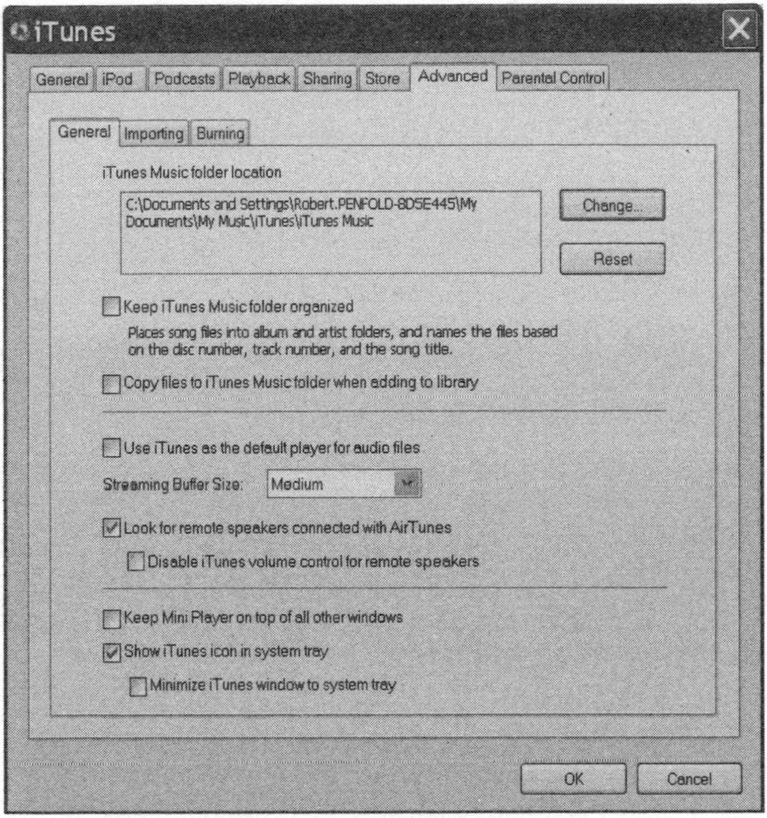

Fig.4.34 The Advanced section of the Preferences window

The location of the folder used to store iTunes music files is shown in the top section of the window. For a PC running Windows this will usually be a subfolder of the My Music folder, which is actually a subfolder of the My Documents folder. The music files are stored in various subfolders of the iTunes folder, and they can be deep in a complex directory structure. For many users it will not really matter that the files are buried deep in a complex file structure. Provided iTunes does not lose track of where the files are stored, users of the program will have no problem in finding and playing them.

It only becomes an issue if you wish to use the files with another program or copy them to another computer. You should be able to locate them

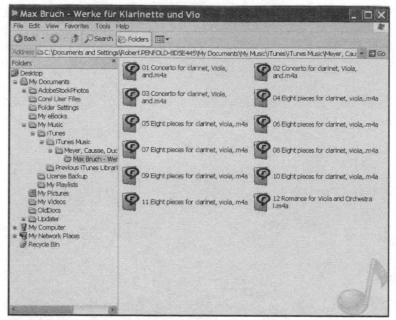

Fig.4.35 Some files in the library located using Windows Explorer

with Windows Explorer (Figure 4.35) or another file browser. However, it might be more convenient to have the files in a folder directly off the root directory of a hard disc drive. This should make it quicker and easier to navigate a browser to the files. There are two buttons in the top section of the Advanced preferences window, one of which enables a different folder to be selected. Operating this button produces a browser (Figure 4.36) that can be used to select a different folder, and there is a button that enables a new folder to be produced. The second button enables the music folder to be reset to its original setting.

Ripping

Probably the way most users obtain music for iTunes and their iPods is to rip it from their collection of CDs. Fortunately, the iTunes program makes it very easy to rip CD tracks into formats that are compatible with iPods. The first step is to place the CD into the computers CD or DVD drive. If there are two or more CD/DVD drives it will probably make no

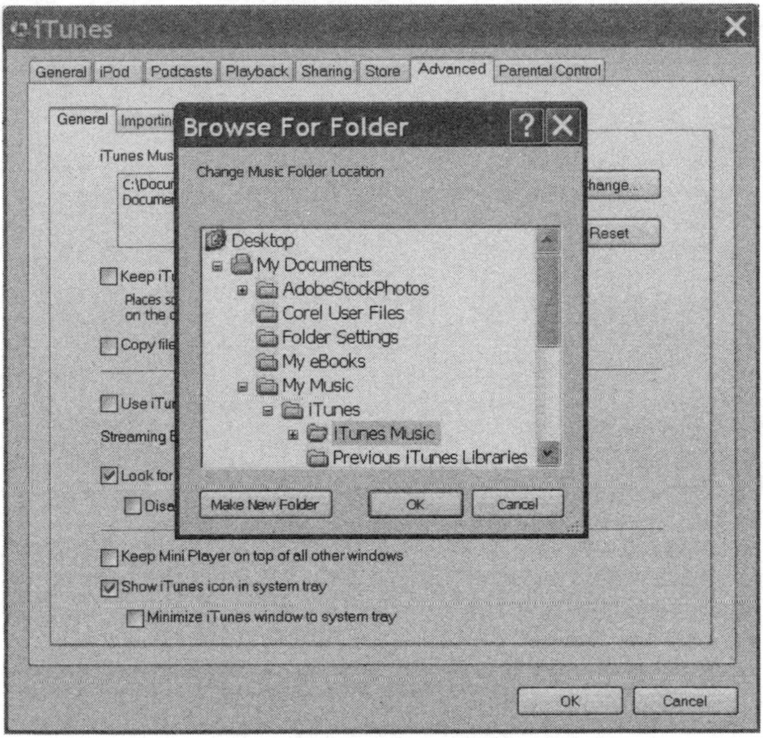

Fig.4.36 Use this browser to select a new folder for the library

difference which one you use. The iTunes program should find and use the disc without any problems. It is generally best to use the drive that has the highest speed rating, as this will help to keep the time taken to rip the CD as short as possible.

In Figure 4.37 an audio CD has been placed in one of the drives and iTunes has responded by giving the disc an entry in the column on the left-hand side of the window. It has also listed the tracks in the main section of the window. By default, the little blue checkbox for each track is ticked, and every track of the CD will be ripped. Remove the ticks from the checkboxes of any tracks that you do not wish to rip. The button in the top right-hand corner of the window (Figure 4.38) is called the Action button, and its exact purpose varies to suit the way in which iTunes is being used. In this case it is labelled "Import CD", and operating it will start the ripping process.

Fig.4.37 The iTunes program has detected the CD and responded to it

The program keeps you informed about the progress that is being made while the tracks are being read and converted (Figure 4.39). An orange coloured icon appears between the track number and the checkbox while a track is being converted, and this is replaced by a green tick icon when the conversion has been completed.   The banner at the top of the window also provides some basic information, such as the name of the track that is currently being processed. The small button at the right end of the banner is

Fig.4.38 The Action button (or Import CD button in this case)

Fig.4.39 The banner keeps you informed about progress

Fig.4.40 The ripping process has been successfully completed

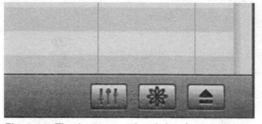

Fig.4.41 The button on the right ejects the disc

operated if you need to stop the process. Eventually the process will be completed, and there will be a green tick to the right of each track number (Figure 4.40). There are three buttons in the bottom right-hand corner of the window (Figure 4.41), and the button at the right end of the row is used to eject the disc once the ripping process has been completed. Left-clicking the Library entry in the left-hand column of the window results in the contents of the library being shown in the main part of the window (Figure 4.42), and the newly ripped tracks should appear here.

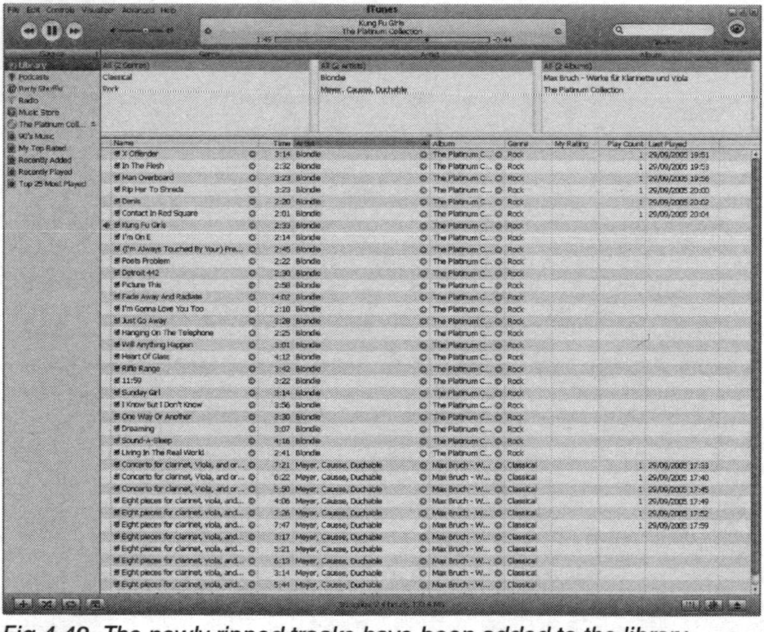

Fig.4.42 The newly ripped tracks have been added to the library

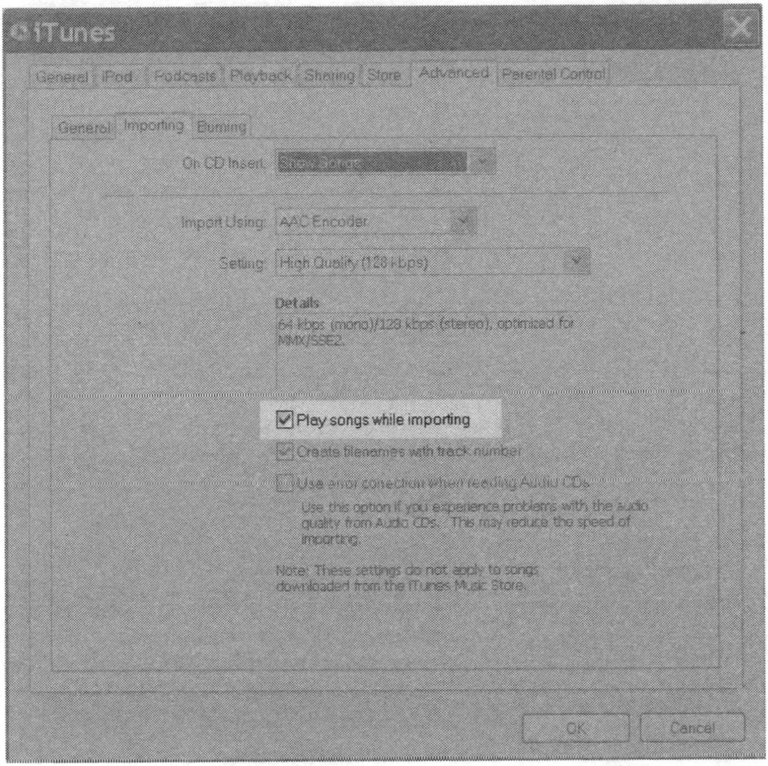

Fig.4.43 You can opt not to play songs as they are imported

By default, iTunes plays each track as it is ripped. This could be useful, but in practice it is often just an annoyance. This feature can be switched off by going to the Advanced section of the Options window and operating the Importing tab within this window. Remove the tick from the checkbox that is labelled "Play songs while importing" (Figure 4.43).

Formats

The iPods are compatible with several audio file formats, and the iTunes program can convert CD tracks to any of them. With the default settings it converts tracks to AAC format with a bit rate of 128 kilobits per second (or 64 kilobits per second for monophonic recordings). This is a good

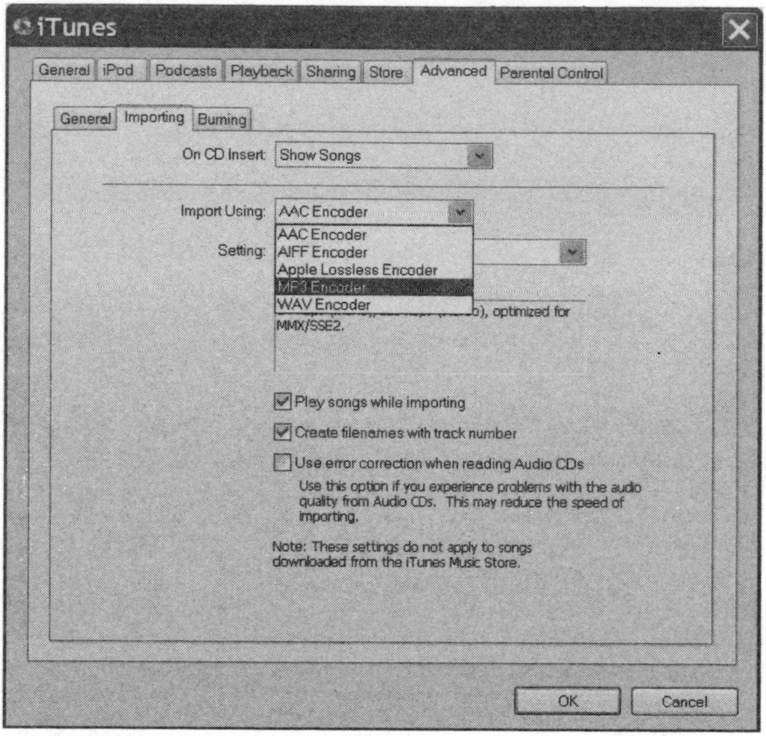

Fig.4.44 Five types of encoding are available

choice since it gives excellent sound quality and quite small file sizes. However, a different file format could be better suited to the particular way in which you will be using the program.

One problem with the AAC format is that it is little used with portable players other than iPods. Clearly this is of no importance if you and your family only use iPods. If other types of player are in use it could be necessary to rip each CD twice. Once to produce AAC tracks that are usable with an iPod, and again to produce files that can be used with an MP3 player. The obvious way around this problem is to use the iTunes program to rip tracks to an MP3 format that can be used with the iPod and the MP3 player. In order to change the type of encoding it is again a matter of using the Advanced section of the Preferences window, and the Importing section within that page of the window.

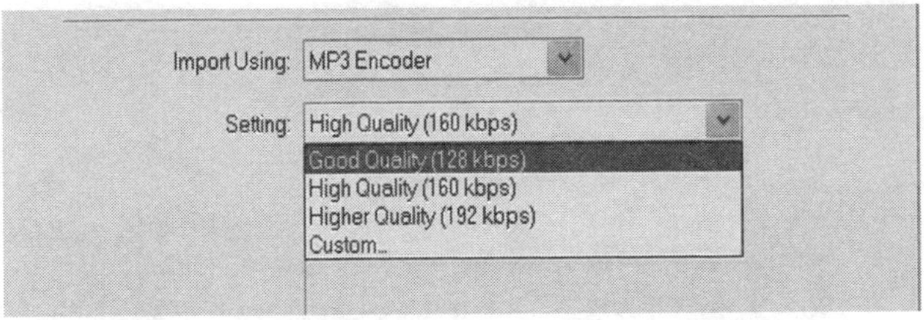

Fig.4.45 Preset bit rates plus a custom option are available

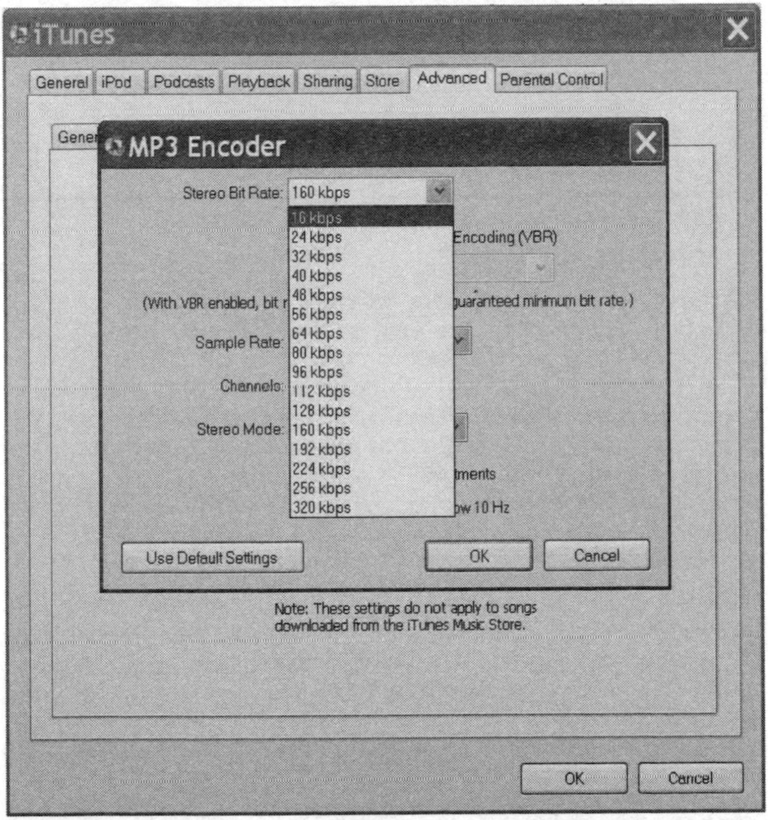

Fig.4.46 The Custom option offers a wide range of bit rates

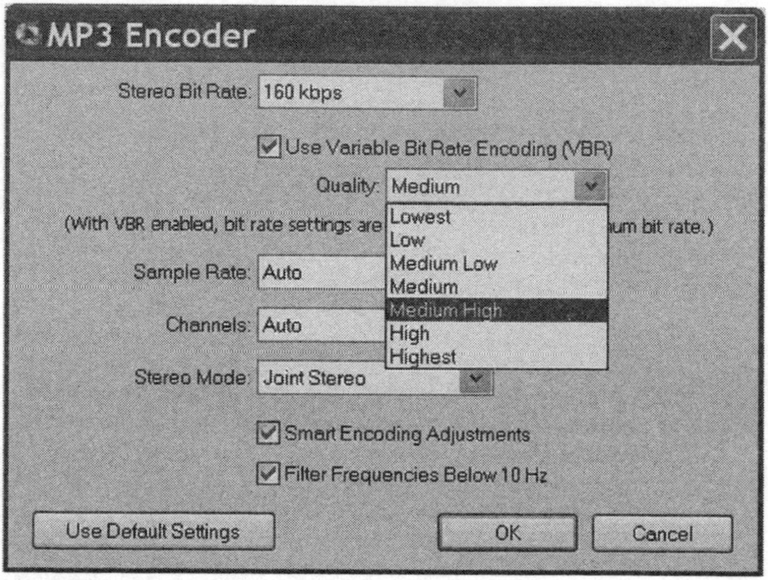

Fig.4.47 A range of seven quality settings are available

The Import Using menu provides five types of encoding, including one MP3 option (Figure 4.44). The Setting menu then provides a choice of three different rates plus a Custom option (Figure 4.45). Preset bit rates of 128, 160, and 192 kilobits per second are available, which are adequate for most purposes. Selecting the Custom option produces a small pop-up window that offers a range of bit rates from 16 to 320 kilobits per second via a menu (Figure 4.46). It is not advisable to use a bit rate of less than 128 kilobits per second for recordings of music. Bear in mind that high bit rates produce relatively large files and that not all MP3 players can handle them.

There is a checkbox near the top of the Custom window that enables variable bit rate (VBR) files to be produced. A menu then gives a choice of quality settings (Figure 4.47). Using a variable bit rate gives excellent quality while keeping file sizes as small as possible. Unfortunately, this type of MP3 encoding is not compatible with all MP3 players, so it might not be a usable option if you need to use the files with a portable MP3 player.

If you decide to use AAC encoding there are some useful options available via the Custom option. This includes a full range of bit rates (Figure

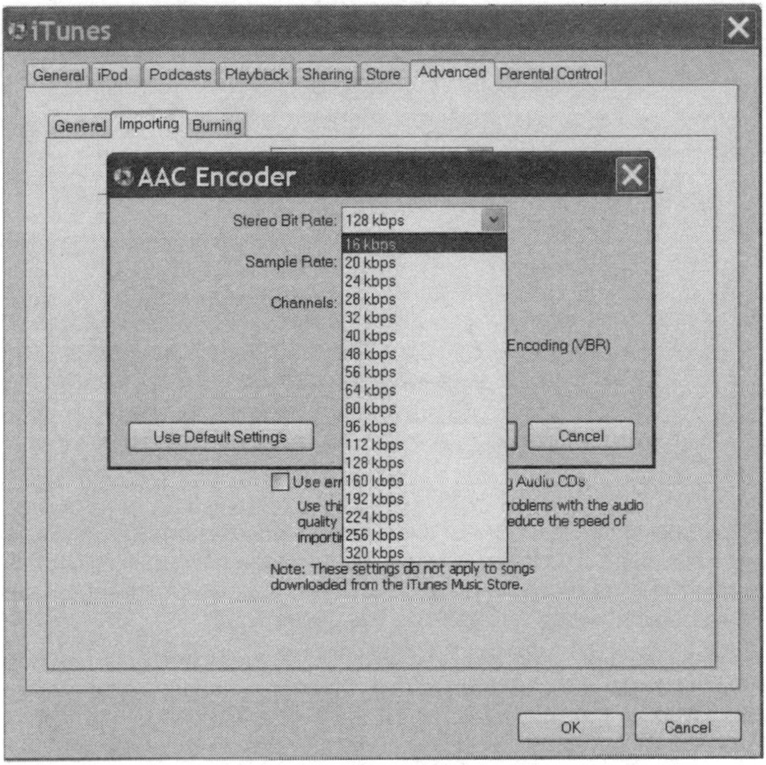

Fig.4.48 A wide range of bit rates is available for AAC encoding

4.48). There is a checkbox that enables variable bit rate encoding to be used (Figure 4.49), and this is active by default. It is unlikely that you will encounter something that can handle AAC files, but not the variable bit rate variety. However, if this should happen it will be necessary to remove the tick from this checkbox in order to produce compatible files.

WAV and ALE

Tracks can be ripped to Wave (WAV) files, which is a format that offers no loss of quality during the conversion. It also offers no compression, so file sizes tend to be very large and it is of little use with portable players. In the current context, WAV files are mainly used as a "halfway house"

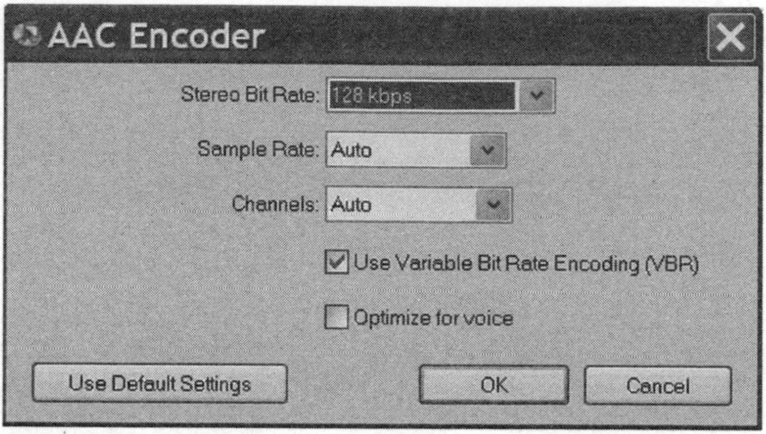

Fig.4.49 There is the option of using variable bit rate encoding (VBR)

when ripping tracks to one of the less common file formats. It is also possible to rip tracks to the ALE (Apple Lossless Encoded) format. This gives some compression, but produces files that are much larger than those obtained when using MP3 or AAC encoding.

However, as it gives no loss of quality it is a good choice for use with iPods that have large disc drives and can accommodate plenty of large files. The AIFF (Apple Interchange File Format) option is probably of little interest to most users. It is a format that was designed by Apple for use with their Mac computers, and it is not used significantly with PCs and portable players.

Note that the encoding options only apply to files ripped from CDs. They do not have any effect on files that are downloaded from the iTunes store or other online music download services. Neither do they apply to audio files that are imported into the iTunes library.

Buying from iTunes

If you wish to buy music via downloads you are not tied to using Apple's iTunes store. On the other hand, many of the companies selling music downloads provide protected WMA files that are not compatible with iPods, or most other portable players come to that. Consequently, the iTunes store is not your only option, but it is likely to be the most convenient one, and it has the advantage of providing files that are guaranteed to be compatible with your iPod and the iTunes program.

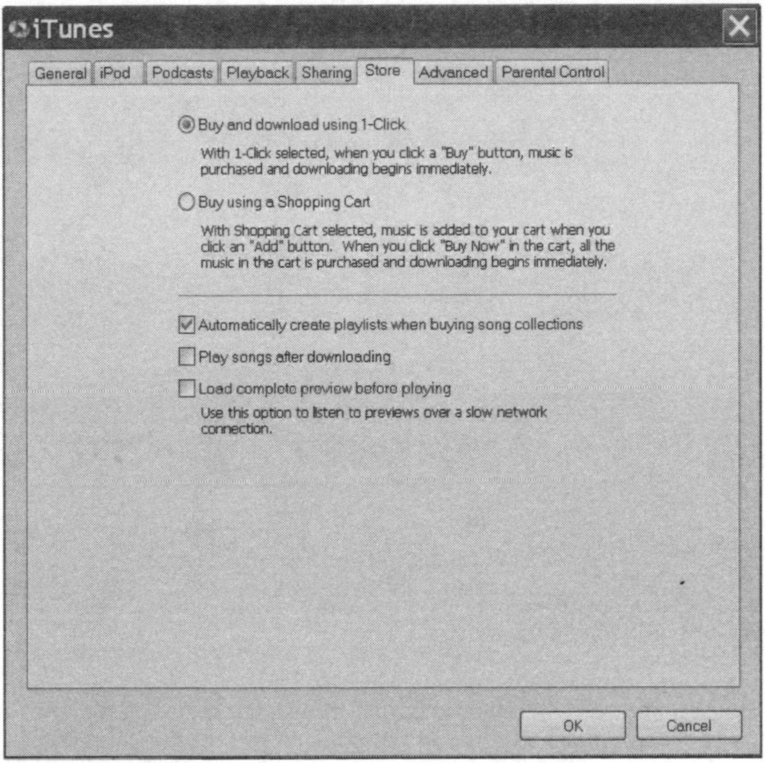

*Fig.4.50 The radio buttons give a choice of normal or one-click
          ordering*

Before trying the iTunes download service it is a good idea to check that
the iTunes program is set to use the store in the way that best suits your
requirements. Select Preferences from the Edit menu and then operate
the Store tab of the preferences window. The Store section of this window
is shown in Figure 4.50, and it is the two radio buttons at the top of the
window that are of most importance. These give the option of one-click
ordering or the conventional method of using a shopping basket and a
checkout. With one-click ordering you can literally order downloads
with a single click of the mouse. This gives the ultimate in convenience,
but it is not necessarily the best approach.

One obvious problem with any one-click ordering system is that you
have to be careful that you do not accidentally order something. It is
probably not a good choice for those who are not very expert at using a

Fig.4.51 The iTunes homepage

mouse. Perhaps of greater importance, with the one-click option the selected track starts to download as soon as you order it. This can be inconvenient, particularly with a slow dial-up connection. Ordering more music can be virtually impossible until the download has finished and there is sufficient free bandwidth to continue using the Internet.

The shopping basket method is relatively slow and cumbersome, but it provides an opportunity for you to check that you have not accidentally ordered the wrong track before committing yourself to the sale. You can also choose everything you require and then download it. The shopping basket method is the safer option until you have gained some experience with the iTunes service. As with any music download service, bear in mind that downloading more than a few tracks can take a very long time when using a dial-up Internet connection. Try not to get carried away.

In order to enter the iTunes store it is just a matter of left-clicking the Music Store entry in the left-hand column of the iTunes program. Of course, there must be an active Internet connection so that the program can connect to the iTunes site. There will be a short delay while the

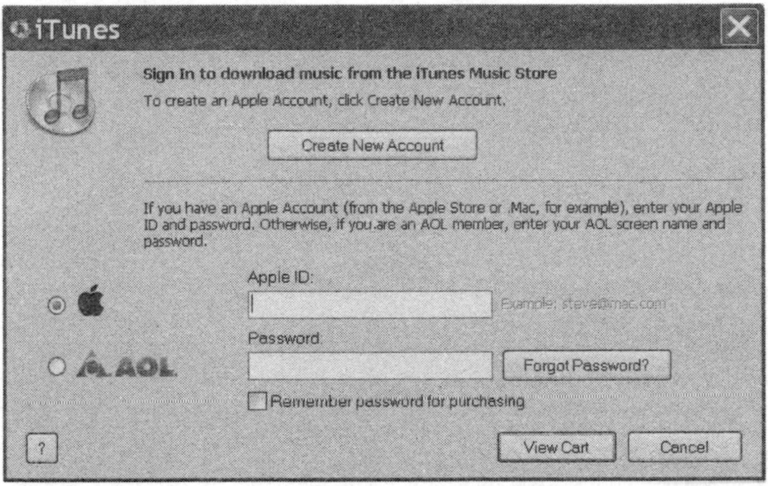

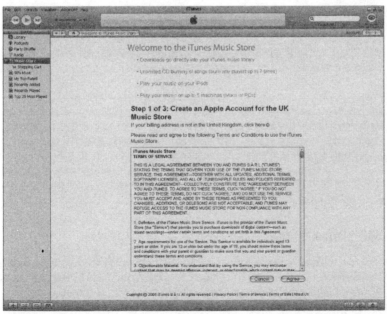

Fig.4.52 An Apple ID and password are needed to place an order

Fig.4.53 A new account can be created from within the iTunes
program

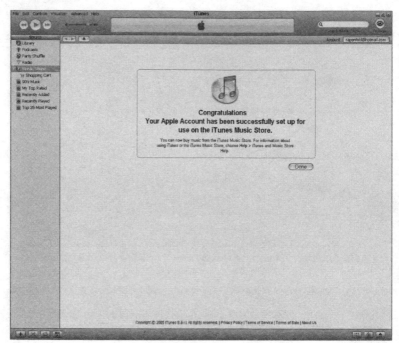

Fig.4.54 *The account has been created and an order can be placed*

program makes the connection to the Internet, contacts the iTunes site, and downloads the homepage, but the latter should soon appear in the main panel (Figure 4.51). If the shopping basket method of ordering has been selected, there will be a Shopping Cart entry in the right-hand column of the window. Left-clicking this entry will usually show the contents of the shopping cart, if any. However, initially it will produce the pop-up window of Figure 4.52.

Registration

In order to use the Apple iTunes store it is necessary to first register with this service. Once registered, you can sign on to the iTunes site using your Apple ID and password. You can sign up with iTunes by operating the Create New Account button and going through the usual Internet sign-up process. This is all done from within the iTunes program (Figure 4.53), which effectively becomes a web browser when using the iTunes

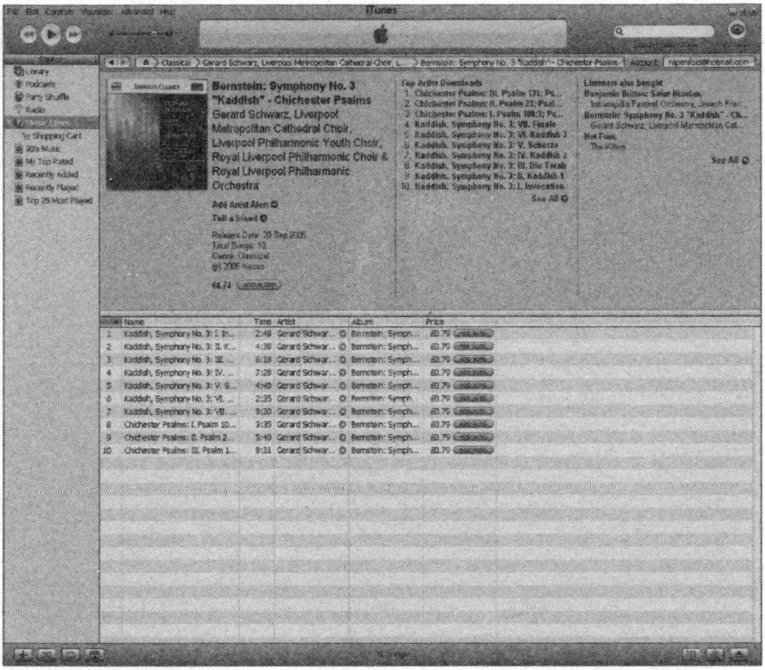

Fig.4.55 The CD's details are shown in the upper section of the window

store. Note that you have to provide credit or debit card details in order to register with the iTunes store even if you will be using the shopping cart method of ordering. Assuming all goes well you should end up with the page shown in Figure 4.54, and you are then ready to proceed.

The iTunes store has the usual range of music categories plus a search facility. Having found a likely CD, its details will be provided in the upper part of the main panel (Figure 4.55). There is a button here so that you can order the entire CD. The individual tracks are listed in the lower section of the main panel, with a button for each one so that individual tracks can be ordered. All the individual tracks are not available for some CDs. Note that there are three buttons in the top left-hand corner of the main panel, and these provide the usual browser function of going back one page, forward one page, and going to the homepage. Of course, in this case the homepage is the iTunes homepage and not the one used for your normal web browser.

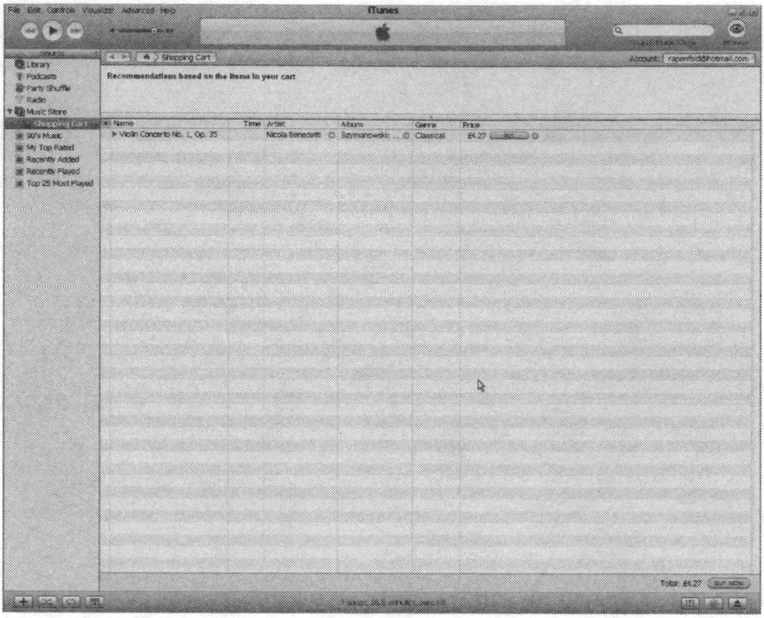

Fig.4.56 Here one item has been added to the shopping cart

Having ordered something, it should be shown in the shopping cart (Figure 4.56). You did not operate the ordering button or something has gone wrong with the system if it does not appear here. If you change your mind and decide not to go ahead and buy something, just operate the tiny button marked with an "X" that is just to the right of the item's Buy button. It will then be removed from the list (Figure 4.57) and you will not have been charged anything.

In order to go ahead and buy something from the shopping cart it is just a matter of operating the Buy button. This will produce the message of Figure 4.58, which is your last chance to back out before committing yourself to buying the track or CD. Assuming you wish to go ahead with the transaction, operate the Buy button. The iTunes program then starts to download the track and the item disappears from the shopping cart. The banner at the top of the window keeps you informed about the progress made with the download (Figure 4.59). If the item you have ordered consists of several tracks, these will be downloaded as separate items. However, this is all handled automatically by the program, so you just sit back and wait for the download process to be completed.

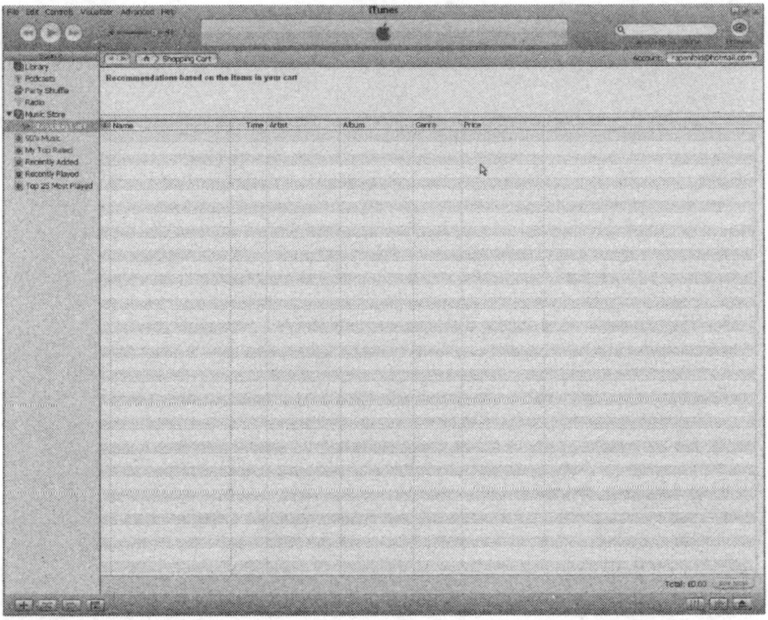

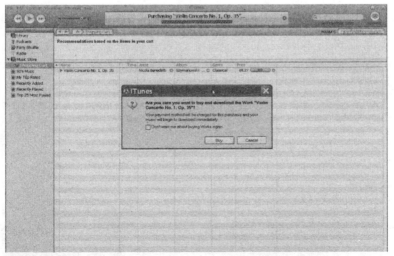

Fig.4.57 Operating the "X" button removes an item from the basket

Fig.4.58 You are asked to confirm the purchase of an item

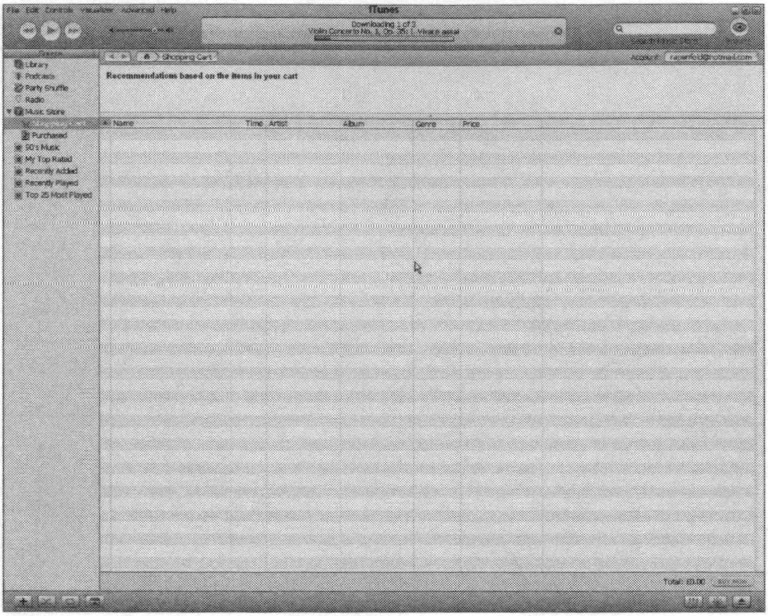

Fig.4.59 The information banner shows how the download is
          progressing

The banner at the top of the window will return to its normal state with
the Apple logo once the downloading has been completed (Figure 4.60).
The downloaded track or tracks should have been automatically loaded
into the library. If you go to the library view it should be possible to
locate the new entry or entries. In this example the three newly
downloaded Nicola Benedetti tracks are present and·correct at the bottom
of the track list (Figure 4.61). Delving into the file structure of my hard
disc drive located the actual files that were downloaded (Figure 4.62).
Note that these have an M4p extension, with the "p" presumably being
used to indicate that these are in protected AAC/MP4 format.

iMix

Most of the categories in the iTunes store are self-explanatory, but the
iMix section (Figure 4.63) perhaps requires a little explanation. An iMix
is basically just a collection of music that someone has put together and
uploaded to the iTunes site. You can look through the iMix collections
out of idle curiosity, or in the hope of finding a list by a like-minded person.

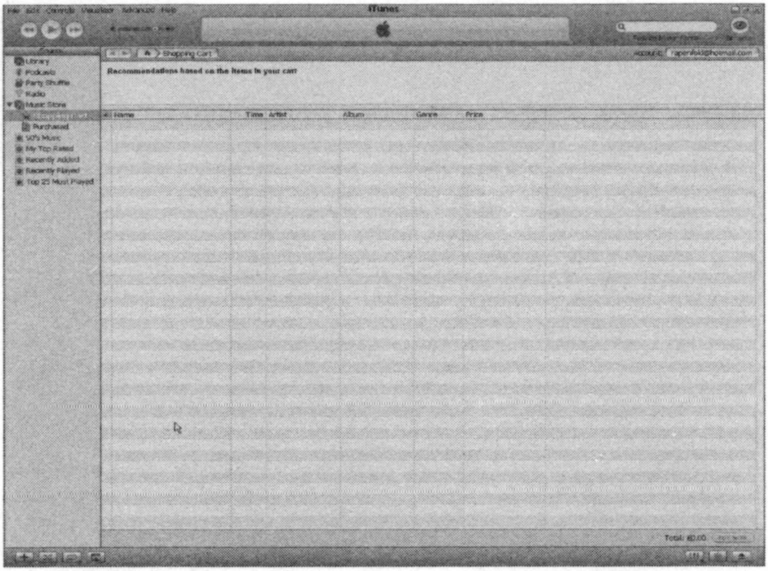

Fig.4.60 The Apple logo indicates a successful download

Fig.4.61 The tracks have been added to the library

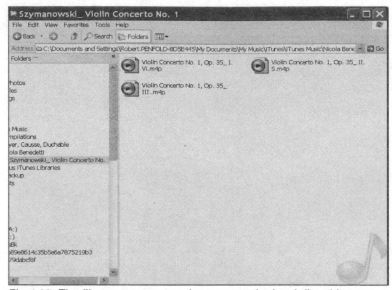

Fig.4.62 The files are present and correct on the hard disc drive

Fig.4.63 The iMix section of the iTunes store

Fig.4.64 An iMix is treated much like an ordinary album

If you can find an iMix by someone that has broadly similar tastes it is likely that their list will contain tracks that you like, but have never heard before.

If you select an iMix it is treated much like a music album, and you have the option of purchasing all the tracks as a "job lot" in the upper half of the window, or the individual tracks in the lower half (Figure 4.64). When purchasing music from the iTunes store you will often be familiar with the music you are buying, having heard it a few times on the radio perhaps. With the music in an iMix it is likely that most of the tracks will be songs you have not heard before, and that they will be performed by artists that are new to you. Fortunately, the iTunes store has a preview facility that enables you to listen to a 30 second excerpt of each track. This actually works with any tracks and not just with those in an iMix, but it is probably of most use in the current context.

In order to preview a track it must first be selected by left-clicking its entry in the lower section of the window. The track should then be

Fig.4.65 You can play a 30 second excerpt of any track

highlighted (white text with a blue background). You can then play it as if it was an ordinary track in the iTunes library. Just left-click the triangular Start/Stop button near the top left-hand corner of the window and the track will play for 30 seconds (Figure 4.65). A preview facility is not a unique feature of iTunes, but the preview systems of some other sites do not work as well as the iTunes version.

There is no need to download any special software since everything needed is already there in the iTunes program. There are no long delays, and the selected track will start playing almost immediately. Some systems only provide a low quality monophonic preview that is of limited value, but the iTunes preview is in high quality stereo. Of course, if you are using a dial-up connection it is likely that the relatively low speed of the connection will introduce some compromises into the iTunes preview facility. However, this is due to the limitations of the Internet connection rather than any shortcoming in the preview facility.

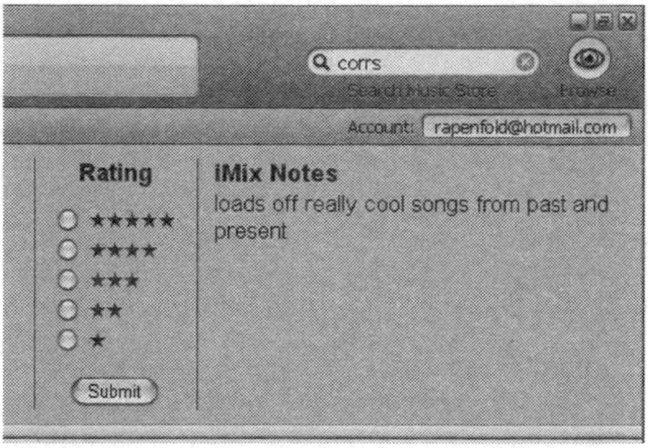

In the top section of an iMix window there are five radio buttons and a Submit button (Figure 4.66). This enables you to register your rating of the collection, and the system has the usual one to five stars with five stars being the best. Each iMix is given an overall rating that is derived from its submitted ratings. As

Fig.4.66 You can give an iMix your star rating

with any system of this type, a high rating means that the selected music is popular, but it will not necessarily match your tastes. Similarly, an iMix that has a low rating contains unpopular music, but that is not to say that you will not like it.

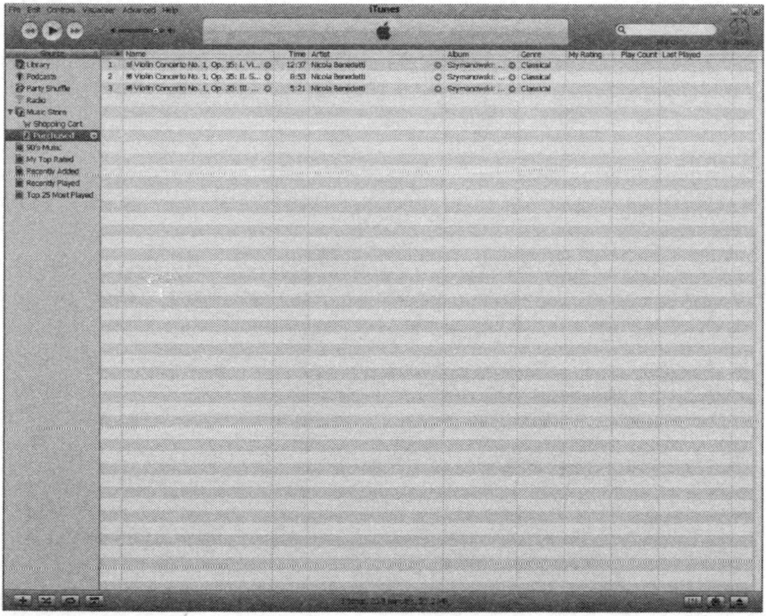

Fig.4.67 The Purchased play list shows the items bought from iTunes

Limitations

When downloading music from iTunes you have to bear in mind that the music is in a protected format and that there are consequently some limitations on the way it can be used. This is the case with practically every site that sells legal downloads, and it is not something that only affects downloads from the iTunes store. Music downloaded from the iTunes store is to a large extent used just like any other music, but you need to be aware of the differences.

The most important difference between an iTunes download and non-protected music is that an iTunes track can only be played on a computer that is authorised to use it. This operates with a licensing system, similar to that used with DRM protected WMA files. When you buy music from iTunes it is, as we have already seen, added to your iTunes library. Once in the library it can be used in the normal way, so you can play it, use it in playlists, and even burn it onto a CD. The difference between a track from iTunes and non-protected tracks is not immediately obvious.

When you purchase music from iTunes it is placed in a special play list that is added to the left-hand column of the program. It is placed immediately below the Music Store and Shopping Cart entries. Selecting it will result in the main panel listing the music that you have purchased from the iTunes store (Figure 4.67). When you first access this play list the message shown in Figure 4.68 will pop up. This simply explains that deleting items from the play list will not delete the music that you have purchased. It will remain in the library and files will remain intact on the computer's hard disc drive. It is probably best to tick the checkbox so that this message does not appear each time you access the Purchased play list.

The Purchased play list can not be edited as freely as other play lists. Most types of editing are not permitted. You can delete items and add tracks that were not purchased from the iTunes store, but it is inadvisable

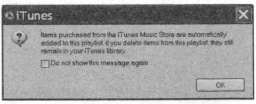

Fig.4.68 This message appears when you access the Purchased play list

to do so. The idea of this list is to make it easy to keep track of the music you have purchased from iTunes and to make it easy to access these pieces of music.

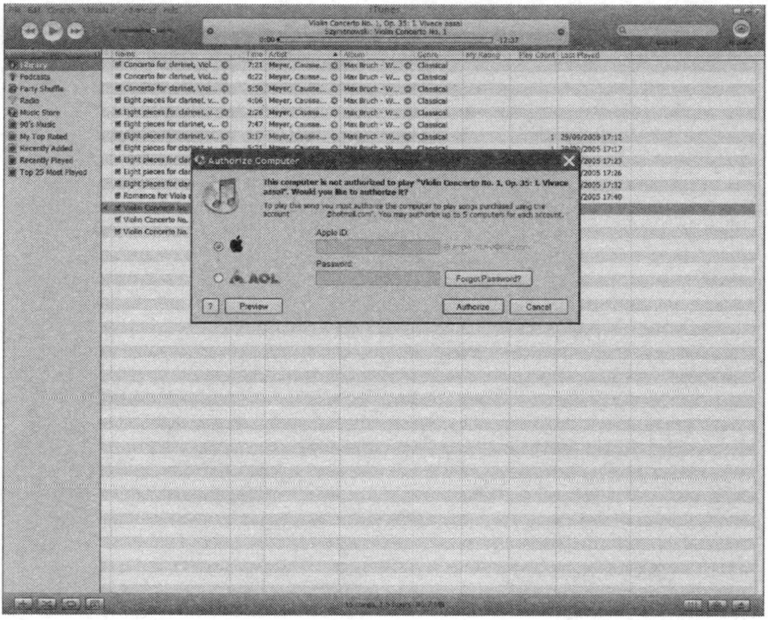

Fig.4.69 This message appears if you try to play a protected track on a computer that is not authorised

Five machines

The main limitation on music purchased from iTunes is that it is restricted to use on five machines, which will probably not be much of a limitation for most users. You can actually copy the music to as many computers as you like, but it will only be playable on a maximum of five machines. In order to play one of these tracks the computer must be authorised to do so. There is no need to obtain authorisation when you buy tracks from the iTunes store and download them to your computer. It will automatically receive authorisation and will be able to play the tracks.

It is necessary to obtain authorisation if the downloaded files are copied to another PC and added to the iTunes library of that PC. Attempting to play any of the files will produce a message stating that the PC is not authorised to play the files (Figure 4.69). You can authorise the computer by entering your Apple ID and password into the textboxes and operating the Authorise button. There must be an active Internet connection so that the iTunes program can obtain authorisation from the iTunes site. If

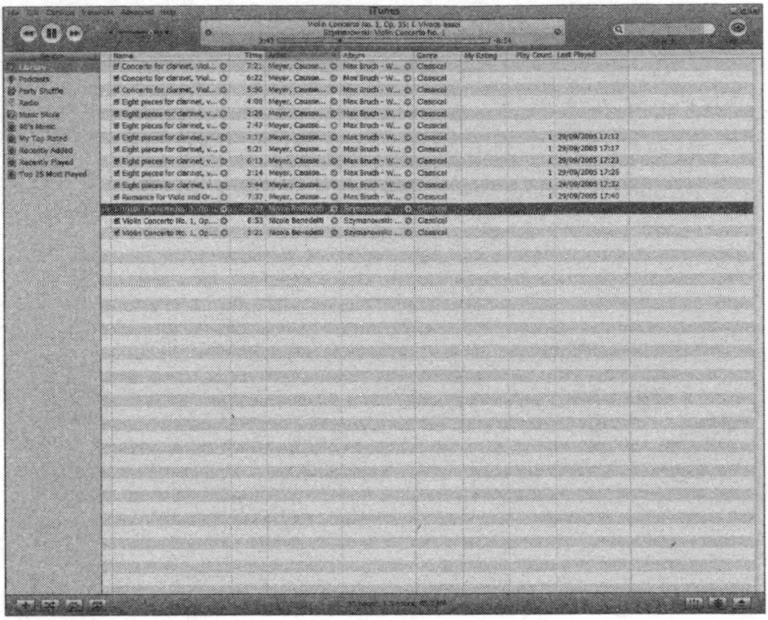

Fig.4.70 After authorisation the track plays perfectly

all is well, a message will appear stating that the computer has been authorised to play the files, and it will also tell you how many machines have been authorised on your account. It should then be possible to play the protected tracks, and everything worked fine in this case (Figure 4.70).

It is not necessary for the iTunes program to connect to the Internet each time you play a protected AAC file. A computer can play any files that you have purchased from the iTunes store once it has been authorised against your account. Therefore, you should have no problem if you load some protected files onto a portable PC and try to play them when there is no available Internet connection. Of course, you must get authorisation for the portable PC before you set off with the portable PC.

Note that Apple does not count an iPod as a "machine". You do not need authorisation to play protected iTunes on an iPod, but they presumably have to be uploaded from a computer that is authorised to play them. An iPod can be synchronised with an authorised PC in the normal way.

Problems?

A potential problem with any authorisation system is that no one uses the same PC forever. Eventually a new PC is bought and the old one is sold or scrapped. Over a period of time the allowance of five machines could be used up and the protected music tracks could become useless. Apple provides a way around this problem by making it possible to "deauthorise" a computer. In other words, authorisation can be removed from a computer so that it no longer counts as part of your quota of five machines. Therefore, you can deauthorise an

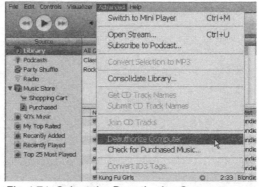

Fig.4.71 Select the Deauthorize Computer option

old PC before selling or scrapping it, and then authorise the new computer. In this way it is possible to go on using the protected tracks indefinitely.

There is a potential problem in that it might not be possible to deauthorise a computer that suddenly goes wrong and is either impossible or too costly to repair. Where possible, it is clearly advisable to deauthorise an ailing computer if it can be made to work sufficiently well to briefly run the iTunes program and connect to the Internet. It is probably worthwhile making some effort to deauthorise an ailing PC if you have a large number of protected AAC tracks. However, the Apple allowance of five machines is quite generous, so it should be possible to go on using protected AAC files for many years even if it proves to be impossible to deauthorise one or two PCs over the years. If you should try to authorise more than five computers on your account, you will simply get a warning message pointing out that you already have the maximum of five machines authorised on your account.

In order to deauthorise a computer you must run the iTunes program and select Deauthorize Computer from the Advanced menu (Figure 4.71). This produces the pop-up window of Figure 4.72 where there are two

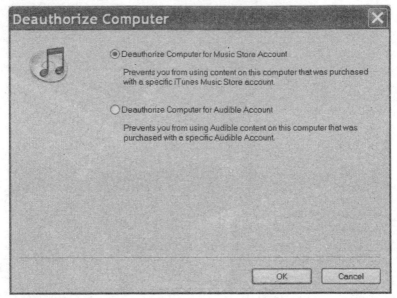

Fig.4.72 The top radio button is used for a music account

radio buttons. Choose the button for the type of account you are using. This will be a Music Store Account, so the upper radio button is selected. Operating the OK button produces the pop-up window of Figure 4.73 where your Apple ID and password are typed into the textboxes. Operating the OK button should produce a message stating that the computer has been successfully deauthorised. Of course, it can only be deauthorised if there is an active Internet connection. Connect to the Internet before starting the deauthorisation process if you do not have some form of always-on Internet connection.

Incidentally, there is no Authorise option in the Advanced menu. The only way to authorise a computer is to try to play a protected AAC track. If the computer already has authorisation to play the track it will do so. If not it will start the authorisation process. When a computer has been deauthorised it is possible to authorise it again, but only if you have not reached your five machine limit.

Note that signing onto your iTunes account and purchasing music does not automatically authorise the computer you are using. This does seem to happen when you set up an account and purchase music from the

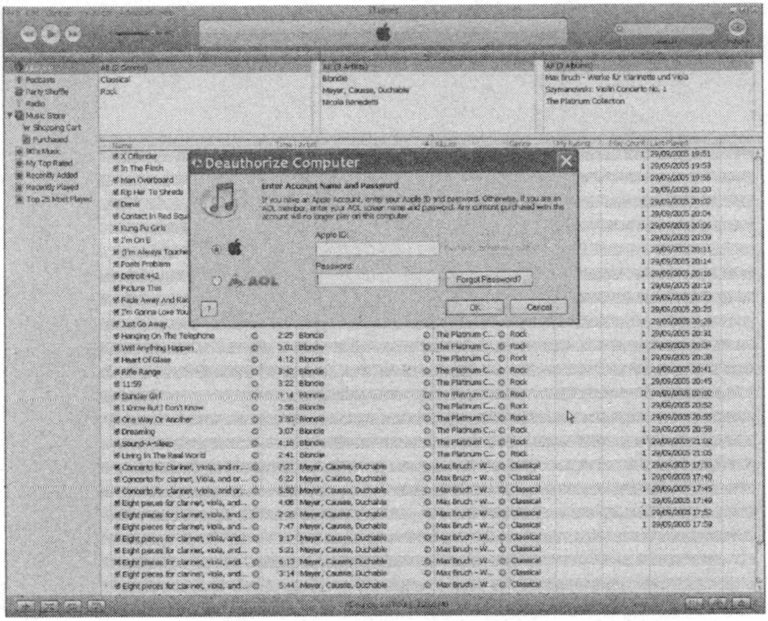

Fig.4.73 Your Apple ID and password are entered in the textboxes

iTunes store, but the PC is presumably authorised as part of the account creation process. When using another computer to purchase music from the iTunes store it is necessary to authorise that computer before it will be able to play the newly purchased tracks.

Networking

These days many home PCs are connected to a small network. By sharing the folder that contains the music tracks it is possible to play the files on any computer in the network. However, the network does not count as one machine. Each computer in the network counts as a separate machine, and must be authorised in order to play any protected ACC files.

Another point to note is that authorising a computer does not render it able to play any protected AAC file. If it is authorised on your account, it will only play tracks that have been purchased via that account. In order to play tracks purchased by someone else it would be necessary for the computer to be authorised on their account as well.

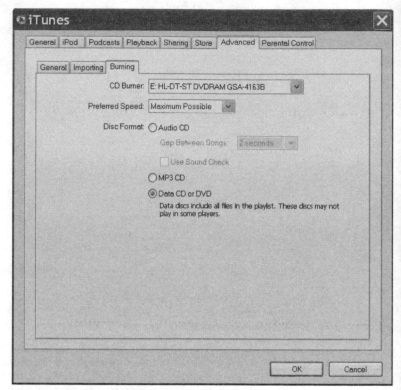

Fig.4.74 There is a choice of three types of CD

Bear in mind that it is possible for someone to buy tracks from the iTunes store using your account if they have your Apple ID and password. Like any password, the one for your iTunes account should be kept secret. If you need to authorise a computer that belongs to someone else it is advisable to do it yourself rather than giving them your Apple ID and password.

Moving files

One way of moving files to another PC is to locate the files on your computer's hard disc and then copy them to any mass storage device that will enable them to be copied over to the destination computer. Locating the iTunes library folder was covered previously. Copying the

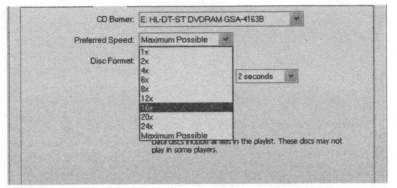

Fig.4.75 The CD writer can be set to record at a lower speed

files to a CD of some sort is probably the best option, since practically any computer can read a data CD. It is possible to burn CDs from within the iTunes program, and it is possible to produce normal audio CDs, MP3 CDs, or data CDs. Audio CDs are produced by default, but the required type can be selected by going to the Advanced section of the Preferences window and selecting the Burning subsection (Figure 4.74). Select the radio button for the required type of CD recording.

There are some other useful settings available via this window. If the computer is fitted with more than one CD/DVD drive, there is a menu here that enables the required drive to be selected. The drive will be used at its maximum speed by default, but another menu provides a range of lower speeds (Figure 4.75). The speeds on offer here will depend

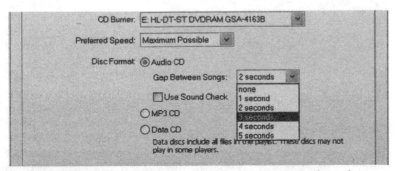

Fig.4.76 The gap between tracks can be zero, one, two, three, four, or five seconds

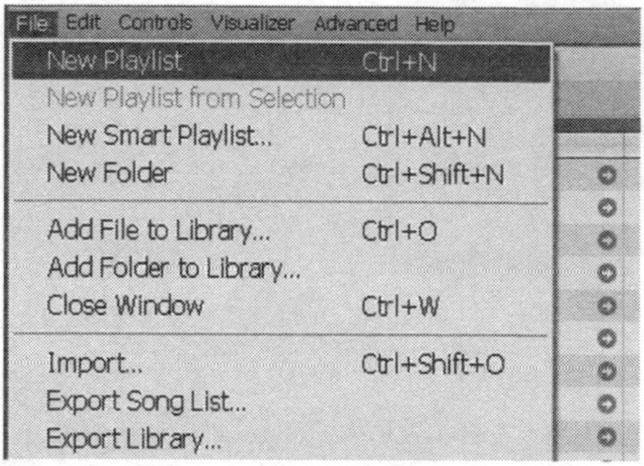

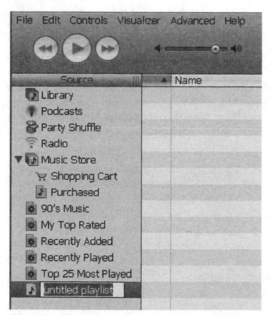

Fig.4.77 Select the New Playlist option

on the maximum speed of the drive. It can be useful to use a lower speed if there are problems with reliability at the maximum speed. A gap of two seconds is normally placed between tracks when producing an audio CD. With the audio CD option selected there is a small menu that enables the gap to be set one, two, three, four, or five seconds, or the gap can be omitted (Figure 4.76).

Fig.4.78 The new play list has been added to the right-hand column

Play list

In order to burn tracks to a CD, regardless of the type of disc that will be produced, you must first produce a play list. The concept of play lists was covered in Chapter 3 and will not be discussed further here. One way of making a playlist in iTunes is to create a blank list and then add files to it. This is probably the best approach when making a play list that will be used to burn a CD. A blank play list can be created by selecting New Playlist

Fig.4.79 The new play list has a name, but it is still empty

from the File menu (Figure 7.77), or by operating the New Playlist button. This is the one in the bottom left-hand corner of the iTunes window that is marked with a "+". The new play list will appear in the right-hand column of the window (Figure 4.78), and its name can be changed to something more appropriate. The names of most play lists can be edited by first selecting its entry and then left-clicking it again. This effectively turns the entry into a textbox that can be edited in the usual way.

You now have a new play list with a suitable name, but it is empty (Figure 4.79). In order to add tracks you must first find their entries in the library or another play list. Select a track or several tracks using the normal methods and then drag them to the new play list's entry in the right-hand column (Figure 4.80). Further tracks can be added to the play list using the same method, but in this case the play list is a burn list for an ordinary audio CD. These have limited capacity so only a limited number of tracks can be selected. For this example I settled for the three tracks that were earlier downloaded from the iTunes store (Figure 4.81).

Fig.4.80 Tracks can be selected and dragged to the play list

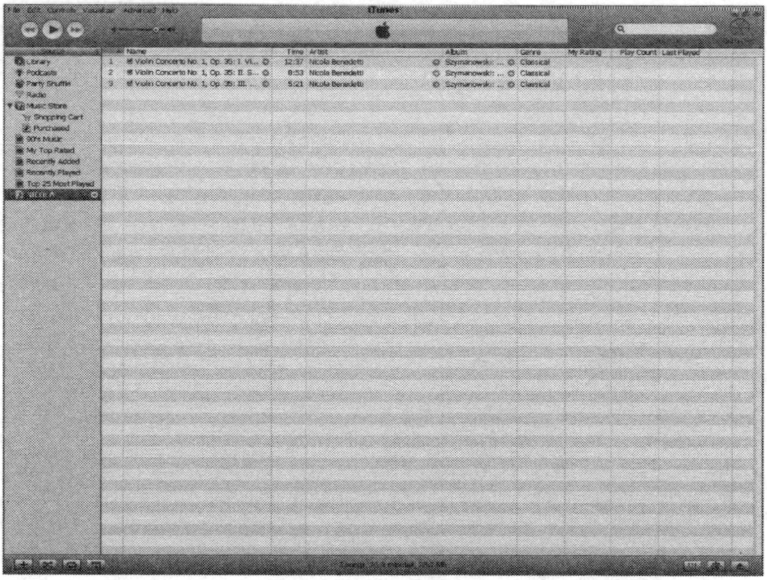

Fig.4.81 The tracks have been duly added to the new play list

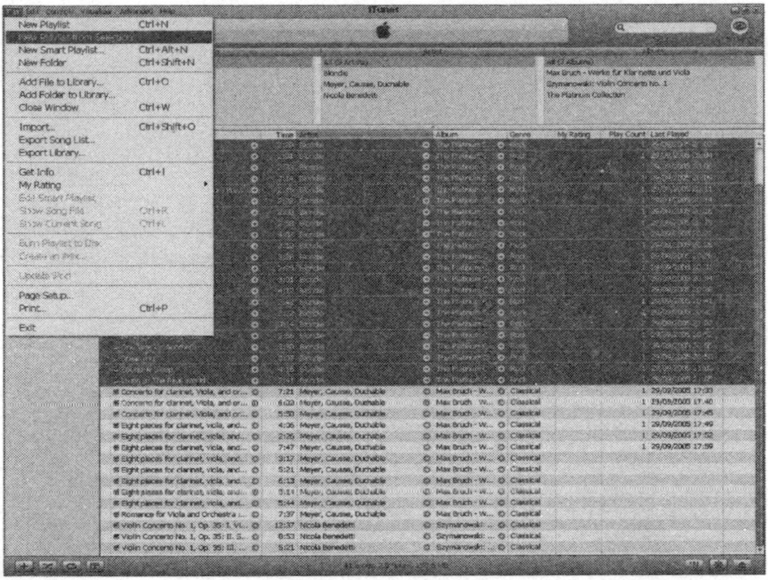

Fig.4.82 This time New Playlist from Selection has been used

Fig.4.83 The selected tracks are included in the new play list

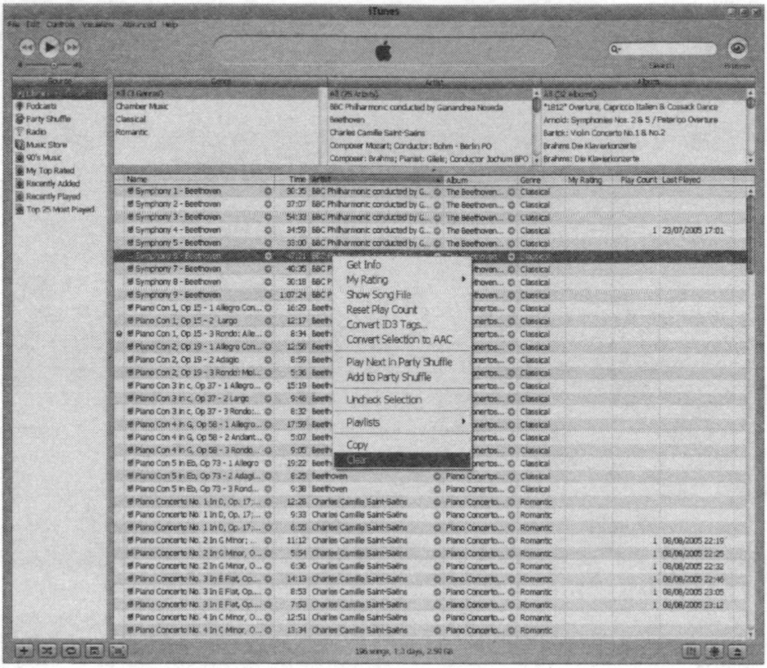

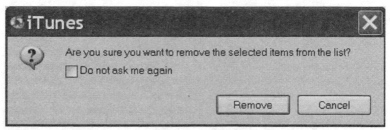

Fig.4.84 A track is easily removed from a play list

An alternative way of producing a play list is to select some tracks first, and then choose New Playlist from Selection from the File menu (Figure 4.82). The new play list will then be populated with the selected tracks (Figure 4.83). With any play list it is possible to add tracks at any time using the dragging method. A track can be removed from a play list by

Fig.4.85 Operate the Remove button to erase the track from the list

right-clicking its entry and selecting Clear from the pop-up menu (Figure 4.84).

This method will also work if a number of tracks are selected and you right-click on one of them. If the warning message of Figure 4.85 appears,

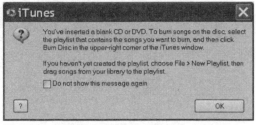

Fig.4.86 *Inserting a blank CD in the drive produces this message*

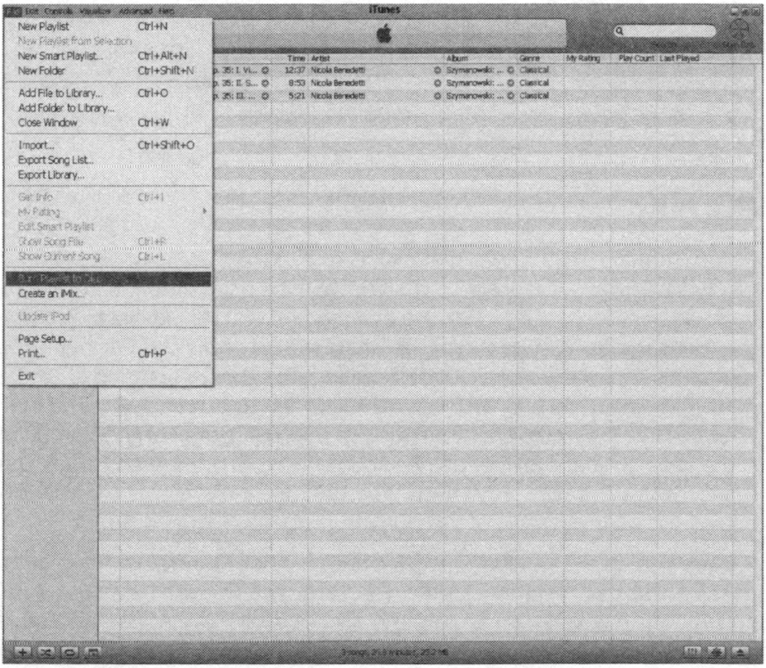

operate the Remove button to delete the entries from the list. Tick the checkbox if you would do not wish this message to appear in the future. Note that you are only removing entries from a play list, and the files themselves will remain in the library. Tracks can be moved to a new position in the list by simply dragging them to the new position.

Fig.4.87 *Choose Burn Playlist to Disc from the File menu*

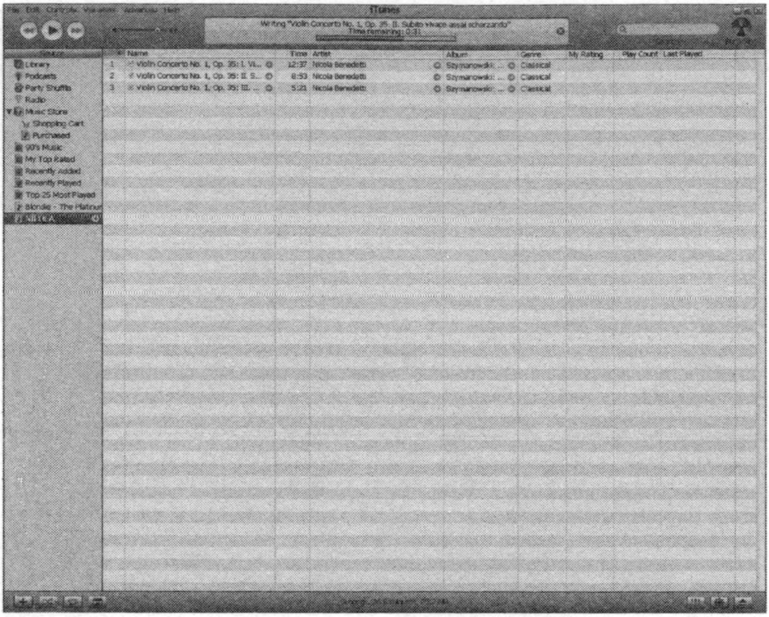

Fig.4.88 As usual, the information banner shows how things are going

Burning

Before burning a CD, check that the correct preferences are set. Place a blank disc in the appropriate CD/DVD drive, which will produce the helpful message of Figure 4.86. Tick the checkbox if you would like to prevent the message from appearing in the future, and press the OK button to remove it from the screen. Once you are sure that everything is set up correctly, select the play list that you would like to burn to a CD and then choose Burn Playlist to Disc from the File menu (Figure 4.87). The button in the top right-hand corner of the window turns to orange and black and rotates while the disc is burned. The banner at the top of the window shows the current status of the burning process (Figure 4.88).

It does not take a genius to work out that once the tracks have been burned onto an ordinary audio CD they not longer have the AAC protection. It is possible to play the disc on any PC that has a suitable drive, and the five machine limit can not be enforced. However, you are bound by the licensing conditions and should not use an audio CD as a means of using protected AAC tracks on more than five computers.

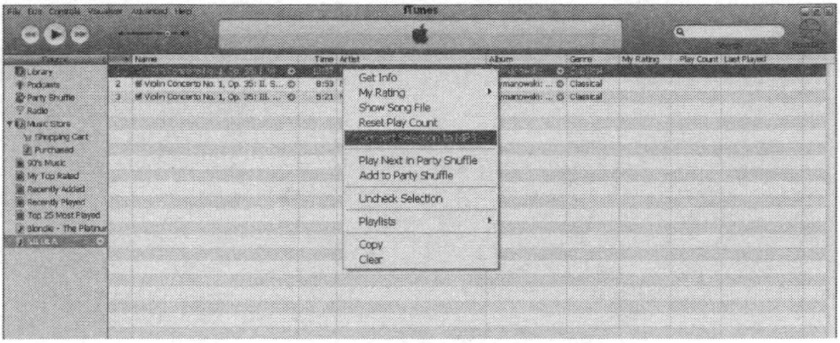

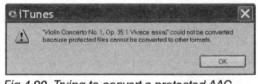

Fig.4.89 There is an option to convert tracks to MP3 format

If a track is right-clicked, the pop-up menu includes an option to convert it to MP3 format (Figure 4.89). Attempts to convert protected audio files to another format are usually unsuccessful, and this is method is no exception. The error message of Figure 4.90 appears if your try to convert a protected AAC file to MP3 format. Trying to burn protected tracks to an MP3 data CD would be equally unsuccessful. Again, it does not take a genius to work out that it is possible to burn protected tracks to an audio CD and then rip them into MP3 or some other format. However, this is outside the licensing agreement. This is a pity, because it renders iTunes downloads incompatible with most MP3 players apart from iPods, which can play the protected AAC files.

Fig.4.90 Trying to convert a protected AAC file produces this error message

Playing

So far we have covered getting music into the iTunes program and uploading it to an iPod. Tracks can, of course, be played by the iTunes program which is a well-specified media player. In the top left-hand corner of the window there are the usual controls for skipping backwards and forwards, and a Stop/Start button (Figure 4.91). The slider control is for adjusting the volume. When playing a CD, the button in the bottom right-hand corner of the screen is used when you need to eject it.

The button at the other end of this row of three buttons displays the graphic equaliser (Figure 4.92). This is a 10-band type that is similar to the equivalent feature in WMP 10. This equaliser is in a "floating" window that can be dragged to any desired position on the screen. The checkbox enables the graphic equaliser to be switched on and off. Note that the graphic equaliser does not become active when it is visible on the screen and switch off again when it is removed. It is the setting of the checkbox that determines whether it is active or switched off. The menu provides a range of preset settings for various types of music (Figure 4.93). There are also settings for such things as boosting and reducing the amount of bass, and a Loudness setting (Figure 4.94).

Fig.4.91 The four main player controls

Fig.4.92 The graphic equaliser is in a "floating" window

Fig.4.93 A number of preset equaliser settings are available

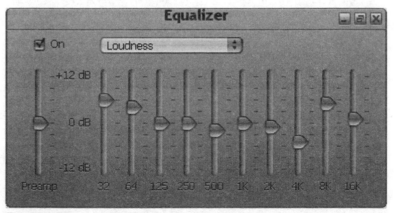

Fig.4.94 The presets include a loudness setting

Fig.4.95 A name for the preset must be entered in the textbox

The can make your own preset settings by first adjusting the sliders to give the required contouring of the sound. There is no need to select Manual from the menu before doing this. Adjusting one of the controls will automatically set the equaliser to Manual mode. Select Make Preset from the menu when you are satisfied with the control settings. This will produce a small window with a textbox so that you can enter a name for the new preset (Figure 4.95). The name that you enter here is the one that will be used for the new preset in the menu. A descriptive name will be more helpful than something like "Preset12". Operate the OK button when a suitable name has been entered, and the new preset should then appear in the menu (Figure 4.96). It can then be selected as and when required, just like any of the existing presets.

Fig.4.96 The new preset has been added to the window

It is possible to edit the list of presets. The list is quite long even with just the supplied presets, but it starts to become slightly excessive if you start adding your own. Things are more manageable if any unwanted presets are removed. To remove a preset, select the Edit List option from the top section of the menu. This produces the pop-up window of Figure 4.97, where the item to be deleted is selected from the list of presets on the left. The two buttons near the top right-hand corner of the window then become active. The Rename button brings up a textbox so that the selected preset can be given a new name. In this case it is the Delete button that is required. This produces the usual message asking if you are sure you wish to delete the item. The message of Figure 4.98 appears if you confirm the deletion. This asks if you wish to remove the selected preset from all the songs that use it. Presumably there will be no songs that use it, so operate the Yes button to go ahead and delete the preset.

Associating a equaliser preset with a track is easy enough, but it requires a column in the play list that is not displayed by default. To display the "missing" column, choose View Options from the Edit menu. The View

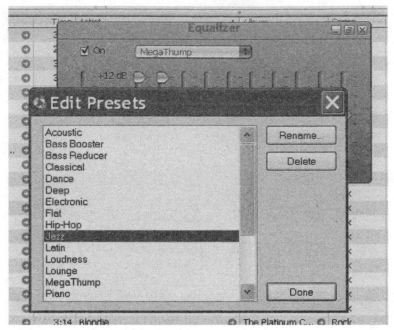

Fig.4.97 Select the preset that is to be deleted

Options window (Figure 4.99) has a number of checkboxes that are used to control the items that are displayed on the screen. Add a tick to the Equaliser checkbox and operate the OK button to close the window.

The play list should now have an additional column on the right, although it might be necessary to scroll the list to the left in order to reveal it. The new column has a button for each track, and left-clicking one of the buttons produces a menu of the available equaliser presets (Figure 4.100). Just select the required preset and it will be

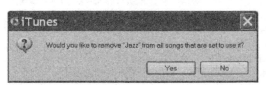

Fig.4.98 Operate the Yes button to confirm the deletion

applied to the track. The name of the selected preset will be added to the right of the button (Figure 4.101). In order to disassociate a track

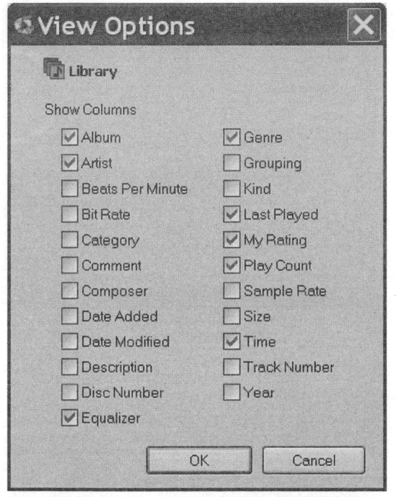

Fig.4.99 *The View Options window is used to select the information that will be displayed. In this case the equaliser checkbox must be ticked*

from the equaliser it is just a matter of left-clicking its equaliser button and selecting None from the menu.

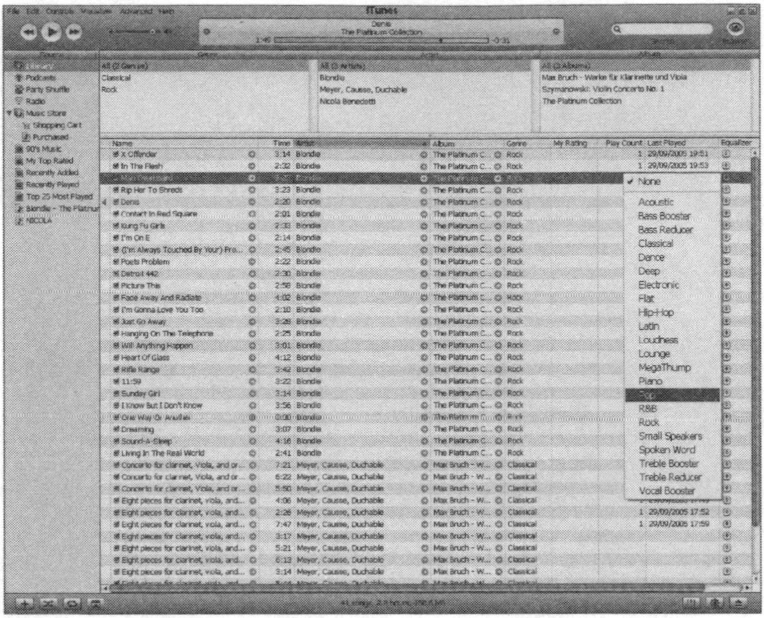

Fig.4.100 The button produces a menu of the available presets

Enhancer

Some useful features are hidden away in the Playback section of the Preferences window (Figure 4.102). The crossfade function enables one track to be faded into the next, and this is essentially the same as the equivalent function in WMP 10 (see chapter 3). The sound enhancer is not active by default, but it can be switched on by ticking its checkbox. I am far from certain about the precise way in which it is supposed to enhance the sound, but it seems to increase the apparent width and depth of the soundstage. It is a bit like a less extreme version of the SRS WOW effect of WMP 10.

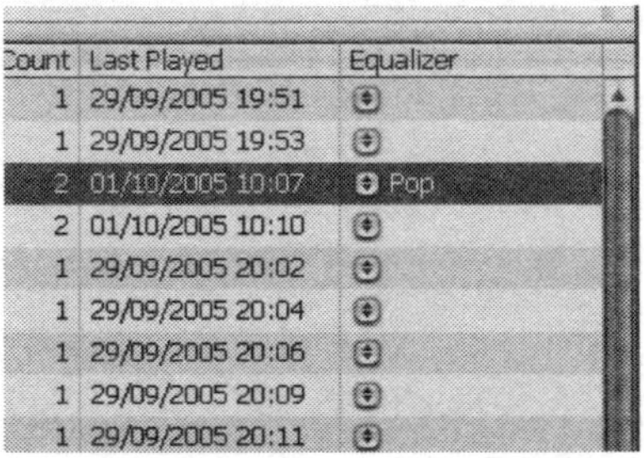

Fig.4.101 The selected preset is shown in the play list

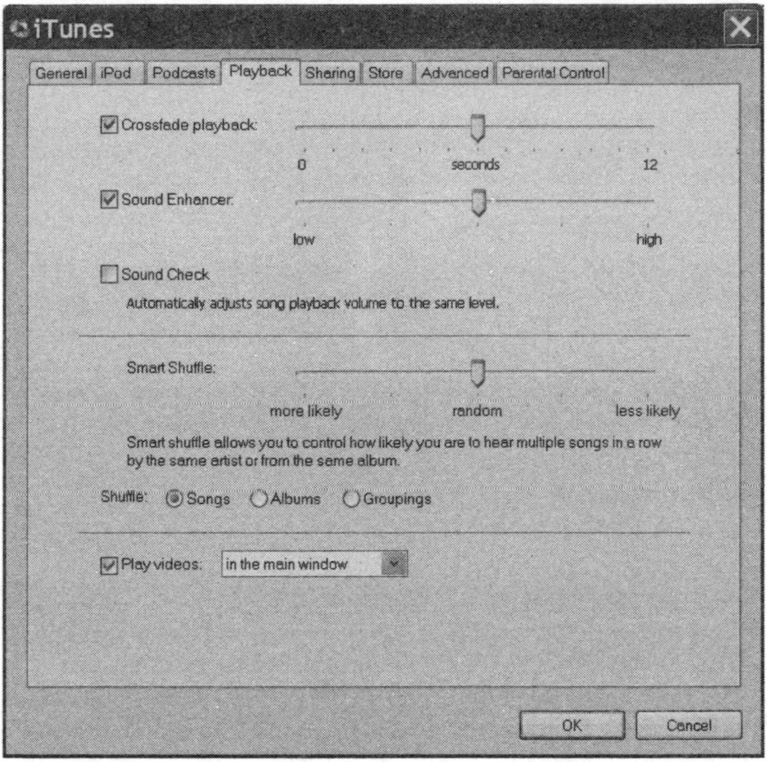

Fig.4.102 Crossfade and a sound enhancer are available

Anyway, it is worth experimenting with this feature, especially for users of headphones or loudspeakers that have limited physical separation.

The slider control and three buttons near the middle of the window give some control over the way in which the Shuffle function operates. This function is switched on via its entry in the Controls menu (Figure 4.103). It can also be toggled on and off via one of the buttons in the bottom left-hand corner of the main iTunes window (the second button from the left). Two versions of a repeat facility are also available here. Repeat All is used if you would like to have a complete play list repeat indefinitely, whereas Repeat One only repeats the track that is currently playing. The Repeat function can also be controlled via the button on the immediate right of the Shuffle button.

Fig.4.103 The Controls menu

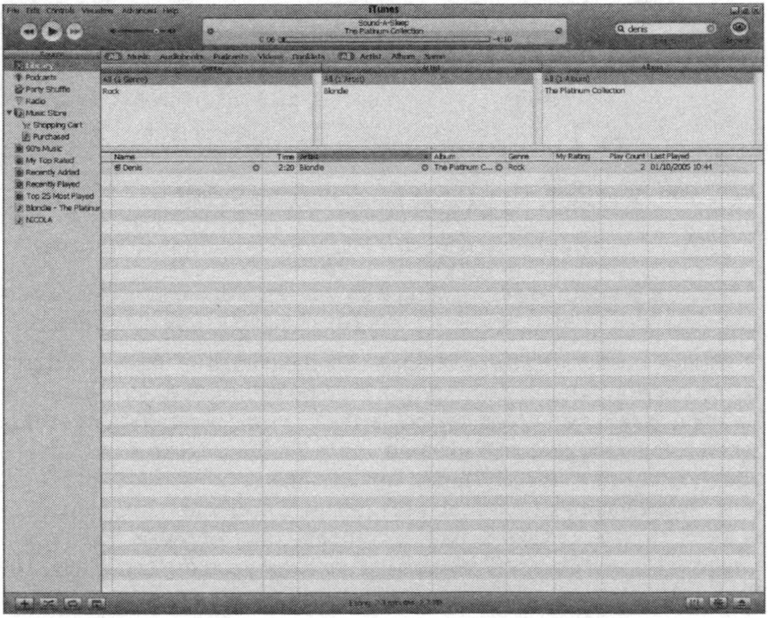

Organising

With only a few tracks in the iTunes library it is not too difficult to find any given track, but it becomes more time consuming as the number of tracks builds up over a period of time. The built-in search function makes it possible to find most tracks almost instantly. Simply type a word that appears in the title of the track and it will be listed in

Fig.4.104 This search has produced just one match

Fig.4.105 This search string matched all the tracks by Blondie

the main panel together with any other tracks that match that search (Figure 4.104). Actually, it is not necessary to type the whole word. The search function will start listing matches as soon as you start typing. You only have to type sufficient letters to reduce the number of matches to something manageable. It is not just the title field that is searched, and matches can be obtained with the artist and the album title provided iTunes has this information. This is very useful for (say) finding all the track by a particular artist or band. In Figure 4.105 for example, using "blo" as the search string was sufficient to display the tracks by the Blondie.

The Action button becomes the Browse button when you are searching the library. This toggles the program between its normal mode (Figure 4.106) and the Browse mode (Figure 4.107). In the Browse mode a new panel appears in the upper section of the window, and this lists the musical genres, the artists, and the albums. Initially the main panel shows everything in each section, but you can narrow things down by selecting

Fig.4.106 *In its normal mode the program lacks the upper panel*

one or more entries in the upper panel. For example, in Figure 4.108 I have selected "Classical" as the Genre and "Arnold" as the artist and this has produced just four matching tracks from one album in the main panel. When the number of tracks in the library starts to build up it is probably best to leave the program permanently in the Browse mode. This mode makes it much easier and quicker to find what you are looking for.

The tracks in the main panel are listed in alpha numeric order, with numbers listed first and then alphabetic sorting. The tracks can be sorted using the data from any field. In Figure 4.107 the sorting of the tracks is based on the Artist field, and the heading of this column is coloured blue to show that this field is selected (it appears darker than the other headings in Figure 4.107). In Figure 4.109 the Album field has been selected instead, and the tracks have been resorted.

Figure 4.107 The screen layout in the Browse mode

Fig.4.108 Only tracks in the selected categories are listed

Fig.4.109 Here the listing order is based on the Album column

Tags

The sorting of tracks is based on information that is attached to each track, and each snippet of information is called a "tag". These tags are extracted from files that you place in the library, or in the case of tracks downloaded from the iTunes store, some of the tags such as purchase information will be provided by the iTunes system. Few if any tracks have a complete set of tags, because some information will not be applicable or will simply not be available. For instance, iTunes purchase information is only applicable to tracks that have been purchased from the iTunes store. The iTunes program enables you to alter some tags, but not all types can be changed. In general, the ones that can not be changed are the tags that provide information that is inherent to the track such as its bit rate and type of encoding.

It is possible that you will be perfectly happy with the tags that the program provides automatically when a track is added to a library. However, it is

Fig.4.110 Select the Get Info option to launch the information window

likely that the occasional track will have tags that are not strictly correct, and probably a bit misleading. For example, with classical tracks you sometimes find that the name in the Artist field is actually the composer of the piece. Most would consider that the artist was the conductor, singer, or some other performer. Errors are not particularly common, but it is a good idea to correct anything like this when it does occur.

A more common problem is when a name is given in a slightly different form in two sets of tracks. For example, you might have one album by "The Beatles" and another where the name of the group is simply gives as "Beatles". These would be treated as albums by different groups by the iTunes search system. Editing this type of thing to give consistent results can be a bit irksome, but it makes the system easier to use.

The information window for a track can be obtained by right-clicking its entry and choosing Get Info from the pop-up menu (Figure 4.110). The first page (Figure 4.111) is a summary that shows some basic information

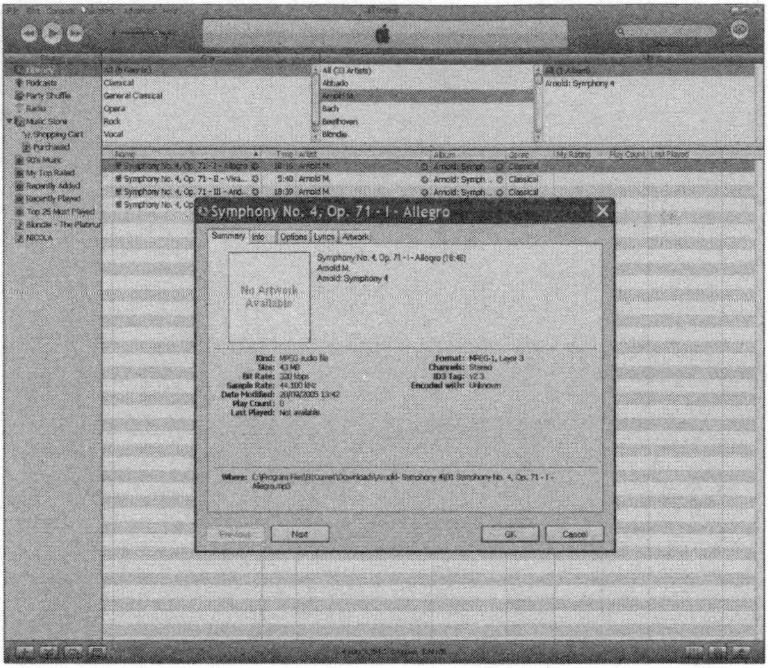

Fig.4.111 The first page is just a summary that can not be edited

such as the location of the file and the bit rate, but it does not allow any editing of the information. Operating the Info tab changes the window to look like Figure 4.112, and here it is possible to edit information such as the artist, album, and composer.

Genre

You can edit any text in the Comments field or add your own comments here. Normally the Genre field can not be freely edited. However, a new genre can be assigned to a track via the menu (Figure 4.113). Also, you can add a new genre by selecting Custom from the menu and then typing the name for the new genre into the textbox, which does then become editable. The new genre will be used just like the ones that are built into the system.

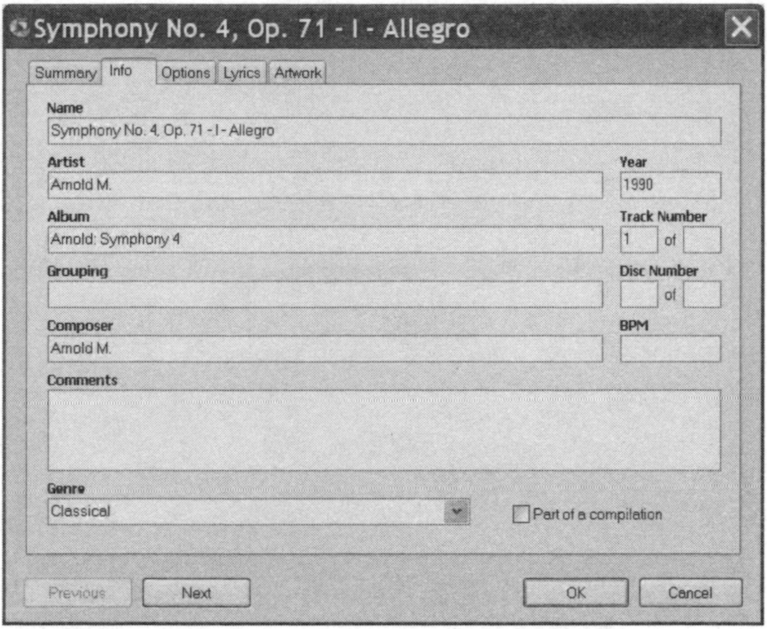

Fig.4.112 The entries on the Info page can be edited

When there is something that needs to be changed on one track it is likely that similar changes will be required for the other tracks of that particular album. Repeatedly closing the Info window and then launching it again for the next track would be a slow and tedious way of handling things. Fortunately it is not necessary to do this. The Next and Previous buttons near the bottom left-hand corner of the Info window respectively move things down and up one track. You can therefore move rapidly from one track to the next, perhaps using the Windows Copy and Paste facilities to almost instantly apply the amended information to each track.

There is an even quicker way of applying the same information to a number of tracks. First select the group of tracks in the normal way, then right-click one of them and select Get Info from the pop-up menu. Left-click the Yes button when asked to confirm that you wish to change the information for a group of tracks. The multiple version of the Info window will then be launched (Figure 4.114). The information is edited much the same as for the standard version, but the information will be applied to all the selected tracks.

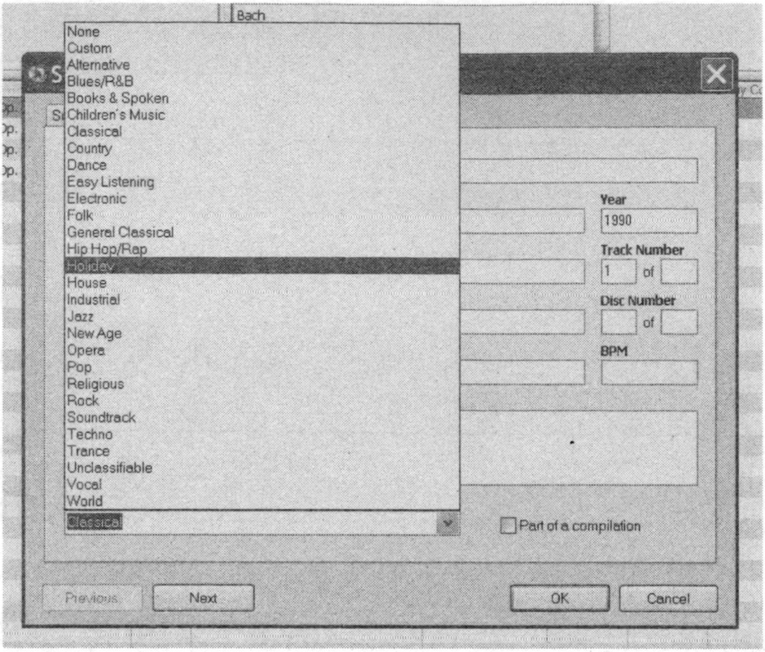

Fig.4.113 A new genre can be assigned via the menu

If you only need to make one or two minor changes it is not really necessary to launch the Info window. The changes can be made directly onto the main panel. In order to change a tag in this way you must first display the track and select it. Left-clicking a tag within that track will then result in the text appearing in an editable textbox (Figure 4.115). It is not an editable tag if you can not get the textbox to appear. Once the tag has been changed, left-click just to one side of it to close the textbox. Note that you can change the star rating by selecting the track and then simply left-clicking at the appropriate point on this tag.

It is worth taking a look at the Options section (Figure 4.116) of the information window. This has a facility to give the track your star rating for it, and an equaliser preset can be applied to the track via the menu. There is also a facility that enables the start and stop time to be adjusted. This can be useful if a track has an exceptionally long blank period at the beginning or the end. The start and stop times can be adjusted to reduce the period of silence to something more acceptable. It can also be used

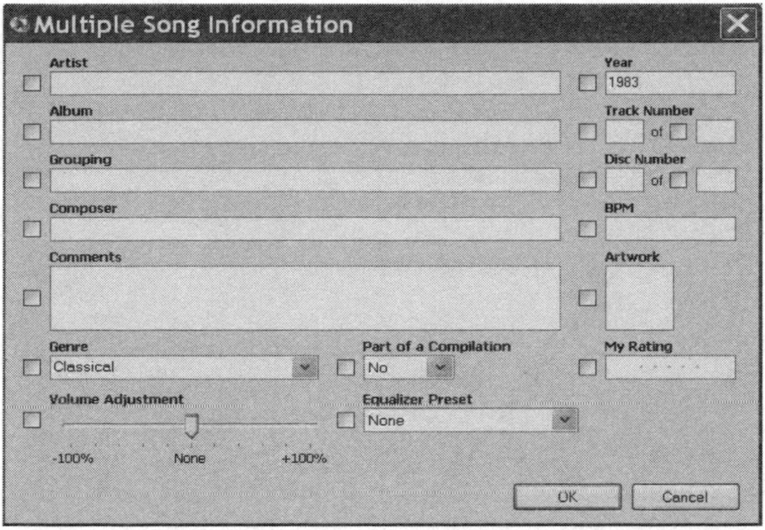

Fig.4.114 The Multiple Song Information window

Fig.4.115 Here the track information is being edited directly

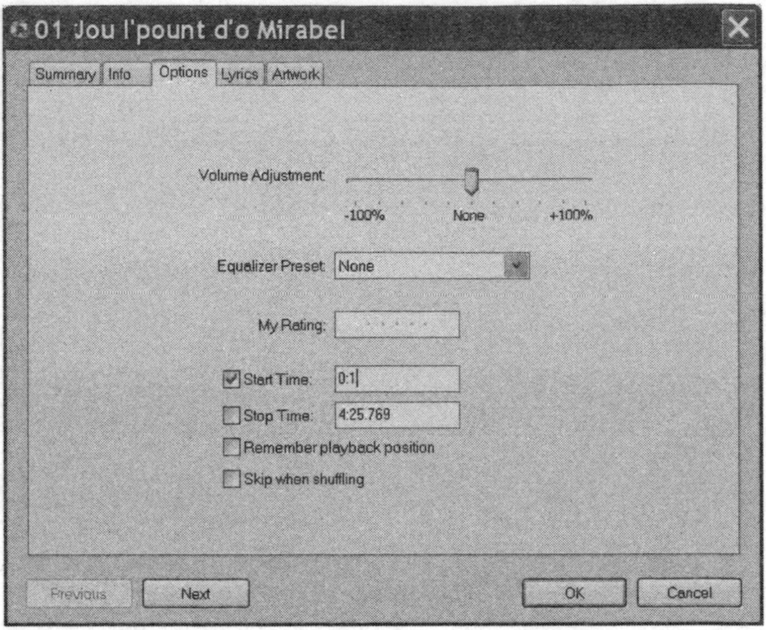

Fig.4.116 The start and stop times can be "fine tuned"

to good effect with tracks that have a spoken introduction that does not really serve any useful purpose once you have heard it a couple of times.

Artwork

The Artwork section of the Info window shows any artwork that is associated with the selected track. This will probably be blank for any tracks that were not purchased from the iTunes store. In the example of Figure 4.117 the selected track is one that was downloaded from the iTunes store in the demonstration provided previously. It therefore shows the cover design for the CD that the tracks were taken from. If the selected track was not obtained from the iTunes store it is still possible to associate some artwork with it, provided you have the necessary image or images. There is an Add button that launches a file browser, and this can be used to associate an image file with the selected track.

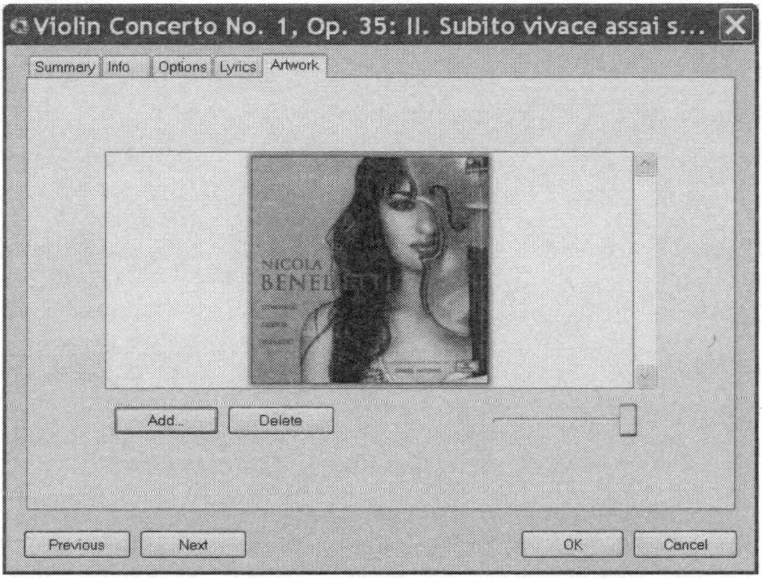

Fig.4.117 The artwork for the track, if any, will be displayed here

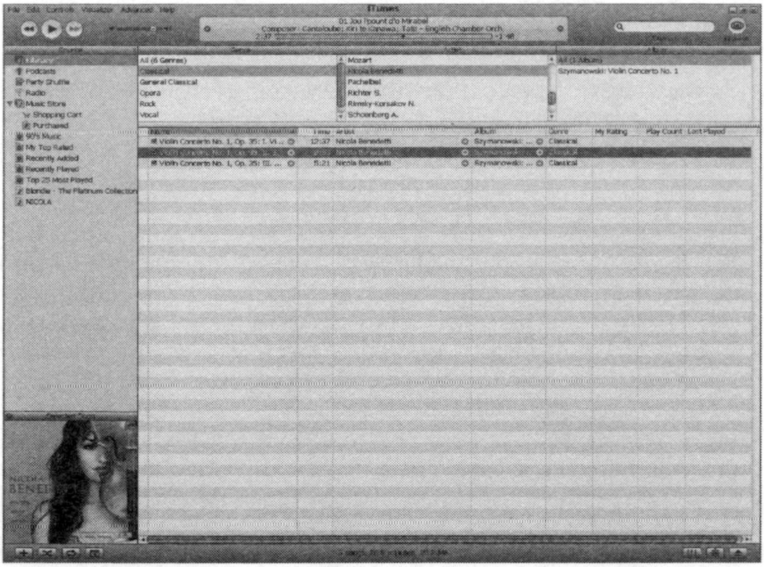

Fig.4.118 The artwork can be displayed in the main window

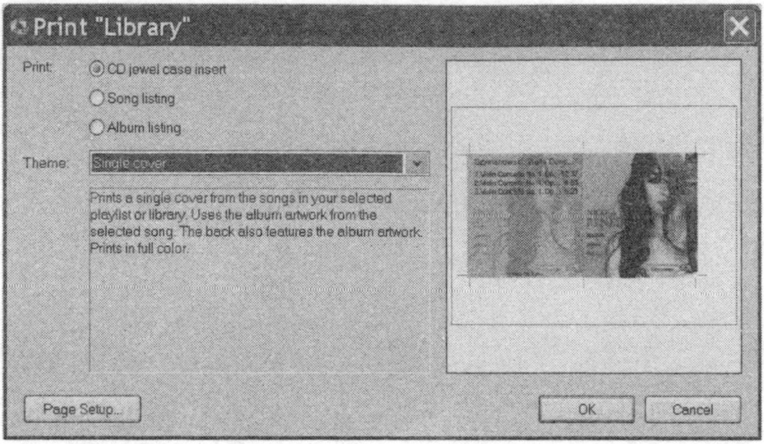

Fig.4.119 The artwork can be printed as a jewel case insert

It is possible to display the artwork associated with the current track in the main iTunes window. In the bottom left-hand corner of the window there are four buttons, and the one at the right end of the row toggles this feature on and off. In Figure 4.118 this feature has been activated, and the artwork is displayed near the bottom left-hand corner of the screen.

There is a facility to print out the artwork, which is very useful if you burn a collection of tracks to a CD. It can be used to print a CD insert, but as yet it is not possible to print a label for the CD itself. Artwork is printed by

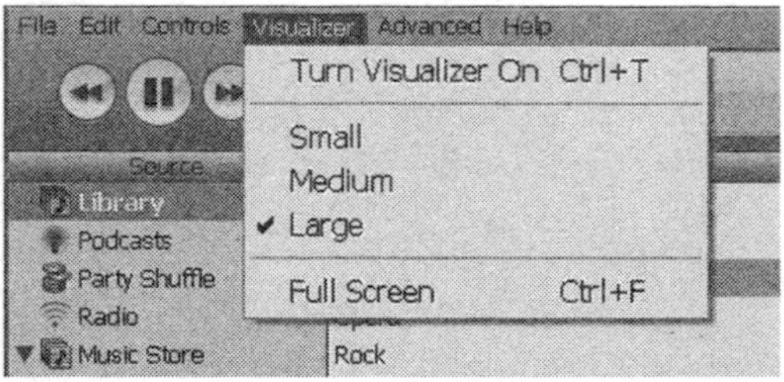

Fig.4.120 The Visualizer options

selecting a track that is associated with the artwork and then choosing Print from the File menu. The Print window (Figure 4.119) has a range of options. For a CD insert it is normally the "CD jewel case insert" radio button that must be selected, together with "Single cover" from the Theme menu. A track listing is included on the rear of the cover, and this will include any tracks that are associated with the artwork.

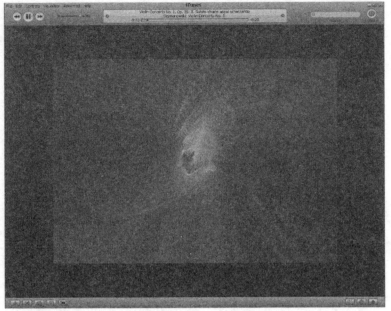

Fig.4.121 The visualizer running in the Medium mode

Visualizer

The iTunes program has a built-in visualisation facility, or Visualizer as Apple call it. The first option in the Visualizer menu (Figure 4.120) enables this feature to be turned on and off. The other four options provide a choice of three display sizes plus the option of running the Visualizer in full screen mode Figure 4.121 shows the Visualizer running in the Medium mode. In the full screen mode it is not possible to switch off the Visualizer via the menu system as it is not displayed (Figure 4.122). In fact none of the onscreen controls are accessible when the Visualizer is running in this mode. However, simply operating the Escape key will return the program to normal operation.

As with any visualisation, bear in mind that the drain on the computer's resources will increase dramatically when this feature is turned on. This will not necessarily matter too much, and the latest dual core processors can no doubt handle the extra load without any difficulty. The situation is different if you are using a relatively old or low specification PC. In general,

Fig.4.122 Press the Escape key to close the Visualizer when it is in Full mode

the larger the active display area, the greater the loading the Visualizer will place on the computer. Using the Full Screen mode is probably not a good idea with an older PC, especially when there are other applications running.

Too much music

Users of the high capacity iPods may well find that the amount of music in the library never becomes too great for their iPods to accommodate.

Fig.4.123 It is all too much for the iPod

With the lower capacity versions it is virtually certain that the library will eventually get too big. The iTunes program will give a warning message if this happens (Figure

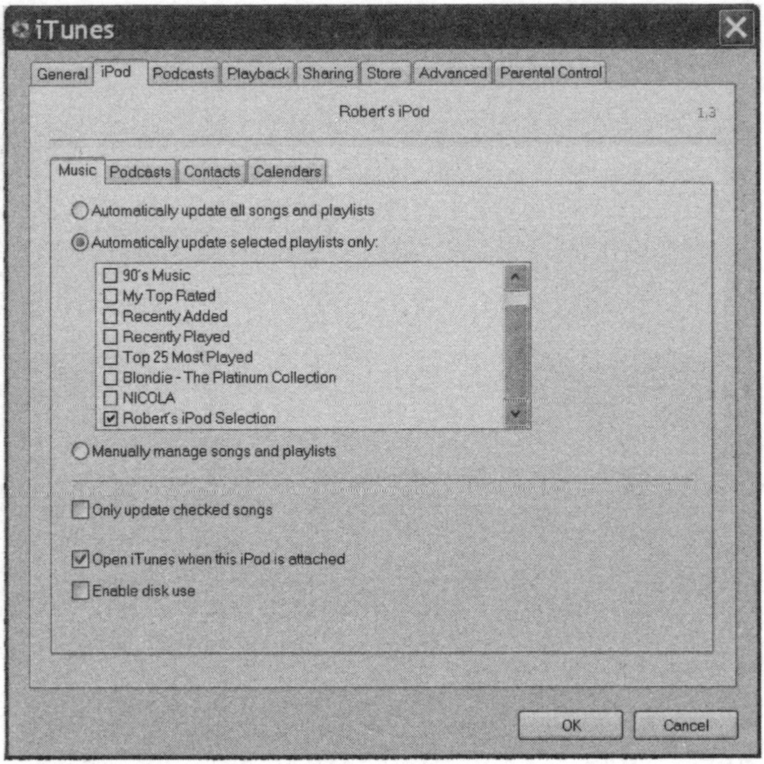

Fig.4.124 When the iPod section of the Preferences window is active it looks like this

4.123), and it will copy as much music as possible to the iPod. Alternatively, it might offer to make a play list consisting of a selection of songs and upload this to the iPod.

Clearly it is better to take proper control and upload the music that you wish to listen to via your iPod. Doing so is quite easy, and the first step is to connect the iPod to the computer. Then select Preferences from the Edit menu and left-click the iPod tab when the Preferences window appears. It should look something like Figure 4.124, but this section of the Preferences window only becomes active if there is an iPod connected to the computer. If it looks like Figure 4.125, the iPod is not connected properly.

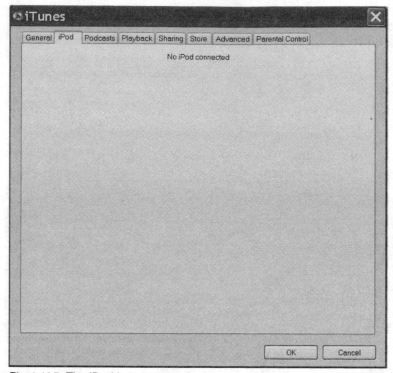

Fig.4.125 The iPod is not connected properly if the iPod section of the Preferences window looks like this

Assuming the active version of the window is obtained, there are three radio buttons that offer two versions of automatic synchronisation and a fully manual mode. Normally the top radio button is selected, and the contents of all the play lists are then uploaded to the iPod. Using the middle button instead results in only the selected play list or lists being uploaded to the iPod. A play list is selected by ticking its checkbox in the scrollable menu. The obvious way of using this facility is to produce a play list that contains the music you wish to have on the iPod. Only tick the checkbox for this play list so that it is the only one that is uploaded to the iPod. Using this method you can easily choose the music to upload, but the actual synchronisation occurs automatically each time you connect the iPod to the computer.

Updating

From time to time you will probably see a message like the one in Figure 4.126 when your iPod is connected to the computer and the iTunes program is running. It is not essential to bother with updating if you are quite happy with the way your iPod is operating. On the other hand, it is probably best to have the latest firmware in the iPod. Opting to go ahead with the update results in the default browser being launched, and the Apple iPod update page being loaded (Figure 4.127). Of course, an active Internet connection is needed in order to update the iPod. The

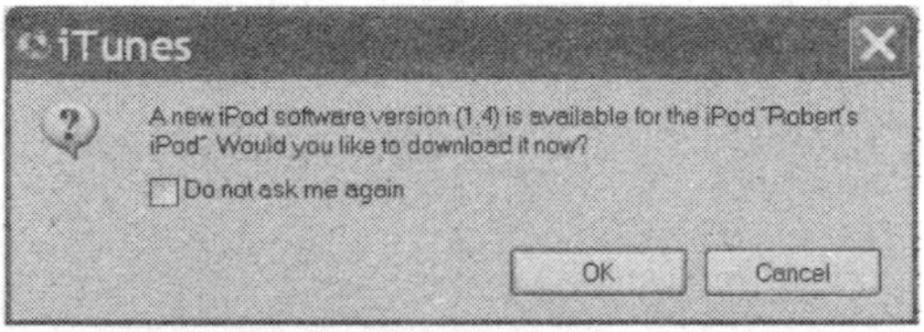

Fig.4.126 ITunes will tell you if an iPod update is available

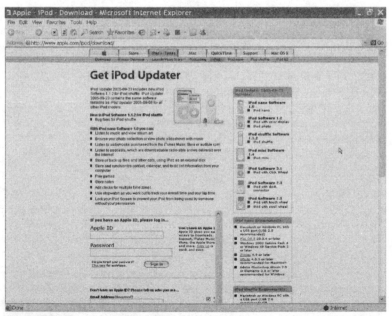

Fig.4.127 You must log in at the update page

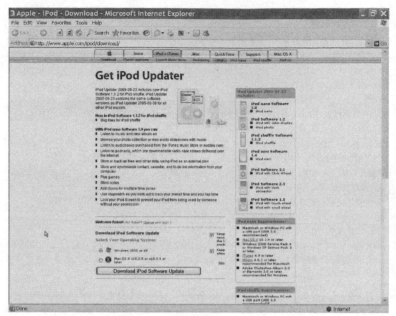

Fig.4.128 Operate the "Download iPod Software Update" button

right-hand side of the page shows the upgrade that is included for each iPod model.

An Apple ID and password are needed in order to obtain iPod upgrades. Enter your ID and password if you have them, or register with Apple in order to proceed. Either way you should end up at a page that includes a download button (Figure 4.128). The two radio buttons enable the appropriate operating system (Windows or Mac OS) to be selected, but the default setting will probably be the correct one. Operating the download button takes things on to the page of Figure 4.129. Left-click the "Click here" link in order to go ahead with the download and update the software. There will be the usual choice of downloading the file to disc or running it. It does not matter too much which you choose, but running the file is probably the more convenient in this case.

After the usual preamble with licence agreements, etc., you should get a message like the one shown in Figure 4.130, stating that the update has been completed successfully. Note that it is the iPod software on the computer that has been updated, and at this stage the iPod itself will be

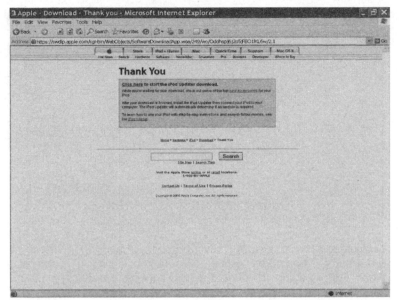

Fig.4.129 Left-click the "Click here" link to start the download

Fig.4.130 The software on the computer has been updated

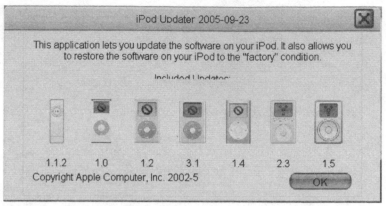

Fig.4.131 This is just an information page

unchanged. The update program might run automatically, but if not it is just a matter of going to the start menu and selecting All Programs – iPod – iPod Updater. Make sure that you choose the updater with the most recent date if there is more than one in the menu.

The Welcome screen of Figure 4.131 appears when the updater is run. Operating the OK button moves things on to the window of Figure 4.132, which confirms that the current firmware version is 1.3 and that it needs to be updated. The two buttons enable the iPod to be updated or restored. Using the Update button results in the iPod receiving a firmware update,

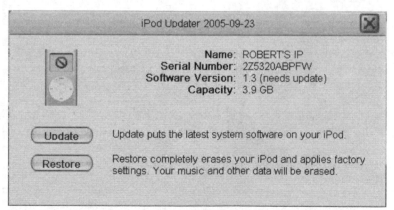

Fig.4.132 It is normally the Update button the is used here. Using the Restore button takes the factory settings and state

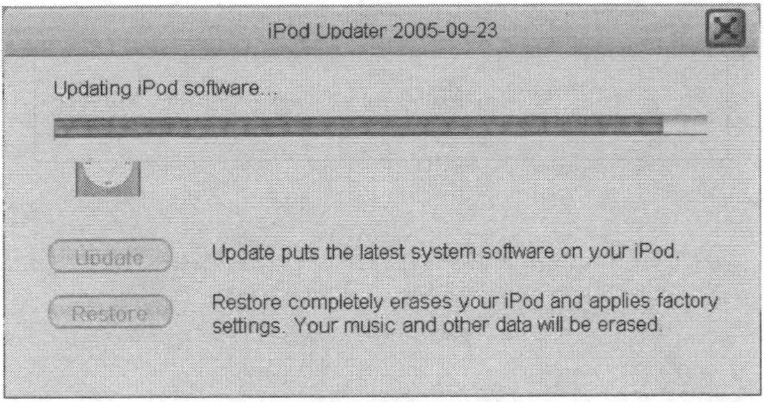

iPod Updater 2005-09-23
Updating iPod software...
Update
Update puts the latest system software on your iPod.
Restore
Restore completely erases your iPod and applies factory settings. Your music and other data will be erased.

Fig.4.133 The usual bargraph shows how the update is progressing

but it is not altered in other respects. In other words, all the settings remain unchanged and the loaded music remains intact.

Using the Restore button results in the iPod's firmware being updated, but it also takes it back to its factory settings and clears the disc or memory. It is normally the Update button that is used. The only reason for using the restore function is if the iPod has become problematic. Resetting an iPod will usually get it working properly, but if that fails it is worth trying to restore it to the factory settings. However, it leaves you with an iPod that must be set up from scratch, just as if it was brand new and just out of the box.

About
ROBERT'S IP
Songs 29
Capacity 3.7 GB
Available 3.6 GB
Version 1.4

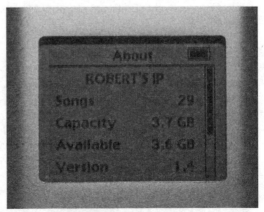

Fig.4.134 The firmware has been updated to version 1.4

Having operated the appropriate button, the program will start updating the iPod and the updater window will show how things are progressing. After a few seconds there

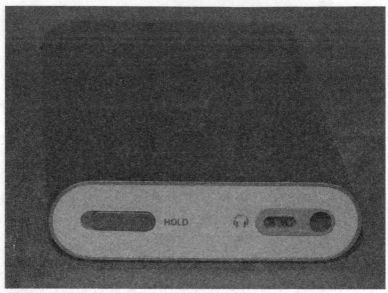

Fig.4.135 *Operating the Hold switch twice is the first step when resetting an iPod*

will be an onscreen message indicating that the update has been completed successfully. You can check that the firmware has been updated by selecting Settings and About from the iPod's menu system (Figure 4.134).

Problems

An iPod is a complex piece of electronics and like any sophisticated gadget there can be occasional problems. When things are not going as expected it is best to start by looking for simple problems. If the controls will not work, make sure that the Hold switch (Figure 4.135) is not set to block the controls. Try moving it firmly from one setting to the other a few times to check that it is not getting into an intermediate position.

The battery could be completely exhausted if the iPod does nothing at all and the display stays blank. Remember that an iPod uses a small amount of power when it is switched off. Even if it is not used at all, an iPod will run the battery down over a period of two or three weeks. Try charging it for a few hours from a computer or the mains charger unit. This will usually restore a "dead" iPod to normal operation.

Where an iPod seems a bit erratic in operation it is a good idea to switch it off, wait a few seconds, and the switch it on again. If that does not help, the next step is to try resetting it. Resetting an iPod is a bit like resetting a computer, with the data stored in temporary memory being cleared, but the data you have stored on the hard disc drive (or Flash memory) being left unchanged. In other words, the music you have uploaded to the iPod should still be there after it has been reset.

Only reset an iPod when it is not connected to a computer. With a recent iPod the reset sequence is to first set the Hold switch to the Hold position and then back to the normal setting again. Then hold down the Menu and Select buttons until the Apple logo appears on the screen (Figure 4.136). The Select button is the one in the middle of the "wheel". The appearance of the Apple logo indicates that the reset has been completed, and it typically requires the Menu and Select

Fig.4.136 The Apple logo appears once the iPod has been reset

buttons to be held down for about five seconds. Note that with older iPods you have to hold down the Play/Pause button instead of the Menu button.

You can try restoring the firmware if the iPod does not work any better after it has been reset. However, as pointed out previously, restoring the firmware results in all the stored data and settings being erased. You are effectively reverting to an iPod that has just been taken out of its box for the first time. It will have to be set up in exactly the same way as a new one. It is likely that the iPod has a hardware fault if restoring the firmware does not cure the problem. It will then have to be returned to an Apple service centre for repairs.

Finally

It is not possible to cover every "nook and cranny" of iTunes here, but most aspects of the program have been covered. With the information provided in this chapter you should be able to load music obtained from various sources into the iTunes program, organise the music, play it, and upload it to an iPod. Additionally you can burn CDs and print out CD inserts. This is really all you need to do in order to use and enjoy the iTunes program and an iPod.

Points to remember

The music stored in an iPod is not organised using the iPod itself. You build and organise a library of music using the iTunes program and then upload it to the iPod, and keep the iPod synchronised with any changes made to the library. The iTunes program has facilities that make it easy to import music to the library and organise it. Music in the library can, of course, be played using the iTunes program.

Most iPods can be used with USB and Firewire interfaces. In general it is best to use a USB interface with PCs and a Firewire interface with Apple Macs, but there can be exceptions. The original USB interface (USB 1.1) is rather slow and is not really suitable for use with iPods. The more recent USB 2.0 interface is required, which is the type fitted to all recent PCs.

One way of getting tracks into the iTunes program is to rip them from your collection of CDs. There are built-in facilities that make it easy to import tracks into iTunes direct from CDs. Any MP3 files you have can also be imported into the library, but WMA files must be converted by iTunes into AAC files that are compatible with iTunes and iPods. Protected WMA files can not be converted and are incompatible with iPods.

Files downloaded from the iTunes store are in protected AAC format. They can be used with up to five computers, and they will not work with a computer unless it is authorised to use them. Protected AAC files can be uploaded to iPods without any restrictions. They can also be burned to CDs using the iTunes program, and the CDs can then be played on any computers and CD players. However, to keep within the licensing conditions the music should still be used on no more than five computers.

Files in the library can be burned to data CDs as well as normal audio CDs. Using data CDs enable far more music to be stored on each CD, making it a good way of backing up music files and transferring them to another PC. Unfortunately, few CD players can handle data CDs or the files that they contain.

Protected AAC files can not be converted to other formats such as WMA or MP3. This means that they are incompatible with most portable players apart from iPods.

The information for tags is read from the music files loaded into the iTunes program and automatically assigned to tracks. In most cases it will be correct but there can be occasional problems. The tags that are likely to problematic are easily edited.

Assuming your PC is connected to a suitable printer, it is possible to print CD case inserts for music downloaded from the iTunes store. It is possible to produce inserts for other tracks provided you can load suitable artwork into the iTunes program.

If the library contains too much music for your iPod to accommodate, it is possible to select the playlists that will be used to synchronise the iPod. One way of using this feature is to have only one play list selected, and to load this with the tracks you wish to use on the iPod.

Choosing an MP3 player

MP3 player?

A few years ago there was a clear-cut distinction between MP3 players and iPods. An MP3 player stored its music in Flash memory that was usually built into the player, but in some cases was provided by plug-in Flash cards of the types used with digital cameras and some other portable gadgets. An iPod had a built-in hard disc drive that was much the same as the drives used in computers, but in a miniature form. The iPod hard disc drives were actually quite similar to the CompactFlash II micro-drives sometimes used with upmarket digital cameras, but with an even higher capacity.

Although the differences between an iPod and a conventional MP3 player appeared to be minor, there was a huge and crucial difference. The early MP3 players mostly had quite limited amounts of storage space. At that time the cost of Flash memory was quite high, so any technical problems governing the use of large amounts of Flash memory were irrelevant. Anything more than a few hundred megabytes of memory simply cost too much for the vast majority of potential customers.

Although the cost of Flash memory has substantially reduced in recent years, it remains relatively expensive where large amounts of storage are required. At the time of writing this there are plenty of players that have one gigabyte (1024 megabytes) of Flash memory, and a few that have two or four gigabytes. Even so, players having really large amounts of Flash memory still seem to be some way off.

The hard disc drives of the early iPods provided a much higher storage capacity than the Flash memory of an ordinary MP3 player. With the player having many gigabytes of storage capacity and the music stored in a highly compressed form it was possible to transfer the contents of a few hundred CDs to the player. With an ordinary MP3 player you could

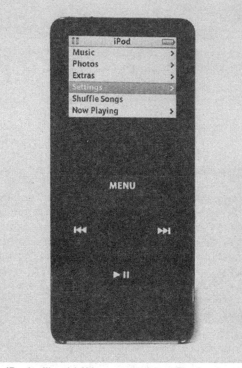

Fig.5.1 Some iPods, like this Nano, now have Flash memory rather than a miniature hard disc drive

only have a few CDs worth of music stored on the player at any one time. In fact some players could only accommodate the equivalent of one or two CDs. You had to be prepared to do a fair amount of shuffling around, with existing tracks being erased to make way for new ones. The iPod rendered this type of thing unnecessary. Most users were able to transfer their entire music collections to their iPod. Any track on any CD was then almost instantly accessible, and could be taken with you wherever you went.

The current situation is not that different to the way it was when the iPod first appeared. There are still plenty of conventional MP3 players that have relatively little storage capacity. The average amount of storage capacity is undoubtedly much higher than it was a few years ago, but it is still far too low to permit a music collection to be transferred to these players. IPods having miniature disc drives are, of course, still available and as popular as ever.

There is a major different in that other manufacturers now produce MP3 players that have built-in disc drives, and Apple produce iPods that have Flash memory rather than a disc drive. These are the iPod Shuffle and Nano (Figure 5.1) players. The Shuffle presumably derives its name from the fact that it requires the music to be shuffled around instead of being stored on the player in its entirety. This shuffling is not necessarily needed with the higher capacity Nano.

Anyway, the current situation is good for buyers of portable music players, since there is now much more choice than in the past and fierce competition has forced prices down. Many pundits were of the opinion that the original iPod stood no chance of becoming a market success due to its high price. As we now know, this was not the case and huge numbers were sold. At their current prices, MP3 players and iPods have to be regarded as great bargains.

Choice

A drawback of having so many different players to choose from is that selecting a suitable player can be a daunting task. Reviews in magazines and on the Internet can be more than a little helpful in sorting out the good from the bad. Reviews also give you a good idea of what is currently available and the current prices. With any reviews it pays to bear in mind that "one man's meat is another man's poison" and that to a large extent you are getting a subjective assessment of each player.

Like many people, I have occasionally bought something that received rave reviews, but on trying to use it have been left wondering if it was actually the same product as the one in the review! I have also had years of sterling service from a poorly reviewed device that was being sold off cheap. Whether a hi-tech product is perceived as good or bad is largely guided by your expectations. There is a tendency to become disappointed if something is not quite what you expected. A little perseverance will often show that a seemingly poor gadget is actually quite good in practice.

Unfortunately, things can also operate the other way around. A device that seems perfect initially can prove to be very awkward when you start using it in earnest. However much you use it, you always seem to press the wrong button, you find that some of the controls are virtually unusable, the display digits are so small that you can only read them with the aid of a magnifier, and so on. Reviews can guide you towards products that are likely to suit your needs, but they will not necessarily provide a means of selecting your ideal product. Buying electronic gadgets online is generally cheaper than going to a local supplier. However, there is still a lot to be said for actually seeing products "in the flesh" before you buy them, and if possible, giving them at least a brief tryout.

Sound quality

As with most things, when buying a portable music player you tend to get what you pay for. The most obvious way in which this manifests itself with music players is that you tend to get an amount of storage space that is roughly proportional to the cost of the player. You also tend to get better build-quality if you buy a more expensive player. It would be incorrect to assume that the sound quality is more or less proportional to the amount of money paid.

If you were to compare the sound quality of a cheap player with that of the latest upmarket type it is likely that the luxury model would comfortably beat the budget player. Even so, there would not necessarily be much difference in the audio quality of the players themselves. Each piece of equipment tended to have its own "sound" in the days when audio equipment was of the analogue variety. There are still plenty of enthusiasts for audio equipment from this era, but the truth of the matter is that each gadget sounded a bit different to all the others because none of them achieved anything approaching technical perfection.

The situation is different with digitally recorded music, where the level of fidelity is much the same for all equipment of a given type. Some methods of digitally storing and playing back music give better results than others. A straightforward 16-bit digital audio system will give better fidelity than one that utilises large amounts of compression. These are differences between the methods of storage and retrieval though, and several items of equipment when using the same program source and playback method will give practically identical results.

This is not to say that there are no differences in the sound quality of various players. Even where two players are based on the same digital audio chips, one might have better processing circuits at the output, giving slightly lower noise and distortion levels. These days though, the differences tend to be quite small. If you compare an expensive player with an out-and-out budget model it is quite likely that the upmarket player will sound significantly better. However, if you swap the two pairs of headphones the results would probably surprise you. The cheap player will suddenly sound "like a million dollars", and the upmarket one will suddenly produce rather "tinny" sounding results.

Headphones

The headphones are analogue in nature, and the way they sound is governed by a wide range of factors. Some are much better than others, and in general you get what you pay for. Most inexpensive MP3 players come complete with "cheap and cheerful" headphones that sound quite reasonable, but are something less than the last word in audio fidelity. No doubt many would frown at the notion of using a cheap MP3 player with an expensive pair of headphones, but the audio quality of a budget MP3 player should be very high. In fact the output quality will be governed much more by the efficacy of the recordings than by the electronics of the player. Using a cheap player with expensive headphones should provide top quality results. Wiring the output of a cheap MP3 player to the input of an expensive hi-fi amplifier should also give really good results.

The practical consequence of all this is that the important differences between one player and another are things like the storage capacity, battery life, size and type of display, etc. The headphones supplied with budget MP3 players mostly sound quite good, but if you really do not like them you can always buy a replacement pair that is more to your liking. It is a fact of portable audio life that headphones do not generally last as well as the players, and two or three replacements could be required during the working life of a player. Over a period of time this gives plenty of opportunity to try different headphones. There is usually no simple upgrade path if you need more memory in your player, a bigger and better display, or something of this nature. You have to make do with the player you have or buy a new one.

Types

Before buying an MP3 player you must decide on the type you require. One that has built-in memory rather than a hard disc drive is no use if you really like the idea of transferring your entire music collection to the player. Players that have Flash memory do have their advantages though. The obvious one is that they are much cheaper than those that have a hard disc drive. Although the prices of all types of player have fallen in recent years, the reduction in price has been most dramatic with the players that use Flash memory. While they are not quite at the stage where they are given away free if you buy a few packets of breakfast cereal, they are heading in that direction. These days you can get quite a nice player, complete with headphones and batteries, for a very reasonable price.

Another major advantage of players that use Flash memory is that they are generally much smaller and lighter than the type that uses a hard disc drive. This is partially due to the fact that Flash memory is physically smaller than a miniature hard disc drive. Another factor is that Flash memory uses less power than a miniature drive, which means that it is possible to use a much smaller battery without compromising the battery life.

Jog factor

For those who like to use portable audio while on the move there is the jog factor to consider. There is no need for a player that uses Flash memory to bother with any anti-jog system. Because Flash memory is purely electronic and has no mechanical moving parts, it is not affected by the amounts of vibration produced while running, jogging, or whatever. If the level of vibration is not high enough to do the user any harm, it should not upset the normal operation of an MP3 player that uses Flash memory.

The situation is very different with portable CD players and MP3 players that have a hard disc drive. It takes very little vibration to make a CD player momentarily "lose the plot". This was a big problem with the early portable CD players, and it remains a major drawback with the low-cost units that are available today. These players are fine if you wish to sit back and relax in the garden while listening to some music, but they do not work well if you start moving around. Even moving around carefully is likely to produce a few glitches, and running while using one of these units will not produce anything worthwhile at all.

The normal solution to this problem is to have a substantial amount of memory built into the player. Data is read from the disc well before it is actually needed by the decoding electronics, and stored in the memory until it is needed. There will typically be something like half a minute or so of data held in the memory circuit, ready to be fed to the decoder circuits. There is no major problem if the player is knocked and the laser takes a few seconds to get back on track. Within a few seconds it will get back "in the groove" and fill the data buffer with data again. In the mean time the decoder circuits can continue to play the data in the buffer, and there is no break in the sound.

Anti-jog solutions are fine in theory, but they do not always work well in practice. They all rely on the fact that the part of the system that reads from the disc can extract the data very fast, and that it can keep the buffer reasonably full provided accurate tracking can be maintained for a reasonable percentage of the time. However, if the player is subjected to a lot of vibration it is possible that the laser reader will not be able to keep on track for a high enough proportion of the time. Anti-jog systems work best if the buffer system is backed up by a laser reader that does not easily "lose the plot".

Buffer

While miniature hard disc drives are not totally immune to tracking problems when subjected to a certain amount of vibration, they seem to be much better in this respect that the laser based optical reading systems of CD players. Portable players that use hard disc drives also have a reasonably large buffer as part of the normal way this type of thing works. In this context a "buffer" is simple some memory that is used for temporary data storage. Reading a continuous stream of data off the hard drive and feeding it to the decoder circuits would be doing things the hard way. It would also give a greatly reduced battery life. The normal way of handling things is to have large amounts of data read from the disc in short bursts and stored in a buffer until they are needed. As far as possible the disc is maintained in an idle state.

The practical consequence of this is that a portable player that has a hard disc drive is much better for use on the move than a portable CD player. It should be smaller and lighter than a portable CD player, and it should also have much better immunity to problems with gaps in the audio output due to vibration. On the other hand, a player that uses Flash memory rather than a hard disc drive has to be regarded as the better choice for a player that will be used while running, jogging, etc. A player of this type can be really small and light, and will not be affected by large amounts or vibration that are maintained for a long period of time.

Inexpensive

You are "spoilt for choice" if a normal MP3 player that uses Flash memory is adequate for your requirements. A very wide range of standard MP3 players are available, at a wide range of prices. As usual, it is generally a case of you get what you pay for, so there is likely to be a good reason

Fig.5.2 This MP3 player was very cheap, but was not supplied with any memory. It takes SD memory cards

for a very low cost player having such a tempting price tag. The least expensive players tend to be very basic indeed, so they might not be quite the bargains that they seem at first glance.

The player of Figure 5.2 cost me more than a tenner, but not much more. The good news is that it came complete with headphones and a battery. The bad news is that it was not supplied with any software other than a driver for Windows 98, there is no built-in memory, the battery is not rechargeable, and the display is extremely basic. This is not to say that the player is of limited use, and not worth the money. I use this player a great deal and often take it with me on photographic expeditions. The fact that it is minute and weighs practically nothing are big points in its favour. When you are already carrying a fair amount of equipment there is a lot to be said for an MP3 player that is as small and light as possible.

A lack of supporting software is quite common with MP3 players. In truth, where some software is supplied with a player it will not necessarily be of much use. Taking the drivers first, peripheral devices need software drivers to integrate them with the operating system. Without this software there is usually no way of accessing the peripheral gadget. However,

Windows has built-in drivers for some types of device, and with many of these the Plug N Play facility will automatically detect the device when it is first connected to the computer. It will then install the appropriate driver software.

As pointed out in some of the previous chapters, many music players are treated as mass storage devices by the operating system. In other words, the operating system "sees" a form of hard disc drive when an MP3 player or iPod is connected to it, and it gives the new drive a drive letter. It can be accessed in the usual way via this drive letter when using Windows Explorer or any other software. No special drivers are needed for this type of mass storage device. You just plug the player into the computer and the operating system does the rest. An onscreen message will inform you that the new hardware is ready for use once the installation process has been completed.

Note though, that Windows 98 has no built-in driver for mass storage devices, and it is for this reason that players are sometimes supplied complete with a driver for Windows 98. Some players are not supplied with drivers for Windows 98, and are only usable with Windows ME, Windows XP, and probably Windows 2000 if it has been fully updated. No version of Windows 95 has proper support for USB 1.1 ports, let alone the USB 2.0 variety, which renders it unusable with practically all MP3 players.

WMP 10

Although players are treated by the operating system as mass storage devices, not all of them can be used via the normal Windows software such as WMP 10 and Windows Explorer. The problem is presumably that some players require the files to be stored on the player in a particular way, and simply placing music files in folders on the player's storage medium will not result in it finding and using them. Where a player is pernickety about the way in which music files are organised, it should be supplied with software to help you organise and upload files.

The Apple iPods and the iTunes software are examples of players that are supplied with matching software, and have no need for the standard Windows programs (see chapter 4). There are other manufacturers that "do their own thing", and Figure 5.3 shows the uploader/organiser program that was supplied with my iRiver MP3 player. If you understand the basics of using a program such as WMP 10 or iTunes it should not take long to master any player or organiser software supplied with your player.

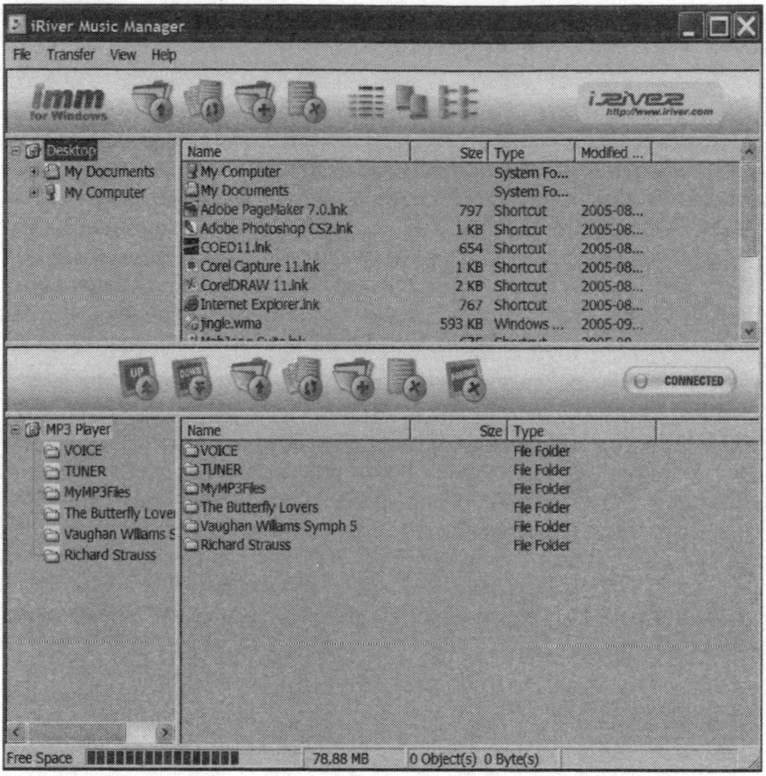

Fig.5.3 The iRiver Music Manager program

If a player is not supplied with any software to help you upload files, it will almost certainly be possible to use the built-in facilities of Windows to upload music and manage the library of music stored on the player. Should a player not be supplied with suitable software or be compatible with the built-in facilities of Windows, it is probably not worth buying it. There would be no apparent means of getting any music stored on the player. However, note that some players are not supplied with software, but that the necessary utilities can be freely downloaded from the manufacturer's web site.

Where no matching software is supplied or made available on the Internet, it is virtually certain that the player will be compatible with WMP 10. Using WMP 10, including synchronising it with an MP3 player, was covered in

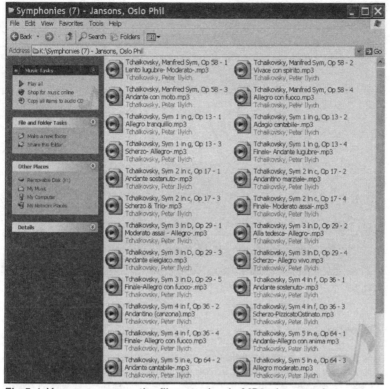

Fig.5.4 You can manage the files on simple MP3 players using Windows Explorer

chapter 3. Consequently, this subject will not be considered any further here. If a player has only a limited amount of memory it is by no means essential to bother with WMP 10. The number of files stored on the player will be relatively small, with perhaps two or three CDs stored on it at any one time. This makes it easy to keep track of what is stored on the player without resorting to some sort of library program. You can simply put the files ripped from a CD into a folder on the hard disc drive, and then use the Copy and Paste facilities of Windows Explorer to copy the files to the player. Using Windows Explorer or any file browser it is easy to see what you have stored on the player (Figure 5.4). The Delete facility of Windows Explorer can be used to remove files that are not needed any more.

Fig.5.5 A simple display is adequate if the player is only used to store a few songs

Display

On the face of it, the display of an MP3 player is not of paramount importance. In practice it can be very difficult to use an MP3 player unless its display is fully up to the task. The simple MP3 player of Figure 5.5 has a very simple display that tells you little more than the number of the track currently selected and the time into that track when it is playing. Ideally the display should be able to display at least a couple of lines of text so that you can deal in tracks by name rather than by number. The more upmarket player of Figure 5.6 has a better display that can display text and simple graphics.

The advantage of a text display is that you know exactly what has been selected, because the player will tell you something like "Dido - Life For Rent - White Flag". This leaves little room for doubt, whereas "03 – 00.00" does not tell you a great deal. The text used by the display might be derived from the names of the files, or it might be taken from the information embedded within the files. Either way, it is far more useful than track numbers, which are largely meaningless in the current context.

The importance of a good display depends on the amount of music stored on the player. The very basic player of Figure 5.5 does not have

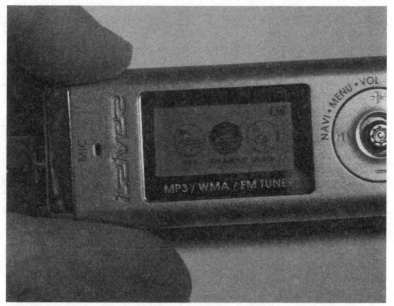

Fig.5.6 Most displays can handle simple graphics, have scrolling facilities, etc.

any built-in memory, but instead uses SD (Secure Digital) Flash cards for storage. Although it will take cards having a capacity of up to one gigabyte, it was probably not designed with such large cards in mind. It actually works best with smaller cards of about 64 or 128 megabytes. These will hold a reasonable number of songs, but not so many that it becomes difficult to find the track that you require. If it comes to it, you can go through the tracks one-by-one, listening to the beginning of each one until the required track is found.

With a player that has a 20 or 40 gigabyte hard disc it is possible to store many thousands of songs on the player. Without a good text display and a well organised library there is little chance of finding any given track reasonably quickly. In fact much of the music transferred to the player would probably disappear and never be heard.

A fair percentage of the more expensive players have a colour display. A colour display certainly looks better than a monochrome type, and they are often easier to read. Good use of colour on the display can make a player easier to use. On the other hand, it is not of great importance

Fig.5.7 CompactFlash, Secure Digital (SD), and XD memory cards

unless the player can also use the display for photographs, videos, or for playing games.   There is a definite trend towards multi-purpose gadgets that are phones, MP3 players, mass storage devices for use with cameras, or whatever.   This type of thing really goes beyond the scope of this. While "do it all" gadgets are very attractive in many ways, bear in mind that they usually involve compromises. Multifunction devices are rarely the best option for any of the functions that they provide.

Memory

At one time the use of memory cards with MP3 players was quite common, but these days the vast majority of players that use Flash memory have it built-in, with no provision for any type of memory card. This is perhaps a pity because the use of memory cards is actually the more versatile method.   If you buy a 256 megabyte MP3 player there is no cheap upgrade path if you later decide that a 512 megabyte or one gigabyte player would be better. You have to buy a new player or make do with the original amount of memory.

With a player that uses memory cards it is just a matter of buying a higher capacity Flash card. Furthermore, the old card can still be used, since taking out one card and putting in another is a very simple matter. Actually, having several small cards with two or three CDs stored on each one is a good way of handling things with a simple player that has only a very basic display. Spreading a large number of tracks across a few memory cards can help to make it easier to find the track you require.

When dealing with any gadget that uses memory cards you have to bear in mind that there are several types of card in common use. CompactFlash cards are probably the most common type, but as they are relatively large they are not used a great deal with MP3 players. SD cards are very small and nearly as widely used as the CompactFlash type, and are often used with MP3 players. XD cards are also quite small and are sometimes used with MP3 players. All three types of card are shown in Figure 5.7.

The type of card used in a player does not matter too much, but you have to be careful that you obtain the right type. Do not assume that a player is compatible with all memory cards of the appropriate type. Cards having capacities from a few megabytes to a gigabyte or more are produced, but MP3 players and other gadgets that use these cards are not usually compatible with a full range of sizes. There will often be maximum and minimum capacities that can be used with a given gadget, and you have to be careful to obtain cards that are within those limits.

One slight drawback of using memory cards is that they are not the toughest of components. When using any Flash memory cards it is essential to observe a few simple rules in order to ensure that the cards do not become damaged. Memory cards are reasonably safe when inside a gadget such as a MP3 player or camera, but they need to be treated with due care when outside a camera. They should be kept away from direct sunlight, moisture, and high temperatures. It is best not to touch any exposed metal on connectors as this could give poor electrical connections. Due to their small size and thinness it is inevitable that memory cards are not very tough, and care must be taken to avoid physical damage. Flash cards are normally supplied with a plastic case (Figure 5.8), and it is best to keep them in this when they are not installed in a player or other gadget.

Fig.5.8 It is best to keep a Flash card in its case when it is not in use

Speed

Players that use some form of Flash memory have lower capacities than those that have a miniature hard disc drive. One could be forgiven for thinking that (say) writing one gigabyte of data to Flash memory would take longer than writing 20 gigabytes of data to a miniature hard disc drive. Unfortunately, Flash memory is rather slow by hard disc standards, and incredibly slow by normal memory standards. Although the Flash name tends to give people the impression that this type of memory is "quick as a flash", the name is derived from the way this type of memory works and is not meant to allude to its speed. Relatively small amounts of data are involved when using an MP3 player that has Flash memory, but the time taken to upload it can be comparatively long.

The miniature hard disc drives used in portable players are unlikely to keep up with the latest super-fast drives used in PCs, but they are not that much slower either. Provided the player is used with a suitably fast interface such as USB 2.0 or Firewire, writing to the disc at 20 megabytes per second or more should be possible. Making comparisons with Flash memory is difficult, because there is no universal speed for this type of memory. The situation is just the opposite of this in fact, with some Flash memory operating many times faster than the "bog standard" variety.

Most Flash memory manufacturers use a speed rating that is essentially the same as the one used for CD-ROM drives. There is a slight difference in that the rating used for a CD-ROM drive is the maximum it can achieve, and the actual speed obtained near the middle of the disc is usually much lower. There is no Flash memory equivalent to this, and the quoted speed should be obtained when writing to any part of the disc.

A speed rating of X1 is equivalent to about 150k (0.15 megabytes) per second. Most memory cards are not actually marked with a speed rating, although this information is usually included in the manufacturer's data. For the built-in Flash memory of an MP3 player it is a figure you might find somewhere in the full specification. A card that has no marked rating usually has a speed of about X4 to x12, and the integral Flash memory of a MP3 player is likely to be within this range. This equates to reading or writing data at very roughly one megabyte or so per second.

Extra cost

At the time of writing this it is possible to obtain memory cards that have speed ratings of up to about X130, although it seems likely that even faster cards will be developed. Unfortunately, very fast Flash cards cost much more than the "bog standard" variety. The premium you have to pay can be more than 100 percent, and the high cost means that you are unlikely to find very fast memory built into anything other than the most expensive MP3 players. Even then it is likely that the Flash memory will still have something less than the ultimate in performance. In order to obtain these very fast write speeds it is probably necessary to opt for a player that uses one of the more popular types of Flash card such as SD.

In terms of the actual writing speeds obtained, a card having a rating of x66 for example, can read and write data at up to 10 megabytes per second. The fastest cards can achieve something in the region of 20 megabytes per second, which starts to rival miniature hard disc drives. In theory at any rate, a gigabyte of data could be written to one of these cards in less than one minute.

Of course, transfer speeds of this order can not be achieved using a USB 1.1 interface. In order to fully utilise the speed of a fast Flash card it is essential to use a player or card reader/writer that supports a high speed interface such as USB 2.0 or Firewire. Using either of these should enable data to be read and written at something very close to the maximum speed rating of the card. Where high-speed operation is needed it is important to check that the player or USB card reader is a genuine USB 2.0 type. Some are described as "USB 2.0 compatible", which means that they are actually USB 1.1 devices that can operate at USB 1.1 speeds with a USB 2.0 interface.

Batteries included

Batteries are an aspect of MP3 players that is probably not given a great deal of thought by most prospective purchasers. However, the type of battery used can have a big impact on the usability of a player and its running costs. What seems like an inexpensive player could be quite costly after a few months of regular use. Rechargeable batteries offer low running costs, but can be a real nuisance if they become exhausted practically every time you use the player. In order to be really usable it is important that a player should be able to operate for a number of hours before it needs either recharging or a fresh set of batteries.

Upmarket players are usually supplied with a rechargeable battery or a set of rechargeable batteries. Sometimes the battery is built into the player and can not be changed by the user. The Apple iPods use this system. An advantage of this method is that it enables the manufacturer to use a battery that is specifically designed to fit the player, which helps to give the highest possible battery capacity within the modest dimensions of the player. The obvious drawback is that the player has to be returned to a service centre for a new battery to be fitted when the battery wears out and no longer holds a worthwhile charge. Apart from the inconvenience of being without the player for a while, this can be quite expensive.

If you intend to take the player out and about with you a great deal there is another drawback. Some players use rechargeable versions of ordinary AA or AAA cells, and in an emergency they will work properly if powered from ordinary AA or AAA batteries. In some cases it is necessary to use "high-power" batteries such as an alkaline type, but many players will work for several hours using a single cell of even the lowest quality. When taking the player on your travels you can take one or two spare batteries with you, or buy a battery if the rechargeable one runs down. It is possible to buy AA and AAA batteries practically anywhere and at virtually any time of day. With a player that has a built-in battery it is unlikely that you would find anywhere to recharge it. Even if you did, it is unlikely that you would be prepared to wait around for a few hours while the battery recharged.

Recharging

There are two ways of recharging the batteries, and one of these is to use a conventional charger that connects to a mains outlet. The alternative is to charge the batteries from a USB or Firewire port of the PC. Charging the batteries from the computer has the advantage of doing away with the need for yet another battery charger/mains power adapter, and its cost. On having a quick count I discovered that our household has more than a dozen of these units. We tend to avoid anything that adds yet another one to the collection. A slight disadvantage of using the computer as a charger is that it means you can only recharge the player when you have access to a suitable computer. Provided you take the charger with you, it is possible to recharge the player anywhere that has a suitable mains outlet. I suppose that ideally you should have both options available.

There is no need to use rechargeable batteries at all if the player will accept ordinary AA or AAA batteries. The initial cost is less if you opt for a player that is not supplied with rechargeable batteries, but the running costs will certainly be much higher if you use primary cells. The cost of recharging small batteries is so low as to be of no consequence. The cost of running a player from ordinary batteries obviously depends on factors such as how much it is used, the particular batteries used, and the power consumption of the player.

Some of the early portable CD players required large numbers of batteries that were short lived. In some cases the cost of the batteries could exceed the value of the CDs that were being played! Fortunately, things have moved on, and modern portable players require just one or two batteries that last a reasonable amount of time. Keeping battery consumption within reason is much easier with an MP3 player than with a portable cassette or CD player because an MP3 player does not have an electric motor to power. It does have some highly complex electronics though, so the power consumption is still significant.

The typical cost of running an MP3 player from ordinary batteries is a few pence per hour. No doubt the cost will mount up over a period of time, but it is hardly likely to "break the bank". A big advantage of this method is that you avoid the hassle of recharging batteries and there is no downtime while batteries are recharged.

Formats

Any MP3 player will of course, play MP3 files, but this is not to say that it will play any MP3 files. As pointed out in chapter 1, MP3 files are recoded at various bit rates and there is also a variable bit rate version of this format. Modern media player programs for PCs can usually play any form of MP3 file, including files that have variable bit rates or high bit rates such as 320 kilobits per second. The same is not true for portable MP3 players. The capabilities vary tremendously from one unit to another, and some are capable of playing a wide range of MP3 files. Others can only handle files that have relatively low bit rates of around 64 to 128 kilobits per second.

An inability to handle anything other than low bit rate MP3 files is not necessarily a major limitation. In order to get as many songs as possible onto an MP3 player it is normal to use the lowest bit rate that gives acceptable audio quality. The lowest usable bit rate that will provide true hi-fi quality is a matter of opinion, but most people are happy with the quality provided by 128 kilobits per second. Any MP3 player should be capable of handling files encoded at this rate.

Of course, you may deem optimum audio quality more important than getting as many songs as possible loaded into the player. Alternatively, you might simply have a lot of MP3 files encoded at high bit rates, and prefer not to spend a great deal of time converting them to operation at lower bit rates. Either way you will need to check the specification of prospective players to ensure that they can handle the bit rates you intend to use.

MP3 is not the only audio file format in common use, and some players can handle other formats. IPods are primarily designed for use with Apples own AAC format, which is also known as MP4. However, they can also play MP3 files having bit rates of up to 320 kilobits per second. Many MP3 players can play WMA files, but once again, the range of bit rates that can be accommodated could be rather limited. WMA has the advantage of being able to produce good audio quality from a relatively low bit rate. Many users are happy with the audio quality of WMA files encoded at 96 or even 64 kilobits per second. This means that you can potentially get 50 or 100 percent more music stored on a player by using WMA instead of MP3.

Note that iPods can not play WMA files, but the iTunes program can convert WMA files into AAC format and upload them to an iPod. Strictly speaking this does not make iPods compatible with WMA files, but if you have or obtain some WMA files they can, in effect, be used with an iPod. There are file conversion programs that can be used to convert WMA files into MP3 types so that they can be played on an MP3 player which does not directly support the WMA format. However, in order to maintain the audio quality it is necessary to use a higher bit rate, and the size advantage of WMA is lost.

Protected files

Note that iPods can not be used with protected WMA files, since they can not be converted into MP3 or AAC format. It follows from this that these files can not be used with MP3 players either. On the face of it, protected WMA files are compatible with portable players that can handle WMA files, but it is not as simple as that. Most portable players are not compatible with the protected versions of WMA files, and might not even work with some non-protected versions of these files.

There are many other audio file formats, but the only one that is supported by a reasonable range of players is the WAV format. This has the potential to produce really excellent audio quality, but the WAV format does not use any form of compression. With a 512 megabyte player it is possible to store something like 10 CDs in MP3 format, and perhaps as many as 20 CDs in WMA format. Using the WAV format you might get a single CD stored on the player if you are lucky.

The ability to play WAV files is not usually included because the manufacturers envisage users playing music in this format. Many MP3 players have a built-in microphone and voice recording facility so that they can be used for recording notes. The WAV files produced from the recordings are quite low in quality, but are adequate for voice recording.

The iPods can use Apple's lossless ALE format, which is useful if you regard sound quality as being more important than storing a large number of tracks in the player. It seems to be little used in practice though. A few MP3 players can handle the OGG Vorbis format, which could be useful if you have access to music in this format. It is probably not a big selling point for most users though.

Finally

When choosing an MP3 player you need to carefully consider the way in which it will be used. The latest top of the range players are impressive pieces of technology but are not necessarily the best choice for you. The previous chapters provide a great deal of information about the way in which players are used, and you really need to digest this before making a choice. Buying an MP3 player and then working out how to use it is a popular way of doing things, but it is a good way of wasting money by buying an unsuitable player. How will you use the player, and which of your prospective choices best "fits the bill"?

Points to remember

Reviews in magazines and on the Internet can be helpful in choosing a player, but the reviewer's perfect player will not necessarily be the best choice for you. Also, bear in mind that reviews on the Internet are not always unbiased and are frequently self-opinionated. Weigh up the facts and make up your own mind.

An expensive player will not necessarily sound better than a cheap one. The players are based on the same technologies and in many cases on exactly the same silicon chips. The sound quality is largely governed by the source files and the headphones. A high price tends to give you more storage space, a better display, etc., rather than better sound.

Having a large amount of storage means that you can load your entire music library onto the player. On the other hand, it is irrelevant if you will never have a huge library of music or will never find the time to upload all your music to the player. A player having a modest amount of Flash memory is a much cheaper and more practical choice unless you are prepared to spend some time organising and uploading music.

Battery life is an important factor. A player will be of little practical value if you frequently have to stop using it so that the battery can be recharged, or it has to be fed with large numbers of ordinary primary cells. A battery life of 12 hours or more is preferable.

All MP3 players are suitable for use on the move and are inherently jog-proof. Players that use Flash memory rather than a miniature hard disc drive are perhaps the better choice for use when jogging, exercising, etc. They tend to be physically smaller and lighter, and will work properly even if subjected to continuous vibration.

The importance of a really good display depends on the storage capacity of the player. It is a desirable feature for any player, but you can get away with something relatively simple with a low capacity player that will store few songs. A good display and menu system is essential for a player that has gigabytes of storage and is used to store a thousand tracks. Without a good display and logical menu system you will never find the song you are looking for!

Ideally a player should be able to handle a wide range of audio file formats. This leaves your options open and reduces the need to convert files to a format that suits the player. Few portable players can handle any form of protected audio file. The iPods are an obvious exception, and they can play the protected AAC files sold by the iTunes store.

If you are an audiophile and require the best possible sound quality, it is important to obtain a player that can handle a lossless audio format. Alternatively, you need one that can handle high bit rates with MP3 or WMA files.

For most users it is a case of size is not important, since all the current MP3 players are quite small and light. However, if you will be taking the player everywhere you go there is a definite advantage in choosing one that is really small and light. With portable devices it tends to be the case that small and light means a relatively short battery life, so make sure that you buy a player that is adequate in this respect.

Index

Index